German-American Genealogical Research
Monograph Numbers 1, 2, and 5

GERMAN MERCENARY EXPATRIATES
IN THE
UNITED STATES AND CANADA
3 Volumes in 1

Clifford Neal Smith

CLEARFIELD

Reprinted, 3 volumes in 1, for
Clearfield Company, Inc., by
Genealogical Publishing Co., Inc.
Baltimore, Maryland
2006

International Standard Book Number: 0-8063-5305-8

Made in the United States of America

German–American Genealogical Research
Monograph Number 1

BRUNSWICK DESERTER–IMMIGRANTS OF THE AMERICAN REVOLUTION

Clifford Neal Smith

Original edition distributed by
  Heritage House, Thomson, IL, 1973   ±√ʃ
Reprint, May 1985, Westland Publications   √
Reprint, May 1986   √
Reprint, December 1986   {
Reprint, July 1987   ±ʃ

Reprint, March 1988   qz
Reprint April 1989   · qz
Reprint, February 1993   u
Reprint, May 1993   u
Reprint, November 1994   u
Reprint, May 1996   u
Reprint, April 1997   u

BRUNSWICK DESERTER-IMMIGRANTS

OF THE AMERICAN REVOLUTION

Clifford Neal Smith

The Staatsarchiv at Wolfenbuettel, Germany, in which the records
of the former Duchy of Brunswick-Lueneburg are preserved, contains numer-
ous documents of interest to German-American genealogical researchers.
One of the most valuable, catalogued 38 B Alt Nr. 260, is a summary report on the Brunswick mercenaries sent to America in British service during the American Revolution, prepared after the return of the units to
Germany.

Brunswick troops were sent to America as follows:[1]

In 1776	4,300
March 1777	224
April 1778	475
April 1779	286
May 1780	266
April 1782	172
Total	5,723
Returned to Germany in autumn of 1783	2,708
Did not return	3,015

Hans Helmut Rimpau has published, in the *Archiv fuer Sippenforschung*, the names of over 1,700 soldiers who failed to return to
Brunswick in 1783.[2] Since the *Archiv fuer Sippenforschung* is hardly
available to American researchers,[3] the names therein have been reprinted hereinafter as they appear in his article. Rimpau did not
list those soldiers presumed to be dead, although it seems likely that
some so listed were, in fact, deserters. The Duke of Brunswick received a special indemnity from the British for every soldier killed,
so it was advantageous to report some deserters as dead, when possible.

The places where soldiers deserted afford a clue as to the possible states in which these deserters might be found at the time of the 1790 federal census (United States), a prerequisite for linking these deserters with their descendants. The Brunswick troops served mainly in Canada and northern New York; Brunswick prisoners of war were interned as far south as Virginia. Battlefield deserters are likely to be found in the state of New York in 1790; former prisoners of war must be sought in all the states southward to North Carolina. Unlike British deserters, there was no way for the Germans to lose themselves in the general populace; consequently, the German deserters are likely to have tried to reach German-speaking settlements in the Mohawk Valley or in Pennsylvania. This is stated as a working hypothesis only. American researchers still have too little data to make a more positive assertion.

Brunswick military units participated in the following battles and skirmishes with American revolutionaries:

Military Unit	Battles
Regiment of Dragoons (dismounted; under Baum)	Bennington
Grenadier Battalion (under Breymann)	Bennington; first & second Stillwater, Saratoga
Regiment Prinz Friedrich	Remained at Ticonderoga during the Saratoga campaign
Regiment von Riedesel	First Stillwater, Saratoga
Regiment von Rhetz	Two companies at first Stillwater, Saratoga
Regiment von Specht	Saratoga
Jaeger [Chasseur] Battalion, or Battalion Barner	First Stillwater, Saratoga

At the battle of Bennington (August 1777) the Americans took 400 German, mainly Brunswick, prisoners of war. A great many other Germans apparently took the opportunity to desert.[4] As a result of the defeat at Saratoga, 2,431 Germans became prisoners of war (the so-called Convention

Army) and 1,122 were killed, wounded, or missing.[5] It seems likely that the missing Germans were mainly deserters, possibly to be found later in the Mohawk Valley of New York.

The Convention Army prisoners of war were held near Cambridge, Massachusetts, from November 1777 to November 1778 (the Germans being quartered at Winterhill barracks). Thereafter, the Army was marched southward, via Rutland, Massachusetts, through Connecticut, New York, New Jersey, Pennsylvania, Maryland, to Charlottesville, Virginia, which they reached in January 1779. Opportunity to desert the column was provided by American militia escorts along the route, and it seems probable that many Germans did so in Pennsylvania while on the march through Pennsylvania-German settlements. After another year, many prisoners were transferred to Winchester, Virginia, and then to Frederick, Maryland. In the summer of 1781 remaining prisoners were moved to Easton, Pennsylvania, and back to Rutland, Massachusetts. All these locations became the scenes of desertions.

The Rimpau list shows the places of desertion for most of the troopers. These places are not always identifiable. Those which this writer has found reference to in early Brunswick memoirs[6] are as follows:

Great Barrington	In New England, near Nobletown, Tyrington
Kinderhook	In New York
Marlborough	In New England, near Northborough & Shrewsborough (Shrewsbury)
New City	Now Lansingburgh, New York
Rutland (formerly Grootland)	In Massachusetts
Shetecock (Scaghticoke)	Near Hudson River
Shrewsbury	In New England, near Marlborough, Northborough
Staunton	In Virginia
Soarts Haus = Sword's House	In Saratoga County, New York
Syrington or Tyrington	Near Nobletown and Great Barrington in New England

Winterhill   Barracks in Cambridge, Massachusetts

* * * * *

The following list contains an age column. Apparently years
and months of age are computed from some fixed date in 1780 not stated
in the original document. It is, of course, regrettable that this
reference date is now unknown, because the age column would then pro-
vide valuable information as to birth month.

Researchers finding names of interest in the list are encour-
aged to write to this writer, care of the publisher, for further information which may be available on a number of other muster rolls of the
Brunswick units in America in his possession. Likewise, this writer
would like to collect data on the places of early settlement for
deserters in order to establish the validity, or invalidity, of his
hypothesis regarding the places of early refuge which these deserters
sought.

CODE

A   Deserted

B   In the service of the (American) enemy

C   Discharged (when in Canada, look for
settlement and land grant in Nova Scotia)

D   Prisoner of war at a place known

E   Prisoner of war whereabouts unknown

F   Transferred to civil service (This is
the literal translation of the German
phrase; however, it seems probable that
a disability discharge is often meant.)

Cpl   Corporal
Drm   Drummer
Lt   Lieutenant

Name	Birthplace	Age	Left Service: How Where When		
			How	Where	When
Abraham, Daniel	Schorborn	36/11	C	Canada 1783	
Abt, Heinrich	Braunschweig	55/09	E		
Achilles, Ludwig	Amsen	34/00	E		
Achilles, Joh. Jul.	Braunschweig	22/10	A	Potomac 29.12.1778	
Achilles, Heinrich	Gebhardshagen	30/00	C	Canada 1783	
Ackermann, Aug.Andr.	Dankelsheim	59/06	A	New Hannover 24.12.1778	
Ackermann, Carl Johann	Frankfurt/Main	22/08	C	Canada 1783	
Adel, Hans	Bavaria	26/00	C	Canada 1783	
von Adelsheim, -- (Ensign)	Bodendorf o.d. Tauber	24/00	A	Canada November 1776	
Adenstedt, Georg	Braunschweig	30/00	C	Canada 1783	
Adner, Gottlieb	Stollberg	40/01	B		
Adolph, Christoph	Nordhausen	33/00	C	Canada 1783	
Ahl, Johann	Nuernberg	22/00	C	Canada 1783	
Ahnstedt, Heinrich	Fallersleben	33/05	B		
Ahrend, Johann	Papendorf in Magdeburg [region]	44/08	E		
Ahrend, Johann	Schmiedeburg, Saxony	19/07	A	Penobscot 3.3.1783	
Ahrens, August	Barum	43/10	E		
Ahrens, Johann	Braunschweig	36/00	C	Canada 1783	
Albenstedt, Gottlieb	Bindern	21/07	A	Tyringham 26.10.1781	
Alberti, Rudolf	Seesen	26/00	A	Canada? 20.10.1781	
Albrecht, Wilhelm	Kirchbraak	32/03	C	Canada 1783	
Albrecht, Johann Heinrich	Wolfenbuettel	26/00	C	Canada 1783	
Albrecht, Heinrich	Salzdahlum	31/09	C	Canada 1783	
Albrecht, Anton	Altenburg	23/00	E		
Allé, Jean Francois	Champagne [France]	26/07	C	Canada 1783	
Allenstein, Gottlieb	Apperode, Brandenburg	33/04	E		
Allewelt, Bernhard	Zorge	30/04	A	Frederickstown 28.12.1778	
Alms, Andreas	Schoeningen	23/00	A	Winterhill 19.3.1778	
Alpers, Ant. Ferdin.	Hamersleben in Brandenburg [territory]	21/00	A	Fishkill 1.12.1778	
Amberg, Georg	Ewelde in Coburg [territory]	21/08	A	Canada 17.7.1781	
Andrae, Christoph	Pirna, Saxony	44/03	F		
Angenant, Carl	Wesel	26/08	C	Canada 1783	
Angerer, Andreas	Bernhardswiese in Ansbach [territory]	24/08	C	Canada 1783	

5

Name	Birthplace	Age	Left Service: How Where When
Apitz, Friedrich	Berlin	26/00	A Winterhill 29.3.1778
Appenhausen, Christ- oph Jul.	Lichtenberg	23/10	E
Assmer, Bernhard	Timmerlah	35/01	C Canada 1783
Aue, Wilhelm	Schaumburg, Hesse	24/00	A Charleston [S.C.] 2.4.1781
Aul, Heinrich	Sonneborn, Hannover	28/06	C Canada 1783
Baacke, Heinrich	Braunschweig	53/06	F
Babtist, Jean	France	--	Abandoned on a sandbank by Gasport 18.6.1779
Bachmann, Lorenz	Lauterbach	36/05	E
Bachmann, Franz	Koenigslutter	26/10	A Taunytown 27.12.1778
Baehr, Michael	Zellerfeld	47/07	F
Baehr, Christian	Braunlage	42/00	E
Baehr, Johann Christ.	Braunlage	26/00	A Virginia 6.1.1779
Baehr, Caspar	Nordheim	27/08	C Canada 1783
Baehrcke, Friedrich	Suepplingen	25/08	A Andover Forges 10.12.1778
Baese, Johann Heinr.	Gifhorn	26/07	A Winterhill 2.10.1778
Baese, Bernhard	Schandelah	31/06	A Winchester 8.4.1781
Baethge, Christian	from Hessen-Damm [Hesse-Darmstadt?]	29/00	D Boston
Baldau, Bernhard	Oldenburg, Bavaria [erroneous?]	31/00	A Canada 3.7.1783
Banck, August	Braunschweig	26/05	D Portsmouth
Bandel, -- (Ensign)	Schwedt	30/05	A Winchester 3.2.1781
Bangemann, Johann	Emmerstedt	28/04	D Winchester
Bardhauer, Daniel	Grembsheim	32/11	F
Barner, Zacharias	Wolfershausen	30/09	E
Barnickel, Jacob	Eschenfeld, Nuern- berg	22/07	C Canada 1783
Bartels, Georg	Braunschweig	24/03	A Salisbury 18.12.1778
Bartels, Hennig	Wenden	32/07	E
Bartels, Heinrich	Braunschweig	41/00	B
Bartels, Heinrich	Gross-Himstedt	38/02	E

Name	Birthplace	Age	Left Service: How Where When		
			How	Where	When
Bartels, Christian	Wittmar	25/09	A	Potomac 30.12.1778	
Bartholomae, Johann	Eisenach	38/07	C	Canada 1783	
Bartholomaei, Georg	Hirschfeld	33/04	C	Canada 1783	
Bartholomaei, Johann	Herstelle, Paderborn	17/03	A	Penobscot 19.5.1783	
Bartram, Andreas	Wicksensen	46/05	C	Canada 1783	
Bartram, Julius	Opperhausen	31/06	F		
Bartram, Heinrich	Dassel	52/10	B		
Bartram, Heinrich	Bodenfelde	35/08	C	Canada 1783	
Bauer, Conrad	Braunsburg	21/03	A	Canada 2.7.1783	
Bauer, Christian	Gothenburg	28/00	C	Canada	
Bauer, Wilhelm	Blankenburg	30/00	A	Winterhill 25.5.1778	
Bauer, Friedrich	Buschenbach, Bavaria	24/11	E		
Bauer, Adam	Philippsburg	28/00	C	Canada 1783	
Bauermeister, Johann	Dahlum, Brandenburg	24/09	A	Potomac 30.12.1778	
Bauermeister, Heinr.	Ruehme	30/08	F		
Baumann, Johann	Bavaria	48/06		Dishonorably discharged Canada 9.6.1783	
Bayer, Johann	Zahne, Saxony	22/00	E		
Bebendorff, Valentin	Packenrode	37/00	C	Canada 1783	
Becker, Christian	Hamburg	22/00	A	Winterhill 12.7.1778	
Becker, Adam	Mainz	23/00		Dishonorably discharged Canada 4.9.1778	
Becker, August	Stollberg	26/07	C	Canada 1783	
Becker, Christoph	Huettenrode	42/09	D	Springfield	
Becker, Friedrich	Braunschweig	24/00	A	Sotfield 19.11.1778	
Becker, Christian	Braunschweig	26/00	D	Newbury	
Becker, Johann	Negenborn	18/07	A	Winterhill 17.5.1778	
Becker, August	Oker	41/03	F		
Becker, Franz	Almerode, Hesse	34/07	A	Potomac 30.12.1778	
Becker, Johann	Friedensdorf in Darmstadt [territory]	34/10	B		
Becker, August	Helmstedt	20/08	A	Winterhill 9.11.1778	
Becker, Jacob	Deutersen	28/00	C	Canada 1783	
Becker, Heinrich	Rettmar	23/00	A	Nobletown 24.10.1777	
Beddiger, Franz	Heerte	23/00	C	Canada 1783	
Behle, Friedrich	Bodenburg	39/06	B		
Behrbom, Ludwig	Meyerhausen	24/02	A	Vergére [Canada?] 17.6.1776	

Name	Birthplace	Age	Left Service: How Where When		

Name	Birthplace	Age	How	Where When	
Behrens, Ulrich (medical corpsman)	Aschwerden	24/00	A	Winterhill 14.5.1778	
Behrens, Heinrich	Markoldendorf	22/04	A	Winterhill 7.4.1778	
Behrens, Heinrich	Gebhardshagen	51/01	B		
Behrens, Carl	Wienrode	35/03	E		
Behrens, Gottlieb	Berlin	28/10	C	Canada 1783	
Beller, Friedrich	Lesse	47/03	E		
Bellmann, Christian	Neustadt a. Ruebenberg	32/00	E		
Bellstedt, Heinrich	Halberstadt	24/07	A	Palmer 16.11.1778	
Benecke, Heinrich	Thedinghausen	32/02	E		
Benecke, Conrad	Braunschweig	23/02	C	Canada 1783	
Benecke, Friedrich	Hildesheim	22/00	C	Canada 1783	
Bense, Peter Christ.	Osterwieck	38/00	A	New Hannover 25.12.1778	
Bentrott, Wilhelm	Negenborn	29/00	A	Winterhill 28.9.1778	
Berck, Johann	Hessian [territory]	32/07	C	Canada 1783	
Berckhane, Juergen	Altenkirchen in Altenburg [territory]	40/11	E		
Berger, Adam	Simmershausen, Hesse	25/03	A	Freeman's Farm 39.9.1777	
Bergmann, Heinrich	Neustadt	39/00	A	New Hannover 24.12.1778	
Bergmann, Gabriel	Reinsdorft	38/03	E		
Bergmann, Johann Joseph	Steinbach a. d. Eichsfeld	24/01	A	Potomac 30.12.1778	
Bergmann, Johann	Steinbach a. d. Eichsfeld	29/00	F		
Bergmann, Andreas	Schoeningen	46/11	E		
Bernhard, Christoph	Oesleben, Brandenburg	31/04	F		
Besselmann, Johann Carl	Wolfenbuettel	26/07	C	Canada 1783	
Besserer, Ludwig	Neustadt, Bayreuth	33/01	C	Canada 1783	
Bethge, Heinrich	Zellerfeld	26/10	F		
Bethge, Andreas	Koenigslutter	27/03	C	Canada 1783	
Beuckert, Joseph	Lissa, Poland	32/07	C	Canada 1783	
Beyer, Nicholas	Erfurt	24/06	C	Canada 1783	
Beyer, Heinrich	Braunschweig	20/07	A	Great Barington 25.10.1777	
Beyer, Johann Wilhelm	Jena	36/05	C	Canada 1783	
Beyssert, Wilhelm	from Wuerttemberg [territory]	28/09	C	Canada 1783	
Biehlert, Conrad	Speyer	34/00	E		
Bielefeld, Johann	Magdeburg	29/04	A	Canada 1783	

Name	Birthplace	Age	Left Service: How Where When
Bielstein, Wilhelm, Lt	Braunschweig	41/07	C Canada 1783
Biennommé, Jacques	France	23/04	A Canada 1783
Billhard, Johann Friedrich	Langensalza	41/06	C Canada 1783
Birckner, Joseph	Jachau, Hungary	21/00	A Winterhill 25.5.1778
Birschner, Georg	Kramenau	32/06	C Canada 1783
Bischoff, Johann	Emmerstedt	41/04	E
Blettermann, Andreas	Clausthal	26/00	A New Providence 16.12.1778
Block, Johann	Schoeningen	24/11	C Canada 1783
Bluemchen, Johann (medical corpsman)	Magdeburg	32/06	C Canada 1783
Bluemer, Conrad	Seesen	45/00	D Stoughton
Blumberg, August	Braunschweig	36/00	A Winterhill 5.5.1778
Blumberg, Juergen	Lamme	25/05	C Canada 1783
Blume, Nicolaus	Freyenstein in Riedesel [territory]	29/00	D Boston
Blume, Nicolaus	Wolfershausen	33/09	C Canada 1783
Blume, Caspar	Reinsdorf	46/00	B
Blume, Andreas	Langeleben	29/00	A Winterhill 8.12.1777
Blume, Conrad	Braunschweig	49/00	C Canada 1783
Bobach, Johann	Zellerfeld	21/00	A Worchester 12.11.1778
Bock, Georg	Gotha	33/00	A Rutland 1.4.1778
Bockemann, Lorenz	Bodenstedt	25/00	A Frederickstown 27.12.1778
Bockemueller, Heinrich	Braunschweig	21/01	A Potomac 30.12.1778
Bockemueller, August	Braunschweig	30/11	E
Bockemueller, Georg	Neustadt	28/09	E
Bockmann, Andr. Hr.	Suepplingen	22/00	A Nobletown 24.10.1777
Bode, Heinrich	Weddingen in Hildesheim [territory]	27/00	E
Bode, Friedrich	Gross-Ruehden	32/07	E
Bode, Martin	Ledersburg, Prussia	26/00	A Pennsylvania 24.12.1778
Bodemann, Joh. Heinr.	Alvensleben	33/10	A Ticonderoga 21.9.1777
Bodenstedt, Julius	Oelper	40/11	F
Bodenstein, Heinr.	Schlewecke	33/08	A Virginia 13.1.1779

Name	Birthplace	Age	Left Service: How Where When
Boebe, Simon	Altringen	23/00	C Canada 1783
Boecker, Christian	Greene	36/00	E
Boecker, Andreas	Gandersheim	38/08	E
Boedecker, Johann Friedrich	Ottenstein	32/00	C Canada 1783
Boedecker, Johann	Minden	22/01	C Canada 1783
Boehling, Heinrich	Stade	41/04	C Canada 1783
Boehme, Johann	Braunschweig	31/08	A Winterhill 18.10.1778
Boehme, Joseph	Altenkirchen, Altenburg [territory]	26/11	E
Boening, Johann	Piemont	49/00	C Canada 1783
Boettcher, Gottlieb	Demmer, Gotha	18/00	A Fort Miller September 1777
Boettcher, Andreas	Emmerstedt	38/01	B
Boettcher, Joh. Christ.	Glogau	27/04	C Canada 1783
Boettcher, Wilhelm	Braunschweig	30/00	A Winterhill 9.4.1778
Bohne, Christoph	Voigtsdahlum	32/07	F
Bohnhage, Carl	Wolfenbuettel	23/09	A Freeman's Farm 7.10.1777
Bohnsack, Joh. Georg	Hesse-Kassel [territory?]	24/07	C Canada 1783
Bojack, Martin	Berlin	48/00	C Canada 1783
Bollmann, -- (medical corpsman)	Hammersleben	30/00	A Halifax 18.7.1781
Bollmann, Heinrich	Gross-Elbe	27/03	C Canada 1783
Bollmann, Christoph	Sottrum in Hildesheim [territory]	20/04	A Winterhill 23.7.1778
Bollmann, Heinrich	Blankenburg	23/10	C Canada 1783
Bonse, Adolph	Lichtenberg	28/08	E
Bonse, Heinrich	Osterode	36/00	E
Boos, Caspar	Wallerstein in Ansbach [territory]	24/06	C Canada 1783
Borchers, Juergen	Halle, Amt Wickensen	35/00	B
Borck, Friedrich	Berlin	22/06	A Great Barrington 25.10.1777
Bormann, Carl	Wolfenbuettel	23/04	C Canada 1783
Bormann, Sigmund	Landshut	27/08	C Canada 1783
Borms, Friedrich	Winzenburg	33/11	F
Born, Daniel	Blankenburg	26/07	F
Bornemann, Gottlieb	Frankfurt/Oder	29/00	E
Bornemann, Carl	Harbke	19/00	A Virginia 16.9.1779
Bosse, Andreas	Berssel/Halberstadt	45/05	C Canada 1783
Bosse, Michael	Langelsheim	22/10	D Virginia

Name	Birthplace	Age	Left Service: How Where When
Bosse, Julius	Burgdorf	32/05	A Nobletown 24.10.1777
Braatz, Friedrich	Wiesenthal, Bohemia	25/07	C Canada 1783
Brackhagen, Andreas	Woprechtshausen	35/06	B
Brader, Conrad	Ruehle	50/01	E
Brandes, Andreas	Dibbesdorf	48/07	F Philadelphia
Brandes, Conrad	Dolgen, Hannover	29/03	E
Brandes, Johann	Braunschweig	17/07	A Westfield 28.10.1777
Brandes, Christian	Rueningen	42/07	B
Brandes, Julius	Dettum	44/04	F
Brandes, Christian	Bremen	21/00	E
Brandt, Joh. Friedr.	Clausthal	--	C Canada 1783
Brandt, Friedrich	Amelunxborn	25/05	B
Brandt, Ernst	Boernecke	55/09	E
Brandt, Johann	Bremen	24/00	A Winterhill 24.4.1779
Brandt, Joh. Chris- toph	Grund	26/09	C Canada 1783
Brauer, Andreas	Fallstedt	36/02	E
Braun, Martin	Adern, Saxony	39/10	C Canada 1783
Braune, Georg	Wilsbach in Ansbach [territory]	20/10	A St. Francois 1.1.1777
Braune, Andreas	Schlotheim	30/09	C Canada 1783
Brecht, Georg	Moehringsheim	23/07	C Canada 1783
Breimesser, Christoph	Ottenburg, Wuerttem- berg	48/09	F
Breitschu, Heinrich	Gernrode	25/00	C Canada 1783
Bremer, Ludwig	Hellenthal	27/10	E
Brendel, Franz	Kayserslutter	21/00	C Canada 1783
Brennecke, Johann	Lesse	28/03	C Canada 1783
Brennecke, Joh. Christ.	Ribbesbuettel	21/00	A Canada 1783
Bretbinder, Wilhelm	Tanne	27/04	B
Breusse, Heinrich	from Saxony	19/00	A Charleston [S.C.] 3.4.1782
Breust, Heinrich	Boettgerode	29/01	D Winchester
Breust, Gottlieb	Westerode	35/00	A Virginia 16.11.1780
Breymann, Joh. Christ.	Braunschweig	32/06	A Winterhill 30.6.1778
Breyter, Friedr. Aug.	Muenchhoffen in Mans- feld [territory]	24/01	A from prisoner of war camp 5.6.1781
Brinckmann, Christ.	Gandersheim	32/08	E
Brinckmann, Andreas	Bevern	38/03	B
Broehse, Martin	Braunschweig	27/08	A New Hartford 21.11.1778
Bruecke, Friedrich	Kreiensen	34/01	F
Brueckner, Joh. Christ.	Schwabach	24/06	C Canada 1783
Bruder, Adam	Freyberg	23/06	C Canada 1783
Brumann, Andreas	Wuerzburg	32/00	A Shrewsburg 11.11.1778
Bruns, Gottfried	Braunschweig	48/00	D Albany

Name	Birthplace	Age	Left Service: How Where When		

Name	Birthplace	Age	How	Where When
Bruns, Friedrich	Braunschweig	33/07	A	Saratoga 10.10.1777
Bruns, Christian	Golmbach	28/01	E	
Bruns, Christian	Salzgitter	44/00	C	Canada 1783
Buechs, Johann	Hirschfeld	28/00	C	Canada 1783
Buehrig, Joh. Conrad	Braunschweig	36/00	A	Cambridge 30.11.1778
Buengener, Friedrich	Wolfenbuettel	35/00	E	
Buesterfeld, Esaias	Braunschweig	31/03	A	New Hannover 24.12.1778
Buettner, Carl	Seesen	30/03	F	
Buettner, Gottfried	Andreasberg	28/00	E	
Buettner, Christoph	Saälfeld	23/09	A	Canada 1783
Burchard, Paul Gebhard	Jerichow, Magdeburg [territory]	44/07	C	Canada 1783
Burgdorff, Joh. Peter	Linde	18/05	A	Lancaster 21.12.1778
Burgdorff, Heinrich	Gross-Linde	38/05	E	
Burgdorff, Heinrich	Burgdorf	33/02	E	
Burgdorff, Johann	Schlotheim	24/00	E	
Burghoff, --, Lt	Braunschweig	36/00		Discharged on order of his Serene Highness [the Duke] 28.8.1781
Burholz, Carl	Altona	41/02	A	Lancaster 23.12.1778
Busch, Ludwig	Salzdahlum	26/00	A	Canada 1783
Buss, Caspar	Neustadt/Harzburg	34/08	E	
Cain, Ernst	Wolfenbuettel	32/11	E	
Carl, Gottfried	Naumburg	40/04	C	Canada 1783
Chameau, Pierre (fifer)	Lion [Lyon? France]	40/00	A	Winterhill 1778
Christa, Martin	Biberach, Bavaria	19/08	C	Canada 1783
Christiany, Georg	Nieder Ohms	25/00	A	Freeman's Farm 1777
Cirenius, Christoph	Calvoerde	30/05	E	
Clausius, Johann	Magdeburg	24/00	A	1777
Coelling, Franz	Amelunxen/Corvey	26/06	C	Canada 1783
Collecter, Joh. Wilh.	Golmbach	38/09	E	
Collet, Abraham	Switzerland	48/06	E	
Conrad, Georg	Reichenberg	25/03	C	Canada 1783
Conrad, Stephan	Sachsenhausen	36/01	C	Canada 1783
Constabel, Friedrich	Schoeppenstedt	50/04	A	Pennsylvania 1778
Contermann, Philipp	Weilburg	35/00	A	Lancaster 1778
Cordes, Friedrich	Hamburg	40/00	E	
Creutznacher, Joh. Friedrich	Eisenach	21/00	C	Canada 1783
la Croix, Louis	Lion [Lyon? France]	49/00	A	New City 1777
Crone, August	Braunschweig	42/06	E	

Name	Birthplace	Age	Left Service: How Where When		
Daentzer, Christoph	Andreasberg	43/03	D	Winchester	
Dahlen, Heinrich	Oker	27/01	E		
Dahlenburg, Matthias	Hessen [town of?]	28/07	A	Winterhill	1778
Dahler, Johann	Mainz [territory]	24/11	C	Canada	1783
Dahlheim, Heinrich	Grasleben	39/06	A	Lewisburg	1779
Dammeyer, Christian	Buendheim	36/05	F		
Dankemeyer, Friedrich	Hessen [town of?]	40/10	B		
Dandorff, Heinrich	Burgdorff, Hannover	35/11	C	Canada	1783
Daniel, Gottfried	Buchen, Saxony	39/06	F		
Dauth, Caspar	Rosen, Alsace	26/07	A	Canada	1782
Decker, Friedrich	Schoenstedt, Brandenburg [territory]	28/00	A	Winterhill	1778
Decker, Joseph	Mamorde, Pfalz [Palatinate]	22/04	A	Canada	1783
Degenhard, Joh. Friedr.	Goettingen	29/00	C	Canada	1783
Dehne, Matthias	Altendorf, Hesse	23/11	C	Canada	1783
Dehnert, Jacob	Obergebern, Grafschaft Hohnstein	26/07	C	Canada	1783
Dehnhardt, Ernst	Budstedt, Saxony-Weimar	21/05	C	Canada	1783
Dehnig, Valentin	Wiedelah, Hesse	36/00	A	1779	
Deilhausen, Christoph	Twieflingen	41/04	E		
Dettmer, Friedrich	Gross-Rueden	21/00	A	Virginia	1780
Dettmer, Heinrich	Gross Stoeckheim	26/00	C	Canada	1783
Dettmer, Heinrich	Zellerfeld	36/08	B		
Dettmer, Carl	Wettern, Hesse	37/00	A	Marlborough	1777
Diebel, Eberhard	Stiege	29/11	E		
Diedrichs, Christoph	Solms	28/02	A	Winterhill	1778
Diedrichs, Christian	Wolfenbuettel	53/09	E		
Diedrichs, Johann	Bamberg	27/06	C	Canada	1783
Diedrichs, Franz	Koenigslutter	38/00	F		
Diedrichs, Heinrich	Braunschweig	18/07	A	Saratoga	1777
Dietz, Caspar	Landehausen in Riedesel [territory]	31/00	D	Boston	
Dietz, Johann	Lausitz	26/00	A	Virginia	1779
Dietz, Christian	Amelunxborn	39/08	E		
Dietzell, Johann	Zunderbach	18/08	A	Freeman's Farm	1777
Dillmann, Friedrich	Lang[en] Schwabach	27/00	C	Canada	1783
Discher, Caspar	Wuerzburg	26/11	C	Canada	1783
Doeren, Christian (medical corpsman)	Neu-Haldensleben	29/04	C	Canada	1783
Doerge, Georg	Blankenburg	57/00	F		
Doerge, Levin	Herholzen	32/08	E		
Doerges, Wilhelm	Luerdissen	28/06	A	New Hannover	1778
Doerges, Heinrich	Vorwohle	38/06	E		

Name	Birthplace	Age	Left Service: How Where When		

Name	Birthplace	Age	How	Where When
Doering, Adam	Erzhausen/Eichsf.	19/00	A	Winterhill 1778
Doering, Franz	Ruestringen/Eichsf.	30/00	A	Yorktown 1778
Doering, Heinrich	Thueringen [Thuringia]	32/00	C	Canada 1783
Doerries, Johann	Boettcherode	46/00	A	Frederickstown 1778
Doesenberg, Anton	Sollingen	20/07	A	Sawnytown 1778
Dohmprobst, Friedrich	Frankenfeld	28/05	A	Canada 1783
Donny, Anton	Altkirchen, Alsace	21/00	A	Canada 1783
Dormeyer, Caspar	Bevern	42/00	E	
Dormeyer, Friedrich	Aarholzen, Waldeck	26/01	A	Quebec 1783
Dorsch, Christoph	Meckmuehle, Wuerttemberg	22/06	C	Canada 1783
Dralle, Johann	Braunschweig	28/05	E	
Drechsler, Joh. Georg	Hambrecht	24/06	C	Canada 1783
Dreyer, Friedrich	Hildesheim	40/00	A	Frederickstown 1778
Dreyer, Friedrich	Fuerstenberg	32/00	E	
Dreyer, Conrad Heinr.	Hessdorf, Hesse	26/00	C	Canada 1783
Drinks, Andreas	Coburg	25/00	E	
Dudloff, Joh. Gottl.	Erichswalde, Saxony?	28/07	C	Canada 1783
Duenckel, Heinrich	Naumburg	34/10	E	
Duevert, Andreas	Braunschweig	21/00	A	Kenderhook 1777
Duevert, Johann	Braunschweig	20/00	A	Virginia 1779
Dupenack, Carl	Goerlitz	29/03	C	Penobscot 1783
Durdy, Matthias	Braband [Brabant?]	30/02	C	Canada 1783
Duvinett, Baptist	Franche Comté, [France]	22/00	A	Isle aux Noix 1782
Ebacher, Johann	Strassburg	28/00	C	Canada 1783
Ebeling, Heinrich	Herhausen	45/05	E	
Ebeling, Zacharias	Herhausen	49/06	F	
Ebeling, Sigmund	Herhausen	31/06	F	
Ebeling, Juergen	Bleckenstedt	24/09	A	Virginia 1779
Ebeling, Carl	Boffzen	37/09	B	
Eberhard, Johann	Bayreuth	25/00	A	Frederickstown 1778
Eberhard, Franz	Heiligenstadt	28/03	C	Canada 1783
Ebert, Heinrich	Fritzlar	23/11	B	
Ebert, Caspar	Wathiral	33/06	C	Canada 1783
Eckert, Adam	Meynungen	37/00	A	Worcester 1777
Eckhard, Gottfried	Rothenhaus	23/07	C	Canada 1783
Edeling, Bernhard	Offenbach	42/02	A	Winterhill 1778
Eggers, Julius	Watenstedt	39/00	D	Albany
Eggers, Johann	Wolfenbuettel	19/00	A	Winterhill 1778

Name	Birthplace	Age	Left Service: How	Where	When
Ehlers, Johann	Braunschweig	35/04	E	(got married)	
Ehlers, Julius	Siersse	46/05	F		
Ehlers, Heinrich	Wolfsburg	22/06	A	Soeffield [?] 1778	
Ehlers, Joh. Conrad	Ohrum	20/04	C	Canada 1783	
Ehrecke, Georg	Hannover	43/03	C	Canada 1783	
Eichenauer, Conrad	Lauterbach	35/00	A	from prisoner of war camp 1779	
Eickemeyer, Andreas	Naensen	37/10	F		
Eichenberg, Georg Gottfried	Cassel [Kassel]	35/00	C	Canada 1783	
Eichmann, Johann	Markeldissen	50/08	F		
Eicke, Ludewig	Gross Steinum	43/03	F		
Eicke, Friedrich, Cpl	Stauffenberg	36/00	A	Winterhill 1778	
Eickhoff, Joh. Andreas	Delmissen	25/00	A	Potomac 1778	
Eimecke, Georg	Schoeningen	27/06	C	Canada 1783	
Einselm, Johann, Cpl	Wuerttemberg	32/00	E		
Ellrich, Georg	Eichsfeld	30/00	A	Yorktown 1778	
Elsner, Nicolaus	Magdeburg	29/03	C	Canada 1783	
Elster, Caspar	Windhausen	24/02	A	Winterhill 1778	
Elze, Ernst	Wenzen	26/00	E		
Emong, Jean	St. Onge [France?]	24/06	C	Canada 1783	
Engel, Georg	Northeim	32/06	C	Canada 1783	
Engelcke, Daniel	Hildesheim	24/00	A	Winterhill 1778	
Engelcke, Christoph	Hohlenberg	29/03	D	Virginia	
Engeler, Diedrich	Voelkenrode	55/00	B		
Engelhard, Bernhard	Bargdorf, Oberpfalz [Upper Palatinate]	39/02	C	Canada 1783	
Engelhard, Georg	Schluesselburg, Wuerttemberg [territory]	42/00	A	Shetekok [?] 1777	
Engelhard, Wilhelm	Neuburg, Pfalz [Palatinate]	21/00	A	Canada 1781	
Entrott, Conrad	Braunschweig	19/00	A	Cambridge 1778	
Eppers, Carl	Wolfenbuettel	29/08	A	Canada 1783	
Erck, Andreas	Trautenthal, Wuerttemberg [territory]	25/07	C	Canada 1783	
Erdmann, Joh. Peter	Almerode	43/10	C	Canada 1783	
Erdner, Joseph	Wald-Muenchen	45/01	C	Canada 1783	
Ernst, Andreas	Dankelsheim	20/06	A	New Hannover 1778	
Ernst, Juergen	Dankelsheim	23/04	A	New Hannover 1778	
Ernst, Christian Martin	Fuemmelse	20/00	A	Virginia 1779	
Eulers, Johann	Noerten	24/11	C	Canada 1783	
Eulers, Johann	Lochstedt, Thuringia	37/00	E		
Eylers, Anton	Negenborn	46/06	F		
Eylers, Christoph	Negenborn	33/10	E		

Name	Birthplace	Age	Left Service: How	Where When
Fabricius, Carl August	Berlin	30/07	C	Canada 1783
Fach, Georg (medical corpsman)	Wasungen bei Mainz	26/03	A	Winterhill 1778
Faust, Friedrich	Lauterbach	24/00	A	Canada 1783
Fehrenschild, Johann	Muehlhausen	29/00	E	
Felis, Juergen	Holzminden	37/08	A	1777
Femmeling, Heinrich	Salzgitter	27/05	A	Quebec 1783
Ferbitz, Johann	Thorn	27/08	C	Canada 1783
Fiedler, Andreas	Eichsfeld	40/00	C	Canada 1783
Fieweg, Georg	Schneeberg	37/09	A	Virginia 1779
Finsterwald, Johann	Bamberg	27/06	C	Canada 1783
Fischer, Conrad	Lesse	20/04	A	Winterhill 1778
Fischer, Wilhelm	Koenigslutter	29/07	A	1777
Fischer, Ernst	Hohegeiss	26/10	F	
Fischer, Heinrich	Stadtoldendorf	20/10	A	Nobletown 1777
Fischer, Caspar	Wuerzburg	25/11	A	Canada 1782
Fischer, Joh. Christoph	Konissen? or Kreiensen?	20/00	C	Canada 1783
Fleischer, Andreas	Plute, Saxony	44/00	C	Canada 1783
Flemme, Christoph	Northeim	26/09	C	Canada 1783
Flemming, Christian	Wederstedt	47/00	A	Winterhill 1777
Flentje, Friedrich	Herhausen	34/05	A	Winterhill 1778
Flicke, Georg	Wolfenbuettel	28/00	A	Potomac 1778
Foehr, Christian	Braunschweig	34/02	A	Winterhill 1778
Foehr, Hans	Kingholm, Denmark	40/00	C	Canada 1783
Fohne, Anton	Kaiserswerth	29/05	A	Great Barrington 1777
Foser, Sebastian	Weittendorf, Austria	24/00	A	Canada 1783
Francke, Heinrich	Scheppau	32/02	D	Albany
Francke, Michael	Uthmoeden	19/00	A	Soarts Haus [house] 1777
Francke, Johann	Muenchehoff	45/06	F	
Francke, Joh. Heinrich	Strelitz	26/06	C	Canada 1783
Francke, Johann	Lauingen	36/07	E	
Francke, Peter	Ferstell	28/00	C	Canada 1783
Francisca, Caspar	Naumdorf	21/00	A	Canada 1781
Franz, Joh. Ernst	Bodenfelde	20/11	C	Canada 1783
Frees, Heinrich	Einbeck	25/04	C	Canada 1783
Freund, Adam	Mehrstedt	23/00	A	New York 1780
Freund, Daniel	Tuetissen	34/11	C	Canada 1783
Freymuth, Sigmund	Freystadt, Bavaria	37/04	A	Canada 1783
Fricke, August (cadet)	Wolfenbuettel	27/06	A	Winterhill 1778
Fricke, Wilhelm (fifer)	Wolfenbuettel	27/07	D	Cambridge (got married)
Fricke, Eberhard	Lochtungen, Stift Hildesheim	29/09	C	Canada 1783

Name	Birthplace	Age	Left Service: How Where When
Fricke, Heinrich	Braunschweig	28/05	C Canada 1783
Fricke, Andreas	Braunschweig	26/07	F
Fricke, Georg	Hildesheim	43/03	A New Hannover 1778
Fricke, Christian	Einum	25/05	A Virginia 1779
Fricke, Joachim Christian	Flechtorf	50/00	F
Fricke, Friedrich	Lutter Bbge.	22/00	C Canada 1783
Fricke, Joh. Heinrich	Harxbuettel	20/00	A Penobscot 1783
Fricke, Carl	Voelkenrode	18/06	A Canada 1777
Fricke, Peter	Bahrdorf	53/00	A Yorktown 1778
Friedenreich, Christian	Gruenstadt, Pfalz [Palatinate]	30/01	D (got married)
Friedrichs, Heinrich	Braunschweig	41/05	E
Fromme, Gottfried	Pforten, Saxony	28/02	C Canada 1783
Fruehling, August	Braunschweig	27/05	A Winterhill 1778
Fuchs, Johann	Kothmannsdorf in Ansbach [territory]	22/00	A Canada 1783
Fuhrmann, Henrich Andreas	Buendheim	38/11	F
Fuhrmann, Johann	Berlin	37/06	C Canada 1783
Fuhrmann, Georg Samuel	Fritzen in Brandenburg [territory]	35/00	C Canada 1783
Fuegerer, -- (chaplain)	Garleben	35/03	Dishonorably discharged 1779
Fuetterer, Georg	Muencherode, Pfalz [Palatinate]	37/00	C Canada 1783
Funcke, Zacharias	Grasleben	32/02	E
Funcke, Joh. Heinrich	Lichtenberg	44/01	E
Gabriel, Friedrich	Strasburg	24/04	C Canada 1783
Gabriel, Ferdinand	Dorstadt	26/05	C Canada 1783
Gade, Christian	Wendeburg	28/10	D Multown [?]
Gaertner, Johann	Clausthal	40/00	E
Galland, Joseph	Hotang [France?]	46/00	C Canada 1783
Gangé, Louis	Paris [France]	41/03	C Canada 1783
Gangloff, August	Wolfenbuettel	25/11	A Winterhill 1778
Gastens, Christian	Grabe, Amt Ottenstein	26/00	A Canada 1779
Gauers, Andreas	Campen	29/00	C Canada 1783
Gauers, Johann	Oppenrode	33/02	D Boston
Gazzemann, Andreas	Stiege	40/10	F
Gebbers, Wilhelm	Suepplingen	32/00	D Albany
Gebhard, Johann	Hettehausen/Fulda	50/05	F
Geffers, Ludewig	Braunschweig	31/00	A Winterhill 1778
Geissmer, Bernhard	Timmerlah	33/10	E

Name	Birthplace	Age	Left Service: How Where When
Gelpke, Gottlieb	Zerbst	27/08	A Canada 1783
Gentheler, Anton	Neumarkt, Bavaria	22/07	C Canada 1783
Gerbig, Wilhelm	Obersdorf, Silesia	23/00	C Canada 1783
Gerecke, Johann	Frankenberg	22/01	E
Gerecke, Heinrich	Lesse	24/00	A Yorktown 1778
Gerecke, Heinrich	Neubrueck, Hannover	42/04	E
Gerecke, Friedrich	Kreiensen	34/06	C Canada 1783
Gerecke, Christian	Kreiensen	32/06	C Canada 1783
Gerlach, Joh. Georg	Freystadt, Silesia	35/00	C Canada 1783
Gerloff, Gottfried	Blankenburg	29/10	F
Gerner, Friedrich	Eisenach	33/07	C Canada 1783
Gersky, Joseph	Schoenberg, Saxony	24/00	A Charleston 1781
Gerlig, Carl	Berlin	23/06	C Canada 1783
Gesse, Johann	Endorf, Saxony	21/11	E
Gessler, Samuel	Sangerhausen	24/11	C Canada 1783
von Geyso, Wilhelm, Cpl	Gudensburg	29/00	E
Geyser, Adam	Ellerberg, Hesse	24/00	A Winterhill 1778
Gideon, Heinrich	Erfurt	30/00	A Winterhill 1778
Giesecke, David	Halberstadt	25/10	A Winterhill 1778
Giesicus, Joh. Diedrich, Cpl	Unna	26/00	A Winterhill 1778
Giesser, Heinrich Ernst	Dresden	24/00	A Freeman's Farm 1778
Gille, Friedrich	Uslar	27/07	C Canada 1783
Glackemeyer, Friedrich	Hannover	22/02	C Canada 1783
Glaeser, Christoph	Saalfeld	25/00	E
Glaser, Johann	Deversdorf	32/03	C Canada 1783
Gleichmann, Christoph	Braunlage	29/06	E
Gleichmann, Friedrich	Braunlage	40/00	E
Glitz, Michael	Landenhausen in Riedesel [territory]	31/00	A from prisoner of war camp
Goeckel, Julius	Lichtenberg	34/00	A Simsbury 1778
Goeckel, Conrad	Darmstadt	34/04	B
Goedecke, Heinrich	Stoeckheim	43/09	C Canada 1783
Goerges, Johann	Hohlenberg	35/04	F
Goersch, Andres	from Brandenburg	25/00	A Penobscot 1783
Goettemann, Friedrich	Lithuania	40/01	A Winterhill 1778
Goetze, Andreas (medical corpsman)	Arnshausen (Eichsfeld)	36/01	C Canada 1783
Goetze, Gottfried	Koeppenitz	27/11	C Canada 1783
Goetze, Conrad	Thiede	41/03	D Virginia
Gohse, Christoph	Wolfenbuettel	39/02	C Canada 1783
Graefe, Heinrich	Voldagsen	31/00	A Worcester 1778
Graff, Johann	Arnsberg/Eichsfeld	18/07	A Winterhill 1778
Graff, Heinrich	Hofen, Saxony	46/06	A Winterhill 1778
Grahn, Friedrich	Jerxheim	29/00	E

Name	Birthplace	Age	Left Service: How	Where	When
Graue, Nicolaus	Alt-Muenster/Fulda	22/01	C	Canada 1783	
Greiff, Ernst	Oldenburg	28/00	E		
Grell, Thomas	Breitenstein	23/08	E		
Gremmers, Heinrich	Braunschweig	41/11	A	New Hannover 1778	
Grimm, August (Captain des Armes)	Braunschweig	41/11	A	Winterhill 1778	
Grimm, Martin	Braunschweig	24/00	A	Winchester 1781	
Grimm, Andreas	Hohegeiss	39/11	A	Potomac 1778	
Grimm, Christian	Hohegeiss	27/00	B		
Grimm, Joh. Georg	Stade	30/04	C	Canada 1783	
Grimmig, Joh. Andreas	Merseburg	21/06	A	Canada 1779	
Grimpe, Andreas	Wienrode	24/04	A	Canada 1783	
Grope, Christoph	Schlewecke	39/00	C	Canada 1783	
Gropengiesser, Conrad, Cpl	Suepplingenburg	28/00	A	New Providence 1778	
Grosse, David	Dresden	48/00	A	Winterhill 1778	
Grote, Christian, Cpl	Walkenried	30/06	A	Canada 1783	
Grote, Heinrich	Semmenstedt	41/01	F		
Grotefend, Julius	Rosheim, Brandenburg	33/00	E		
Grotefend, Juergen	Heerte	25/00	A	Winterhill 1778	
Grotefend, Peter	Heerte	26/05	A	Winterhill 1778	
Grotewahl, Andreas	Braunschweig	28/10	A	Cambridge 1778	
Gruendeler, Friedrich	Seweissen, Saxony	26/06	C	Canada 1783	
Gruene, Conrad	Engelade	30/00	D	Templetown	
Gruene, Christoph	Wolfenbuettel	57/01	B		
Gruene, Heinrich	Gittelde	22/05	F		
Gruene, Jacob	Elbingen	28/05	C	Canada 1783	
Gruenebach, Johann	Heerdorf, Ansbach	17/11	A	1777	
Gude, Georg	Bodenfelde	26/00	A	Penobscot 1783	
Gue, Johann	Hildesheim	28/00	C	Canada 1783	
Guenter, Heinrich	Soellingen	46/00	A	Quebec 1780	
Guenter, Friedrich	Koenigslutter	47/00	E		
Guenter, Heinrich	Soellingen	32/07	E		
Guenter, Jacob	Fritzlar	42/11	E		
Guenter, Johann	Glaesersdorf, Silesia	36/07	A	Canada 1783	
Gummert, Christian, Cpl	Koenigslutter	33/07	A	Frederickstown 1778	
Guntermann, Joseph	Heyden/Eichsfeld	24/00	C	Canada 1783	
Gusmann, Ernst	Luedenhorst, Hesse	26/06	A	Springfield 1777	
Gutcke, Joh. Friedrich (Staff corpsman)	Frankfurt/Oder	40/00	A	Canada 1783	
Guth, Friedrich	Halle	28/01	A	Penobscot 1783	

Name	Birthplace	Age	Left Service:		
			How	Where	When
Haacke, Glorian [?]	Braunschweig	30/11	E		
Haacke, Heinrich	Braunschweig	24/11	F		
Haagen, David	Hamburg	18/06	A	Winterhill 1777	
Haase, Ludwig, Cpl	Braunschweig	29/03	B		
Haase, Anton	Braunschweig	25/00	A	Winterhill 1778	
Haase, Georg	Spielberg in Isen-burg [territory]	39/11	F		
Haase, Christoph	Braunschweig	30/05	F		
Habeney, Conrad	Greene	45/06	E		
Habermann, Juergen Paul	Gotha	20/00	A	Canada 1781	
Haeberle, Johann	Grund	26/00	A	Yorktown 1778	
Haeberlein, Matthias	Eichstedt	21/04	C	Canada 1783	
Haemel, Johann	Bemerode in Ried-esel [territory]	23/00	A	Canada	
Hagemann, Arnold	Gross Rueden	30/09	C	Canada 1783	
Hagen, Heinrich	Branderode, Branden-burg	37/07	F		
Hagen, Heinrich	Megnungen	38/09	C	Canada 1783	
Hahn, Christ. Ludwig	Istedt, Thuringia	43/00	A	Winterhill 1778	
Hahn, Georg Friedrich	Altstadt	18/00	A	Canada 1778	
Hahne, Anton	Riddagshausen	45/05	C	Canada 1783	
Hahne, Heinrich	Hohegeiss	30/01	E		
Hahne, Friedrich	Eydorf, Wuerttemberg	20/00	A	Canada 1782	
Hahne, Anton	Brontrueck, Paderborn	29/06	C	Canada 1783	
Halbe, Johann	Braunschweig	30/00	F		
Haldermann, Carl	Wolsdorf	24/05	A	Virginia 1779	
Halleckau, Heinrich, Cpl	Pickelsheim	43/07	F		
Halm, Andreas	Wolbeck	21/00	C	Canada 1783	
Hamburg, Caspar	Steinau	33/00	E		
Hammel, Johann	Thiede	28/00	D	Multown	
Hanekratt, Christian	Braunschweig	30/00	C	Canada 1783	
Hann, Johann	Hunsthagen	23/00	E		
Hanne, Friedrich	Boernecke	35/00	E		
Hannecke, Julius	Braunschweig	33/06	A	Blandford 1777	
Hantell, Johann	Wiesenfeld	32/02	E		
Hantelmann, Heinrich	Linden	23/11	F		
Harbord, Ernst, Cpl	Braunschweig	23/09	C	Canada 1783	
Harbord, Friedrich	Langensalza	23/03	C	Canada 1783	
Harnacke, Conrad	Wienrode	30/11	A	Potomac 1778	
Harras, Gottlieb Ludw.	Braunschweig	25/05	A	Marlborough 1778	
Harries, Heinrich	Osten, Grafschaft Hoya	30/00	A	Yamasca 1782	
Hartjen, Johann	Stadtoldendorf	35/00	E		
Hartmann, Carl, Cpl	Voigtsdahlum	20/09	A	Lewisbourgh 1779	

Name	Birthplace	Age	Left Service: How Where When		
Hartmann, Friedrich	Langelsheim	37/00	D	Boston	
Hartmann, Conrad	Westerode	28/00	B		
Hartmann, Conrad	Langeln	19/09	A	Sawnytown	1778
Hartmann, August	Gandersheim	21/02	A	Winterhill	1778
Hartmann, Friedrich	Langelsheim	33/06	F		
Hartmann, Ludwig	Mackensen	28/00	C	Canada	1783
Hartog, Johann	Hamburg	30/02	C	Canada	1783
Hartung, Rudolf	Halberstadt	43/03	D	Springfield	
Hartung, Joseph	Heiligenstadt	32/06	C	Canada	1783
Hartwig, Christian	from Hildesheim [territory]	25/00	E		
Hasselmann, Andreas	Sommerschenburg	41/00	C	Canada	1783
Hassenbein, Christoph	Wittmarsen	35/00	E		
Hasslinger, Joseph	Roth, Bavaria	32/03	C	Canada	1783
Hassold, Wilhelm	Spandau	28/09	A	Shetekok [?]	1777
Hatschenberger, Johann	Pressburg	26/06	C	Canada	1783
Haue, Joh. Christoph	Wolfenbuettel	33/07	C	Canada	1783
Haue, Georg	Prachtig/Bamberg	25/09	C	Canada	1783
Hauf, Johann	Gernsheim/Darmstadt	34/07	C	Canada	1783
Heckerott, Conrad	Hessen-Homburg	24/06	C	Canada	1783
Heer, Ludwig Christ.	Buschweiler	20/03	C	Canada	1783
Hegenberg, Joseph	Hildesheim	22/06	C	Canada	1783
Heidekamp, Johann	Muenchehof	39/09	F		
Heidemann, Friedrich (medical corpsman)	Clausthal	28/00	A	from prisoner of war camp 1781	
Heindorff, Heinrich	Westerode	26/09	E		
Heindorff, Andreas	Westerode	40/06	F		
Heine, Michael	Pabstorf	56/01	F		
Heine, Christoph	Gersbach in Schwarzburg [territory]	27/00	A	Winterhill	1778
Heinecke, Tobias	Gorna, Saxony	30/06	C	Canada	1783
Heinecke, Christoph	Gross Rueden	29/03	A	Virginia	1779
Heinecker, Anton	Nuernberg	26/00	A	Quebec	1778
Heinemann, Heinrich, Cpl	Braunschweig	32/06	D	Philadelphia	
Heinemann, Lorenz	Erfurt	22/00	A	Winterhill	1778
Heinemann, Heinrich	Halberstadt	47/04	C	Canada	1783
Heinemann, Friedrich	Schoeningen	25/04	C	Canada	1783
Heinemann, Juergen	Wenzen	30/07	A	Frederickstown 1778	
Heinemeyer, Diedrich	Halle, Amt Wickensen	29/00	A	from prisoner of war camp 1781	
Heinze, Gottfried	Loesewitz	31/07	C	Canada	1783
Heise, Johann	Prenzlau	31/06	C	Canada	1783
Heiss, Michael	Ulm	22/00	C	Canada	1783
Held, Joh. Gottfried	Dresden	44/06	C	Canada	1783

Name	Birthplace	Age	Left Service: How Where When		
Hellberg, Johann	Wismar	26/01	C	Canada 1783	
Hellmer, Christoph	Forst	33/05	A	Winchester 1781	
Hellmuth, Heinrich	Weferlingen	38/00	E		
Hellwig, Johann	Gorzheim, Baden-Durlach	36/00	E		
Helmbrecht, Stephan	Goslar	24/00	A	Winterhill 1778	
Helmer, Conrad	Bevern	35/04	E		
Helmsdorff, Franz	Rostock	24/08	E		
Henckel, Julius (medical corpsman)	Braunschweig	22/02	A	Winchester 1781	
Henckel, Gottfried (medical corpsman)	Braunschweig	30/06	C	Canada 1783	
Hendel, Friedrich	Aschersleben	32/00	E		
Hennecke, Heinrich	Burell	33/00	F		
Hennemann, Heinrich	Einbeck	24/07	C	Canada 1783	
Henning, Georg	Paderborn	35/03	C	Canada 1783	
Henninger, Johann	Denstedt in Halberstadt [territory]	29/09	A	Winterhill 1777	
Hepner, Ludwig	Selchow, Silesia	20/00	A	Syringham 1776	
Herbecke, Joh. Georg	Livland [Livonia]	28/06	C	Canada 1783	
Herbst, Heinrich	Dankelsheim	31/02	A	Yorktown 1778	
Herbst, Adam	Varrenstedt, Saxony	25/00	A	Penobscot 1783	
Herchner, August	Leipzig	26/04	C	Canada 1783	
Herhold, Johann	Berendorf/Corvey	39/00	A	Yorktown 1778	
Hermann, Johann	Dorndorf/Eisenach	27/04	B		
Hermsdorff, Carl	Koenigstein	39/00	A	Canada 1783	
Hertlein, Adam	Waldungen, Wuerttemberg	28/04	C	Canada 1783	
Hesper, Friedrich	Braunschweig	23/03	C	Canada 1783	
Hesse, David	Burgdorf	27/08	A	Salisbury 1778	
Hesse, Heinrich	Schlewecke	30/08	E		
Hesse, Carl	Negenborn	22/02	A	Frederickstown 1778	
Hesse, Johann	Biberach [Bavaria]	23/04	C	Canada 1783	
Heuer, Julius	Offleben	49/03	E		
Heuer, Peter	Amt Salzdahlum	35/04	F		
Heuer, August	Sickte	48/06	C	Canada 1783	
Heusinger, Christian	Berklingen	38/11	B		
Heutenschleben, Heinrich	Vorsfelde	32/11	E		
Heyberger, --, Cpl	Teuben, Saxony	39/00	A	New Hannover 1778	
Heydecke, Johann	Gerste/Hildesheim	26/00	D	Northampton	
Heydecke, Christoph	Walkenried	27/09	A	New Hannover 1778	
Heydefuss, Joh. Heinr.	Langelsheim	24/01	A	Canada 1783	

Name	Birthplace	Age	Left Service: How Where When		
Heymert, Johann	Sachsen-Gotha	22/06	C	Canada	1783
Heyne, Conrad	Herzogenbusch	18/02	A	Syringham	1777
Heyne, Maximilian	Muenchen	23/06	A	Canada	1783
Hetzler, Pancrat	Braunau	34/10	C	Canada	1783
Hiep, Bernhard	Eichstaedt/Ansbach	50/03	A	St. Charles	1777
Hilbert, Claus	from Mainz [terri-tory]	28/08	A	New City	1777
Hilkemann, Arend	Northeim	45/06	B		
Hildebrand, Joseph	Duderstadt	29/08	A	Pittstown	1778
Hildebrand, Andreas	Weissenborn, Hannover	20/07	A	Penobscot	1782
Hille, Christoph	Halberstadt	23/07	C	Canada	1783
Hille, Friedrich	Helmscherode	25/03	A	Lewisbourgh	1778
Hillecke, Andreas	Watenstedt	32/02	F		
Hittel, Sigmund Georg	Fuerth	23/04	C	Canada	1783
Himberger, Balthasar, Cpl	Pfalz [Palatinate]	52/00	F		
Hinderkirchen, Johann	Pritzen/Tirol	25/06	C	Canada	1783
Hinte, Heinrich	Braunschweig	19/04	A	Winterhill	1777
Hintersass, Johann[7]	Windersheim	30/00	E		
Hinze, Friedrich	Fuerstenberg	26/06	E		
Hinze, Christian	Elligerode	21/09	A	Hackelstown	1778
Hinze, Christoph	Klein Dahlum	51/06	B		
Hinze, Christian	Deerssen	44/02	D	Virginia	
Hinze, Joh. Friedrich	Altendorf	42/01	E		
Hinze, Anton	Merxhausen	38/02	E		
Hirsch, Rudolf	Braunschweig	31/00	E		
Hirschbach, Friedrich	Braunschweig	46/02	C	Canada	1783
Hirschmann, J. Jacob	Danzig	23/09	C	Canada	1783
Hirte, Christoph	Melberstedt	43/06	E		
Hochmer, Anton	Bernsheim/Mainz	44/00	A	New Hannover	1778
Hoeber, Diedrich	Braunschweig	28/06	C	Canada	1783
Hoefer, Ferdinand Friedrich	Wolfenbuettel	22/03	A	Yorktown	1778
Hoeh, Gottfried	Wittenberg	29/05	C	Canada	1783
Hoepe, Georg	Carlshafen	28/07	A	Cambridge	1778
Hoffmann, Thomas	Wien [Vienna, Austria]	25/04	C	Canada	1783
Hoffmann, Heinrich	Klein Biewende	39/00	E		
Hoffmann, Philipp	Goslar	24/05	A	Hackelstown	1778
Hoff[mann?] Ludwig	Blankenburg	26/07	A	Long Island	1780
Hoffmann, Johann	Hebersheim, Hesse	23/06	E		
Hoffmann, Gottlob	Merseburg	30/00	C	Canada	1783
Hoffmeister, Friedrich	Weddig	36/06	C	Canada	1783

Name	Birthplace	Age	Left Service:		
			How	Where	When
Hoffmeister, Heinrich	Mahlum	28/05	F		
Hoffmeister, Johann	Bockum/Hildesheim	32/09	A	Marlborough 1778	
Hoffmeister, Gottlieb	Nettlingen/Hildesheim	33/06	A	Virginia 1781	
Holland, Christoph	Braunschweig	26/04	A	Winterhill 1778	
Holland, Andreas	Braunschweig	24/00	A	Winterhill 1778	
Holland, Joh. Heinr.	Braunschweig	42/06	C	Canada 1783	
Holle, Gottlieb	Steinbra	33/04	C	Canada 1783	
Holle, Gottfried	Dutsche/Stolberg	22/00	A	Sorel 1782	
Hollemann, Conrad	Dettum	23/00	A	Winterhill 1778	
Hollway, Juergen	Lichtenhagen	22/09	A	1780	
Hollwege, Gottfried	Polzin, Pomerania	43/08	C	Canada 1783	
Holste, Andreas	Lelm	42/00	F		
Holtoegel, Christoph	Einbeck	46/01	C	Canada 1783	
Holzberg, Johann	Gebhardshagen	28/00	E		
Holzberg, Johann	Goslar	32/04	B		
Holzberger, Johann	Cassel [Kassel]	32/02	E		
Holzkamp, Christian	Braunschweig	31/01	E		
Holzwerter, Gottfried	Eisleben	23/02	C	Canada 1783	
Homann, Gottfried	Hirschberg	29/00	C	Canada 1783	
Hommelmann, Johann	Culmbach [Kulmbach]	32/06		Dishonorably discharged at Penobscot 1783	
Hoppe, Caspar	Nazzungen/Paderborn	35/11	E		
Hoppe, Johann	Dettum	30/04	C	Canada 1783	
Horn, Christian	Peine	52/09	B		
Horn, Ludwig	Braunschweig	24/10	B		
Horn, Heinrich	Creutzburg, Saxony	29/06	E		
Hornburg, Christ.	Hoya	35/06	C	Canada 1783	
Hornung, Christoph	Semmenstedt	33/04	E		
Hortus, Georg	Weisseburg, Hungary	36/09	C	Canada 1783	
Hosang, Georg	Braunschweig	46/00	B		
Hottelmann, Hans	Bodenstedt	43/00	C	Canada 1783	
Hoven, Ludwig	Erxleben	34/00	E		
Hoyer, Wilhelm	Helmstedt	20/07	C	Canada 1783	
Hube, Johann	Badersleben	37/01		released at Cambridge 1778	
Hugsmann, Heinrich	Gastorf	48/04	E		
Huebe, Johann	Calvoerde	28/04	A	Winterhill 1778	
Huelle, Christoph	Wernigerode	35/05	F		
Huene, Bernhard	Wolfenbuettel	46/00	E		
Huene, Christian	Grund	35/09	E		
Huenerberg, Georg	Vorwohle	49/11	F		
Hueter, Georg	Erfurt	25/05	E		
Huetting, Michael	Jena	36/00	A	Canada 1783	
Huettinger, Adam	Holkhoven, Bavaria	21/00	C	Canada 1783	
Huettner, August	Northeim	25/02	C	Canada 1783	

Name	Birthplace	Age	Left Service: How Where When		
			How	Where	When
Hummerich, Christ.	Pfalz [Palatinate]	23/00	C	Canada 1783	
Hunstedt, Heinrich	Braunschweig	32/00	C	Canada 1783	
Husung, Friedrich	Walbeck	31/00	A	Potomac 1778	
Hutzel, Nicolaus	Weiss, Pfalz [Palatinate]	46/00	A	Soarts House 1777	
Ifland, Adam	Erfurt	22/09	C	Canada 1783	
Imhoff, Friedrich	Wolfenbuettel	28/00	B		
Immhoff, Ludewig	Wolfenbuettel	27/06	C	Canada 1783	
Immenthal, Christoph	Frankenhausen	28/00	C	Canada 1783	
Isensee, Heinrich	Stoeckheim	22/00	D	Bat Bay	
Iserhoff, Gustav (medical corpsman)	Braunschweig	28/02	C	Canada 1783	
Isselmann, Conrad	Suepplingen	28/00	A	New Providence 1778	
Jacobs, Conrad	Golmbach	27/10	E		
Jahn, Joachim	Uthmoeden	19/00	A	Kenderhook 1777	
Jahns, Martin	Belzig, Saxony	41/04	A	New Providence 1778	
Jahns, Christ.	Glentorf	28/04	A	Freeman's Farm 1777	
Jahns, Conrad	Wolfenbuettel	31/00	A	1777	
Jasten, Christian	Barum	30/00	A	1777	
Jatscheck, Johann	Hungary	37/07	C	Canada 1783	
Jocks, Johann	Luettich [Liège, Belgium]	24/08	C	Canada 1783	
John, Martin	Heiligenstadt	30/06	C	Canada 1783	
Jordan, Johann	Gummern, Saxony	27/02	C	Canada 1783	
Jorns, Johann, Cpl	Ackenhausen	30/09	A	New Hannover 1778	
Juergens, Conrad	Suepplingen	46/04	E		
Juergens, Friedrich	Wolfenbuettel	26/05	A	Quebec 1783	
Juergens, Christian	Bevern	32/02	F		
Juergens, Andreas	Gernrode	27/11	A	Virginia 1779	
Juergens, Heinrich	Watenstedt	25/00	E		
Juncker, Caspar	Stiege	29/05	D	Virginia	
Jung, Georg	Stuttgart	28/00	A	Canada 1782	
Just, Conrad	Carlshafen	28/10	C	Canada 1783	
Just, Friedrich	Stiege	32/02	A	Yorktown 1778	
Kaeseho, Jacob	Illkenrode/Mainz	29/04	C	Canada 1783	
Kaesewieter, Andreas	Harzburg	27/08	E		

Name	Birthplace	Age	Left Service: How Where When		

Name	Birthplace	Age	How	Where When
Kahmann, Heinrich	Braunschweig	38/06	C	Canada 1783
Kalb, Joh. Conrad	Oberheydelbach	31/05	A	Canada 1783
Kalck, Ernst Ludwig	Kuestrin	31/11	C	Canada 1783
Kalckofen, Jacob	Koblenz	24/00	A	New York 1780
Kalossky, Zacharias	Braunschweig	25/00	A	Fishkill 1778
Kaltofen, Friedrich, Cpl	Braunschweig	43/07	A	Winterhill 1778
Kammerer, Andreas	Schwarzenberg, Saxony	39/03	A	Blandford 1777
Kannengiesser, Peter	Elbingerode	46/01	F	
Kappey, Friedrich	Gremsen	24/05	C	Canada 1783
Karpe, Nicolaus	Harburg	32/07	C	Canada 1783
Karweil, Andreas	Aschersleben	35/05	C	Canada 1783
Kassmann, Johann	Aventra/Mainz [terri- tory]	26/04	C	Canada 1783
Kasten, Heinrich	Woltwiesche	28/10	F	Philadelphia
Kastenbein, Christian	Zellerfeld	24/00	A	Virginia 1781
Kauff, Christian	Frankfurt/Main	27/00	A	from prisoner of war camp 1781
Kauffmann, Anton, Cpl	Koenigslutter	22/05	C	Canada 1783
Kaune, Julius	Adersheim	38/00	C	Canada 1783
Kautsch, Gottlieb	Brune, Saxony	22/11	A	Long Island 1781
Kay, Just	Hasselfelde	26/06	E	
Kayser, Wilhelm	Medebach	23/09	A	Penobscot 1782
Kefelder, Valentin	Aspern, Pfalz [Palat- inate]	26/00	E	
Keitel, Johann	Braunschweig	32/06	A	Winterhill 1778
Keller, Joseph	Alsace	24/01	E	
Keller, Carl	Sophienthal	24/06	C	Canada 1783
Kellermann, Friedrich	Lamme	51/04	C	Canada 1783
Kerber, Anton	Ahlshausen	41/01	B	
Kerth, Carl	Walterssen, Silesia	36/08	C	Canada 1783
Kessler, Jacob	Hessian [territory]	24/07		Transferred to the Hessian [troops] 1782
Kestler, Johann	Schuttenburg	22/00	E	
Kestner, Johann	Einbeck	21/00	E	
Kettner, Joh. Andreas	Schaffhausen	33/06	C	Canada 1783
Kinberger, Johann	Ellwangen	48/00	A	Winterhill 1778
Kind, Ferdinand	Zorge	23/06	A	Frederickstown 1778
Kirchhoff, Friedrich	Barmecke	47/00	F	
Kirchhoff, Christoph	Benneckenstein	30/07	E	
Kirchhoff, Juergen	Suepplingen	29/07	E	
Kirchhoff, Aug. Andr.	Helmstedt	40/00	A	Frederickstown 1778
Kirsch, Heinrich	Algermissen	52/09	E	

Name	Birthplace	Age	Left Service:		
			How	Where	When
Klages, Heinrich	Gross Denkte	21/00	A	Nobletown	1777
Klamrott, Heinrich	Blankenburg	40/02	A	Winterhill	1778
Klapproth, Ernst	Nordhausen	26/07	C	Canada	1783
Klatter, Jacob, Cpl	Switzerland	33/01	E		
Kleemann, Adam	Reitlingen	28/02	C	Canada	1783
Kleinbecker, --	Muenden	35/00	E		
Kleine, Matthias	Winnigstedt	25/11	A	Kenderhook	1777
Kleinert, Christoph	Braunschweig	38/10	E		
Kleinert, Carl	Prag [Czechoslovakia]	29/06	C	Canada	1783
Kleinschmidt, Casp. Fr.	Ober-Reussen	41/00	C	Canada	1783
Kletscher, Johann	Merseburg	25/05	C	Canada	1783
Klinge, Arend	from Hannover	22/10	C	Canada	1783
Klingenbrunn, Nicolaus	Wien [Vienna, Austria]	23/00	C	Canada	1783
Klintzmann, Christoph	Calvoerde	30/02	E		
Klosterbauer, Sebastian	Dankhoff	21/00	C	Canada	1783
Kludius, August	Braunschweig	31/00	C	Canada	1783
Kluge, August	Berlin	41/00	C	Canada	1783
Klussmann, Daniel	Erscherode in Riedesel [territory]	26/10	C	Canada	1783
Knabe, Gottlieb	Wellen	25/00	E		
Knackstedt, Ludwig	Greene	22/08	F		
Knauff, Gottfried	Steinbach, Grafschaft Castell	23/07	A	Canada	1783
Kniep, Christian	Schoeningen	24/00	D	Northampton	
Knopf, Christian	Blankenburg	29/05	A	Virginia	1778
Knopf, Heinrich	Wolfenbuettel	30/00	A	Virginia	1779
Knueppel, Heinrich	Gross Buelter/Hildesheim [territory]	32/07	F		
Knust, Andreas	Hohendorf/Hildesheim [territory]	25/06	C	Canada	1783
Koch, Zacharias	Langelsheim	20/00	A	New York	1781
Koch, Andreas	Stiege	20/01	A	Lancaster	1778
Koch, Johann	Einbeck	21/00	A	Winterhill	1777
Koch, Andreas	Quedlinburg	45/00	E		
Koch, Heinrich	Harzburg	44/00	E		
Koch, Anton	Harzburg	31/00	C	Canada	1783
Koch, Daniel	Dankelsheim	43/02	F		
Koch, Joh. Ernst	Salzderhelden	29/06	C	Canada	1783
Koch, Heinrich	Saxony-Weimar	29/00	C	Canada	1783
Koch, Joh. Heinrich	Golmbach	39/06	C	Canada	1783
Koehler, Andreas	Koenigslutter	33/07	E		
Koehler, Nicolaus	Winsheim	44/00	C	Canada	1783
Koehler, Christian	Herzberg	36/00	C	Canada	1783
Koehler, Philipp	Eisenach	27/00	E		
Koehr, Albr. Ulrich	Mannheim	29/08	A	Palmer	1778

Name	Birthplace	Age	Left Service:		
			How	Where	When
Koeller, Franz	Schwalenberg	24/05	B		
Koeller, Phillipp	Hessen-Hanau	29/10	C	Canada 1783	
Koempe, Heinrich	Bernhausen	27/00	E		
von Koenig, Victor, Lt	Osterwieck	29/11	C	Canada 1783	
Koenig, Arnold	Einbeck	38/06	C	Canada 1783	
Koenig, Carl	Magdeburg	28/00	E		
Koenig, Friedrich	Kluempe/Hildesheim	22/07	C	Canada 1783	
Koenig, Johann	Langenfeld/Eichsfeld	22/00	C	Canada 1783	
Koepper, Elias	Einbeck	24/00	A	Winterhill 1778	
Koerber, Johann	Bernburg	36/06	C	Canada 1783	
Koerner, Ludwig	Ahlshausen	45/05	A	Frederickstown 1778	
Kohle, Michael	Sonneborn	24/04	C	Canada 1783	
Kohlenberg, Joh. Andreas	Wickensen	25/10	A	Kenderhook 1777	
Kohlstock, Christoph	Helmstedt	29/03	F		
Kolbe, Christian	from Saxony	46/00	F		
Kolbe, Christoph	Eisleben	20/00		Dishonorably discharged Winterhill 1778	
Koppe, Friedrich	Edissen, Hannover	26/06	A	Canada 1783	
Korreus, Johann	Alsfeld/Hildesheim [territory]	31/00	E		
Kossé, Francois	Franche Comté [France]	47/11	B		
Kowald, Johann	Rostock	32/06	A	Canada 1782	
Krach, Gottlieb	Koenigslutter	25/00	E		
Kraefft, Heinrich	Biewende	39/03	D	Virginia	
Kraefft, Heinrich	Warberg	55/00	F		
Kraehan, Christian	Reindorf/Vogtland	24/01	A	Penobscot 1783	
Kraehane, Heinrich	Braunschweig	32/07	C	Canada 1783	
Kraentzky, Carl	Stettin	38/07	D	Albany (married there)	
Krafft, Franz	Bamberg	25/00	C	Canada 1783	
Kramer, David	Cattenstedt	38/07	E		
Kratikofsky, Friedrich	Marienburg, Poland	24/06	C	Canada 1783	
Kraul, Johann	Nuernberg	37/00	A	Virginia 1779	
Kreickenbaum, Juergen	Gittelde	42/06	A	1777	
Kreickenbom, Diedrich	Emmerborn	45/04	A	New Hannover 1778	
Kreickenbom, Conrad	Wickensen	48/07	F		
Krendel, Heinrich	Cramme	30/06	C	Canada 1783	
Krepper, Christoph	Coburg	26/04	C	Canada 1783	
Kress, Joh. Michael	Lobensbach	23/00	C	Canada 1783	
Kreupe, Johann	Heerte	16/00		Dismissed 1777	
Kreuter, Friedrich	Merxhausen	26/06	F		
Kreutzer, Christoph	Krinderode, Hannover	22/08	C	Canada 1783	

Name	Birthplace	Age	Left Service: How	Where	When
Krieg, Joh. Gottfried	Nordhausen	21/07	C	Canada	1783
Kroeckel, Andreas	Grasleben	37/04	E		
Kroll, Nicolaus	Kiel	29/00	A	Downingstown	1778
Krug, Johann Adam	Eschwege	44/07	C	Canada	1783
Krueger, Georg	Beckenburg	39/09	B		
Krueger, Christoph	Machthausen/Hildesheim [territory]	17/00	A	Winterhill	1778
Krueger, Johann	Braunschweig	24/00	A	Virginia	1779
Krull, Heinrich	Kiel	40/09	C	Canada	1783
Kruse, Caspar	Kalbecht	52/04	B		
Kruse, Georg	Minden	43/00	C	Canada	1783
Krusius, Johann	Bronstedt, Magdeburg	20/00	A	Kenderhook	1777
Kuckuck, Urban	Heynade	25/00	E		
Kuffener, Joh. Ludwig	Pappenheim	41/03	A	Quebec	1783
Kugeler, Caspar	Burg Bamberg	27/06	C	Canada	1783
Kuegelan, Franz	Gebbensleben	33/09	A	Worcester	1778
Kuehne, Christoph	Bevern	26/04	E		
Kuehne, Caspar	Darmstadt	35/00	A	Virginia	1779
Kuehnholz, Christoph	Huettenrode	28/02	E		
Kuemmel, Friedrich	Fuerth	32/04	C	Canada	1783
Kuenne, Peter	Gevensleben	27/09	F		
Kuenstler, Christoph	Breitenworbis	24/00	A	Montgomery	1778
Kulemann, Geghard	Negenborn	49/09	E		
Kulemann, Johann	Braunschweig	40/02	F		
Kumpff, Christoph	Niedorf, Bohemia	43/08	C	Canada	1783
Kundelach, Joh. Christ.	Delligsen	28/08	C	Canada	1783
Kunert, Friedrich	Froesen, Brandenburg	26/03	B		
Kunst, Heinrich	Suepplingen	27/00	D	Boston	
Kunstmann, Bernhard	Koethen	39/00	C	Canada	1783
Kuny, Georg	Ansbach	22/00	A	Canada	1783
Kupfer, Georg	Wilsstein, Ansbach	23/04	C	Canada	1783
Lahr, Jacob	Alshey? [Alzey?] Pfalz [Palatinate]	31/05	A	Saratoga	1777
Lamar, Anton	Normandy [France]	36/02	C	Canada	1783
Lambert, Nicolaus	Picardy [France]	44/00	C	Canada	1783
Lampe, Heinrich	Lichtenberg	20/09	A	Potomac	1778
Lampe, Matthias	Fuemmelse	34/08	F		
Lampe, Balthasar	Thiede	50/11	E		
Lampe, Rudolph	Blankenburg	44/04	F		
Lampe, Friedrich	Roethel/Hildesheim [territory]	40/02	A	Castletown	1777
Lampers, Franz	Striegau	27/00	E		
Lange, Johann	Lauterbach, Riedesel [territory]	24/01	A	Cambridge	1778

Name	Birthplace	Age	Left Service: How Where When
Lange, Wilhelm	Harderode	29/03	D Salem
Lange, Heinrich	Seesen	23/09	A Salisbury 1778
Lange, Martin	Halberstadt	17/00	A Canada 1778
Lange, Matthias	Kloster Scheuren, Bavaria	23/00	Dishonorably discharged Canada 1783
Lange, Conr. Christ.	Hannover	25/07	C Canada 1783
Lange, Christoph	Halle	24/06	C Canada 1783
Lange, Franz	Wien [Vienna, Austria]	41/04	B
Lange, Sigmund	Eisleben	30/07	B
Langelueddcke, Heinr.	Berlingen	32/00	A Bennington 1777
Langemeyer, --, Registrar	Braunschweig		C Canada 1783
Langemeyer, Wilhelm	Immendorf	27/06	A 1780
Langens, Valentin	Holzen	29/00	C Canada 1783
Langheld, Wilhelm	Kniestedt	28/00	E
Langkop, Heinrich	Kneitlingen	35/04	C Canada 1783
Langzeddel, Andreas	Neuwerk	52/07	F
Lanzinger, Johann	Schrobingen, Bavaria	23/04	C Canada 1783
Lappe, Heinrich	Geitelde	19/04	A Winterhill 1778
Larsch, Johann	Schweidnitz	26/03	C Canada 1783
Lattermann, August	Langelsheim	22/00	C Canada 1783
Lattmann, Heinrich	Wolfenbuettel	43/00	C Canada 1783
Lauer, Joh. Conrad	Holzheim	27/10	C Canada 1783
Leepcke, Joachim	Elsebeck	33/00	A Springfield 1777
Leffert, Joh. Philipp	Potsdam	25/00	C Canada 1783
Lehmann, Gottfried	Dessau	60/00	E
Leibheit, Heinrich	Braunschweig	28/06	B
Leich, Ludewig	Wandersleben, Saxony	30/01	E
Leiste, Andreas	Hornhausen, Brandenburg [territory]	23/00	A Peterlittletown [?] 1777 [?]
Lelle, Johann	Goeppingen	27/08	A Freeman's Farm 1777
Lemberger, Andreas	Bennenrode, Riedesel [territory]	24/00	A Canada 1776
Lentz, Jacob	Brume, Prussian [territory]	50/00	C Canada 1783
Leonhard, Caspar	Schwaebisch Hall	29/09	C Canada 1783
Lessmann, Wilhelm	Deensen	34/01	F
Leydolff, Johann	Walkenried	37/00	C Canada 1783
Leyer, Johann Anton	Faulenbach	21/07	C Canada 1783
Leywald, Christ.	Ahlshausen	24/02	A Winterhill 1778
Leywald, Christ.	Haretehausen	28/03	A Winterhill 1778
Liebau, Heinrich	Schlottheim, Schwarzberg [territory]	27/08	A Nobletown 1777
Liebau, Christian	Saxony-Gotha	32/06	C Canada 1783

Name	Birthplace	Age	Left Service: How Where When		
Liebheit, Christian	Hennham	51/02	E		
Lieffert, Lorenz	Trier	24/04	C	Canada	1783
Liess, Wilhelm	Twuelpstedt	50/03	F		
Lilly, Gottfried, Cpl	Wolfenbuettel	36/08	C	Canada	1783
Linckert, Heinrich	Wasserborn/Eichsfeld	34/06	E		
Lindau, Joh. Heinrich	Amt Hessen	21/07	A	Canada	1783
Lindwurm, Wilhelm	Stockhausen, Riedesel [territory]	28/09	C	Canada	1783
Linne, Johann	Stumpfwedel	21/08	A	Canada	1783
Lipcke, Joachim	Zoebenitz	40/09	E		
Lippelt, Heinrich	Helmstedt	35/10	F		
Littge, Gebhard	Harlingerode	34/01	E		
Loebegruen, Alexander	Stockholm [Sweden]	46/00	E		
Loede, Gottlieb	Liebenau, Saxony	25/07	C	Canada	1783
Loedell, Christian (medical corpsman)	Braunschweig	30/03	C	Canada	1783
Loefferer, Carl	Dresden	29/00	C	Canada	1783
Loefferer, Johann	Dannhausen, Bavaria	42/01	C	Canada	1783
Loehmann, Johann	Stoessingen	30/06	C	Canada	1783
Loehr, Heinrich	Braunschweig	28/09	B		
Loehr, Heinrich	Semmenstedt	40/03	F		
Loehrs, Conrad	Grosselbe	26/03	B		
Loewe, Johann	Lauffen, Switzerland	24/10	A	Canada	1783
Loewe, Joseph	Niederode	31/00	C	Canada	1783
Lohmann, Peter Heinr.	Deerstorff, Hannover	29/04	A	Blandford	1777
Loine, Francois	Besancon [France]	41/03	A	New City	1777
Longenhoff, Johann	from Hessian [territory]	39/06	E		
Lorberg, Johann	Oppershausen	20/02	A	Newbury	1778
Lorenz, Christian	Erzhausen	33/00	A	Hampton	1778
Lorz, Heinrich	Zellerfeld	26/09	A	Cambridge	1778
de Loux, Jacques	Flanders [Belgium]	26/07	C	Canada	1783
Lucht, Gustav	Stralsund	23/09	C	Canada	1783
Luechau, Conrad Christ.	Eickendorf, Prussia	20/00	A	Hackelstown	1778
Luecke, Conrad, Cpl	Koerbecke/Paderborn	29/02	A	Freeman's Farm 1777	
Luecke, August	Blankenburg	25/03	E		
Luecke, Friedrich	Grosselbe	26/06	E		
Luecke, Christian	Boffzen	24/00	E		
Luedde, Conrad	Vorsfelde	28/09	A	Lewisburgh	1779
Luedecke, Joh. Philipp	Hildesheim	37/00	A	Canada	1781
Luehe, Christoph	Thiede	34/04	E		
Lueneburg, Friedrich	Braunschweig	22/00	A	New Hannover 1778	
Lueters, Gottlieb	Salzfeld, Saxony	22/04	C	Canada	1783
Luettge, Johann	Gardelegen	28/03	C	Canada	1783

Name	Birthplace	Age	Left Service: How Where When		
			How	Where	When
Luettge, Christian	Landsberg	21/00	E		
Luettge, David	Amitz, Brandenburg	16/06	A	Canada	1783
Luttmann, Johann	Schwegau	21/00	E		
Lutz, Johann	Erbach/Wuerzburg	25/06	A	Canada	1783
Maasberg, Joh. Heinr.	Hohenassel	30/00	A	Virginia	1779
Mackewitz, Johann	Braunschweig	38/04	F		
Maenner, Christoph	Immendorf	37/01	E		
Maertens, Heinrich	Gandersheim	32/09	A	Lewisbourgh	1779
Mahnert, Julius	Braunschweig	42/06	B		
Mahrenholz, Johann	Wolfenbuettel	19/00	A	New England	1779
Mandel, Christoph	Hohenkirchen, Hesse	28/01	B		
Mandel, Christoph	Dreutzendorf	22/00	A	New Hannover	1778
Manecke, Johann, Cpl	Brockshausen	30/00	C	Canada	1783
Marckworth, Conrad	Salder	43/04	E		
Martens, Johann	Salzliebenhall	23/00	E		
Martini, Ernst	Gandersheim	25/10	A	Virginia	1780
Marx, Johann	Goslar	30/00	A	Winterhill	1778
Marx, Daniel	Scharfoldendorf	35/01	F		
Maschweg, Michael	Nuernberg	27/09	C	Canada	1783
Mast, Moritz	Harzburg	31/10	A	Lancaster	1778
Matthaes, Johann	Bruessel [Belgium?]	51/09	C	Canada	1783
Maucke, Joh. Friedrich	Breslau	23/06	A	Winterhill	1777
Maue, Christian	Gadenstedt	22/09	A	Staunton	1779
Meck, Friedrich	Sewesten/Hannover	25/09	A	Winterhill	1778
Mecker, Franz	Marienburg	27/00	C	Canada	1783
Meffert, Franz	Schwabach	23/00	A	Canada	1783
Meinecke, Hans	Belzerode	38/00	E		
Meinecke, Johann	Gummern, Saxony	31/06	C	Canada	1783
Meinschein, Anton	Wolfenbuettel	25/08	A	Soffield	1778
Meisner, Theodor	Striegau	19/00	A	Winterhill	1778
Meisner, Gottfried	Anhalt/Dessau	39/00	A	Peterstown	1778
Melzheimer, Carl	Negenborn	32/00	A	New England	1779
Mentzel, Johann	Christiansstadt	26/00	C	Canada	1783
Merckel, Christoph	Waldkappel	37/00	A	Rappahannock	1779
Merckel, Heinrich	Leutefeld/Eichsfeld	31/05	C	Canada	1783
Merckel, Johann	Heidelberg	24/03	C	Canada	1783
Mertens, Jacob	Winzenburg	27/09	C	Canada	1783
Mertens, Christ.	Deensen	47/05	A	Worcester	1778
Mertens, Georg	Calvoerde	45/06	F		
Messing, Christoph	Elbingen	26/06	C	Canada	1783
Metsch, Johann	Schindeben	23/03	A	Canada	1783
Metzdorff, Gottl.	Berlin	18/00	A	Canada	1783
Metzger, Lorenz	Ober-Eschbach	25/00	C	Canada	1783
Meyer, Joh. Georg	Braunschweig	34/06	C	Canada	1783

Name	Birthplace	Age	Left Service: How Where When		
Meyer, Heinr. Wilh.	Wolfenbuettel	36/00	A	Canada 1783	
Meyer, Gottfried, Cpl	Braunlage	42/00	E		
Meyer, Christ.	Boettcherode	18/00	A	to enemy 1778	
Meyer, Johann	Eschenau	19/07	C	Canada 1783	
Meyer, Julius	Wolfenbuettel	25/00	E		
Meyer, Franz	Welle/Paderborn	31/00	F		
Meyer, David	Wallstorff, Churpfalz [Electoral Palatinate]	24/10	A	St. Charles 1777	
Meyer, Franz	Gross Denkte	40/00	F		
Meyer, Johann	Wickensen	30/11	E		
Meyer, Heinrich	Wickensen	32/04	F		
Meyer, Heinrich	Braunschweig	28/10	E		
Meyer, Daniel	Brechhausen, Westphalia	39/06	A	Freeman's Farm 1777	
Meyer, Heinrich	Deensen	30/11	B		
Meyer, Christian	Ahlshausen	39/04	F		
Meyer, Heinrich	Hohlenberg	29/07	A	Virginia 1779	
Meyer, Friedrich	Bornumhausen	29/02	A	Canada 1783	
Meyer, Georg	Braunlage	36/00	A	Virginia 1779	
Meyer, Philipp	Loewenstedt	40/01	F		
Meyer, Adam	Muehe	19/00	A	Marlborough 1777	
Meyer, Johann	from Mainz [territory]	33/03	C	Canada 1783	
Meyer, Johann	Coelln	22/02	C	Canada 1783	
Meyer, Jacob	Wolkersdorf	26/06	C	Canada 1783	
Meyer, Wilh. Nic.	Cassel [Kassel]	21/04	A	Canada 1783	
Meyer, Heinrich	Lichtenberg	28/00	A	Sawnytown 1778	
Meyer, Johann	Jerxheim	26/00	A	Marlborough 1778	
Meyerding, Georg	Breistedt	45/02	E		
Meylers, Ant. Nic.	Amberg/Pfalz [Upper Palatinate]	43/09	A	Winterhill 1778	
Meyne, Christian	Ottenstein	25/07	C	Canada 1783	
Michael, Friedrich	Hannover	29/06	C	Canada 1783	
Mitterbusch, Heinrich	Kirchbrak	24/00	E		
Moegel, Gottlieb	Grimma, Saxony	20/11	C	Canada 1783	
Moehling, Ludewig	Braunschweig	19/00	A	Winterhill 1778	
Moehlmann, Christoph	Negenborn	33/00	A	Winterhill 1778	
Moehring, Heinr., Cpl	Moerum	29/02	A	Potomac 1778	
Moennecke, Friedr.	Liebenburg	31/00	A	Canada 1783	
Moennecke, Daniel	Salzdahlum	36/03	A	New Hannover 1778	
Mohr, Hr. Simon	Ansbach	24/00	A	Winterhill 1777	
Molle, Michael	Ohrenforth, Saxony	20/07	C	Canada 1783	
Mordt, Hr. August	Ebensdorf, Vogtland	22/01	C	Canada 1783	
Moritz, Samuel (medical corpsman)	Rittkau, Saxony	22/00	A	Winterhill 1778	

Name	Birthplace	Age	Left Service: How Where When
Moritz, Friedrich	Naumburg	48/00	E
Moro, August	Bayreuth	43/01	C Canada 1783
Mortag, Andr.	Jena	25/00	A from prisoner of war camp
Moses, Joh. August	Nordhausen	30/09	C Canada 1783
Muess, Heinrich	Grestedt/Hildesheim	26/04	C Canada 1783
Mueckerling, Friedrich	Bodenburg	47/00	A Yorktown 1778
Muehlhan, Johann	Clausthal	44/00	A Worcester 1778
Mueller, Johann, Drm	Comorra, Hungary	29/01	C Canada 1783
Mueller, Daniel, Drm	Goslar	46/06	B
Mueller, Juergen, Drm	Breitenworbis	23/07	
Mueller, Georg	Angersbach, Riedesel [territory]	26/00	A from prisoner of war camp 1779
Mueller, Heinrich	Burgdorf	28/00	A Winterhill 1777
Mueller, Nicolaus	Eichsfeld	33/05	C Canada 1783
Mueller, Peter	Elsbeck	44/00	F
Mueller, Friedrich	Illmershausen/Darm-stadt	19/00	A Winterhill 1778
Mueller, Friedrich	Braak	25/08	F
Mueller, Heinrich	Greene	29/03	F
Mueller, Andreas	Eger	24/06	C Canada 1783
Mueller, Georg	Osterwieck	37/09	Dishonorably dis-charged 1782
Mueller, Joh. Christ.	Seesen	33/01	E
Mueller, Andreas	Stadtoldendorf	40/05	E
Mueller, Johann	Riga [Latvia]	27/00	Dishonorably dis-charged 1782
Mueller, Franz	Liebenburg	30/06	A Canada 1782
Mueller, Johann	Osterwieck	29/00	E
Mueller, Ernst	Einum	43/07	E
Mueller, Joh. Christ.	Breitenkamp	37/07	C Canada 1783
Mueller, Christian	Wolfenbuettel	35/08	B
Mueller, Christian	Leipzig	40/06	C Canada 1783
Mueller, Friedrich	Brandenburg [terri-tory]	31/06	A Canada 1782
Mueller, Johann	Kummersdorf, Silesia	53/09	C Canada 1783
Mueller, Samuel	Frankfurt	20/07	C Canada 1783
Mueller, Ulrich	Jerxheim	22/01	A Canada 1783
Mueller, Heinrich	Westfelde/Hildesheim	19/00	C Canada 1783
Mueller, Heinrich	Bromberg, Saxony	25/04	A Penobscot 1782
Mueller, Andreas	Parchim, Brandenburg	20/07	A Penobscot 1782
Muente, Heinrich	Zellerfeld	38/00	A Frederickstown 1778
Mumendeich, David, Drm	Wernigerode	41/00	E
Mund, Carl	Braunschweig	44/02	C Canada 1783
Munte, Jacob	Vorsfelde	36/11	A Sawnytown 1778

Name	Birthplace	Age	Left Service: How	Where When
Naacke, Gottfried	Thorn, Saxony	25/06	C	Canada 1783
Nagel, Christoph	Zorge	27/11	E	
Naumann, Sigmund	Magdeburg	24/06	A	Winterhill 1778
Nebel, Johann	Tollmuetz	30/05	C	Canada [1783?]
Neddermeyer, Conrad	Stoetterlingenburg	30/00	E	
Nehrengardt, Joseph	Lothringen [Lorraine, France]	36/10	C	Canada 1783
Neuhoff, Joh., Cpl	Braunschweig	43/06	E	
Neuhoff, Heinrich	Nette/Hildesheim	21/10	A	1777
Neumann, August Friedr.	Langensalza	40/00		Abandoned on a sandbank near Gasport 1779
Nickel, Johann	Wuerzburg	22/09	C	Canada 1783
Niemann, Ludewig	Nordsteimke	44/09	F	
Niemeyer, Heinrich	Astfeld	24/06	A	Springfield 1777
Nienstedt, Conrad	Amsen	24/00	A	Iveritt 1778
Nietz, Johann	Hannover	33/02	C	Canada 1783
Niewand, Heinrich	Braunschweig	24/06	A	Springfield 1777
Nissky, Anton	Neustadt, Saxony	26/08	C	Canada 1783
Noa, Conrad	Holzminden	30/09	A	Frederickstown 1778
Noack, Erdmann	Berlin	28/00	E	
Nolte, Johann	Westborn	34/10	A	Soffield 1778
Nolte, Ernst	Westerhoff	36/03	E	
Nolte, Adolf	Lueneburg	27/00	E	
Nordtmeyer, Heinrich	Freyenhagen, Waldeck	44/00	A	From prisoner of war camp 1779
Noth, Christoph	Krumrode	27/00	C	Canada 1783
Nothnagel, Friedrich	Hamburg	20/00		Killed by wild animals 1777
Nothwehr, Georg	Hessen [town of?]	22/10	A	Saratoga 1777?
Nuennemann, Friedrich	Eichsfeld	38/00	F	
Obermann, Julius	Tanne	41/98	F	
Ochsenkopf, Andreas	Wuelperode	20/10	A	Soffield 1778
Ockam, Heinrich	Dettum	42/02	E	
Oelmann, Heinrich	Klein Vahlberg	31/10	E	
Oelmann, Friedrich	Gebhardshagen	31/01	E	
Oelschlaeger, Johann	Burgsdahl, Brandenburg	34/00	C	Canada 1783
Oelze, Johann	Gandersheim	34/11	E	
Oertel, Christoph	Aschersleben	33/08	C	Canada 1783
Ohle, Gottfried	Berlin	24/03	C	Canada 1783
Ohme, Friedrich	Wienrode	27/08	C	Canada 1783

Name	Birthplace	Age	Left Service: How Where When
Ohms, Michael	Langenstein, Brandenburg	38/05	D Enfield
Ohse, Johann	Papenrode	38/01	E
Opitz, Michael	Neustadt/Orla	30/06	C Canada 1783
Oppenhausen, Heinrich	Rischingen, Lippe	19/10	A Springfield 1777
Oppermann, Franz	Braunschweig	26/00	E
Oppermann, Andreas	Schapen	24/00	A Canada 1783
Oppermann, Heinrich	Bodenhausen	34/11	A New Hannover 1778
Orthner, Franz	Hopfgarten/Salzburg	35/04	C Canada 1783
Osterodt, Heinrich	Hessen [town of?]	40/04	C Canada 1783
Osterwald, Caspar	Starkel, Hesse	19/00	C Canada 1783
Ostwald, Heinr. Conrad	Braunschweig	18/00	A Virginia 1779
Othmann, Johann	Elbingen	23/01	A Quebec 1783
Othmer, Heinrich	Barwecke	51/00	A New Hannover 1778
Othmer, Ernst	Emmerstedt	38/00	E
Otte, Johann	Schoeppenstedt	38/07	E
Otto, Christian	Braunschweig	31/04	A Lancaster 1778
Otto, Caspar	Neisse	24/04	C Canada 1783
Otto, Carl	Hannover	31/00	C Canada 1783
Otto, Gottfried	Braunschweig	30/01	F
Otto, Tobias	Stoetterlingenburg	27/06	C Canada 1783
Ottobusch, Jacob	Weissmann/Bamberg	30/06	C Canada 1783
Paetz, Andreas	Neuwallmoden	23/01	A Sawnytown 1778
Paetz, Conrad	Walkenried	49/06	E
Paetzel, Joh. Christ.	Schoeneben, Brandenburg	29/06	C Canada 1783
Pape, Christian	Lichtenberg	36/00	B
Pape, Andreas	Lesse	29/00	B
Pape, Johann	Lesse	30/09	C Canada 1783
Pasche, Carl, Drm	Goslar	21/07	C Canada 1783
Pasche, Heinrich	Twuelpstedt	31/00	F
Pasemann, Heinrich	Vorsfelde	40/00	A Sawnytown 1778
Patzmann, Wilhelm	Bremen	38/00	E
Paul, Jacob	Bahrdorf	32/02	C Canada 1783
Paul, Friedrich	Weimar	32/02	C Canada 1783
Paul, Joh. Georg	Reval [Estonia]	31/03	C Canada 1783
Paulsen, Christian	from Silesia	42/08	C Canada 1783
Pechow, Andreas	Raebke	30/08	E
Pecht, Johann	Laubach	36/00	A Winterhill 1777
Pechter, Johann	Stuttgart	21/00	A Cambridge 1778
Peitsch, Heinrich	Braunschweig	27/05	C Canada 1783
Penzer, Gottfried	Fuerstenberg	25/00	A Frederickstown 1778
Perlinger, Paul	Kostheim	63/06	C Canada 1783

Name	Birthplace	Age	Left Service: How Where When		
			How	Where	When
Peters, Friedrich	Muensterforth	45/07	C	Canada	1783
Peters, Johann	Rostock	19/09	A	Cambridge	1777
Peters, Daniel	Vorsfelde	32/10	C	Canada	1783
Peters, Joachim	Gargel/Altmark	24/08	A	Winterhill	1778
Peters, Heinrich	Weddelnstedt	38/00	A	Winterhill	1778
Peters, Lud. Rudolf	Boltzum/Hildesheim	25/03	C	Canada	1783
Petersdorff, Tobias	Rostock	31/00	A	Assomption [Ascension?] 1781		
Peterson, Johann	Christiana [Oslo? Norway?]	48/00	A	Canada	1782
Petri, Ludewig	Seesen	47/03	F		
Pfaender, Christoph	Schwabach	24/06	C	Canada	1783
Pfanner, Peter	Wuerzburg	31/06	C	Canada	1783
Pfannkuchen, Conrad	Cassel [Kassel]	26/00	C	Canada	1783
Pfaudt, Friedrich	Stickholm [Stockholm?]	31/06	C	Canada	1783
Pfeiffer, Ernst	Herzerode/Zerbst	24/04	C	Canada	1783
Pfeiffer, Christian	Altenburg	29/02	C	Canada	1783
Pfengel, Friedrich	Culmbach [Kulmbach]	32/00	E		
Pfuhl, Gottlieb	Kemberg, Saxony	25/00	C	Canada	1783
Philipps, Joh. Heinr.	Bodenburg	19/06	C	Canada	1783
Pieper, Johann, Cpl	Linden	32/00	A	Montreal	1781
Pieper, Heinrich	Gross Buchholz	23/01	A	Canada	1783
St. Pierre, Jean Marie	St. Rocques [France]	23/00	A	Quebec	1783
Pilgert, Joachim	Schoenhagen, Prussia	26/00	A	Long Island	1780
Piscand, Nicolaus	Indelheim	19/07	C	Canada	1783
Plaetz, Christian	Herhausen	31/08	C	Canada	1783
Plagge, Johann	Hellerdorf	39/06	E		
Plate, Bernhard	Ollenrode/Hildesheim	35/06	C	Canada	1783
Plettner, Heinrich	Appenrode, Brandenburg	26/06	C	Canada	1783
Plincke, Johann	Burgwedel	38/00	A	New York	1782
Plumbom, Conrad	Wolfenbuettel	37/10	F		
Plumhoff, Heinrich	Kueblingen	41/10	E		
Pohle, Heinrich	Geistdorff/Hannover	32/09	A	Winterhill	1778
Pomerenne, Julius	Woltwiesche	26/00	A	Yorktown	1778
Pongs, Johann	Isenburg	20/00	E		
Poppe, Caspar	Landehausen, Riedesel [territory]	35/00	D	Reading	
Poppe, Julius	Lutter/Barenberg	37/00	A	Yorktown	1778
Poppenberg, Carl	Sophiendahl	30/00	A	Hampton	1778
Potthoff, Heinrich	Holzminden	26/06	F		
Prein, Georg, Cpl	Braunschweig	37/10	F		
Presson, Johann	Lion [Lyon? France?]	26/09	C	Canada	1783
Preuss, Heinrich	Bogau, Saxony	17/00	A	Charleston	1781
Preussner, Friedrich	Berlin	20/11	A	Winterhill	1777

Name	Birthplace	Age	Left Service: How Where When
Probst, Heinrich	Gandersheim	51/00	B
Proche, Rudolf	Dangelsleben, Branden-		
	burg	28/00	A Winterhill 1778
Puckel, Johann	Rothenburg	28/00	A Canada 1783
Pueckel, Johann	Nuernberg	24/03	C Canada 1783
Pueckel, Georg	Wilmersdorf	23/02	C Canada 1783
Radeloff, Friedrich			A From prisoner of
(medical corpsman)	Quedlinburg	28/00	war camp 1778
Rademacher, Bernhard	Braunschweig	29/10	A Winterhill 1778
(Captain des Armes)			
Rademacher, Conrad	Ingeleben	45/00	E
Raeckau, Johann	Lucklum	47/00	A Soffield 1778
Raecke, Nicolaus	Magdeburg	30/00	E
Raecke, Heinrich	Bettmar	22/00	A Kenderhook 1777
Rahmann, Hermann	Delmenhorst	33/06	C Canada 1783
Ramcke, Friedrich	Hamburg	25/02	A Winterhill 1778
(medical corpsman)			
Ramler, Friedrich	Dresden	24/05	C Canada 1783
Rannefeld, --, Cpl	Luettich [Liège,	28/00	A Sawnytown 1778
	Belgium]		
Rasehorn, Christ.	Timmenrode	31/05	A Canada 1783
Rauch, Joseph	Innsbruck [Austria]	45/00	C Canada 1783
Raul, Heinrich	Nette/Hildesheim	27/07	C Canada 1783
Rausch, Heinrich	Lobmachtersen	26/00	B
Rausch, Adam	Freyberg	37/03	C Canada 1783
Rauschenberg, Johann	Hohenhameln	23/06	A Canada 1783
Rehse, Andreas	Braunschweig	27/08	C Canada 1783
Reichenberg, Heinrich	Winsen/Luhe	44/02	C Canada 1783
Reichers, Nicolaus	Wickensen	37/07	A Frederickstown
			1778
Reiffert, Heinrich	Netz/Paderborn	30/09	C Canada 1783
Reinboth, Joh. Christ.	Kredig, Saxony	33/00	C Canada 1783
Reinecke, Johann	Frohse, Brandenburg	27/05	C Canada 1783
Reinecke, Heinrich	Westerode	34/00	A Virginia 1779
Reinecke, Heinrich	Thune	36/01	E
Reiners, Heinrich	Nadungen	47/05	A Saratoga 1777
Reinhard, Heinrich	Olzhofen, Saxony	26/00	C Canada 1783
Reinhard, Jacob	Gernrode/Eichsfeld	28/00	C Canada 1783
Reinhard, Christian	Duderstadt	23/06	A Winterhill 1778
Reinholz, Conrad	Blankenburg	27/07	A Saratoga 1777
Reinwald, Wilhelm	Frankfurt/Main	19/05	A Winterhill 1778
Reiss, Christoph	Braack	21/08	A New Hannover 1778
Reissig, Heinrich	Gadenstedt	33/00	C Canada 1783
von Reitzenstein,	Conradsreith, Saxony	39/10	C Canada 1783
Gottl. Chr.			

Name	Birthplace	Age	Left Service: How Where When		
Remm, Johann, Drm	Haholzen/Bayreuth	24/00	A	Frederickstown 1778	
Remmet, Franz	Neustadt, Silesia	39/00	C	Canada 1783	
Repcke, Hr. Christ.	Barum	35/05	F		
Ressing, Andreas	Hundrungen, Saxony	38/01	C	Canada 1783	
Reumann, Friedrich	Braunschweig	53/04	B		
Reupcke, Christian, Cpl	Volkersheim	30/00	D	Stoughton	
Reussing, Georg	Aschaffenburg	25/06	C	Canada 1783	
Reussner, Carl	Kirchheim, Swabia [Wuerttemberg]	40/08	C	Canada 1783	
Reyn, Heinrich	Allendorf/Ohm	41/06	A	New Hannover 1778	
Rheinfelder, Johann	Bamberg	21/00	A	Winterhill 1778	
Richelmann, Heinrich	Thune	30/03	A	New York 1782	
Richter, Christian	Leipzig	26/02	C	Canada 1783	
Richter, Jacob	Leipzig	30/00	C	Canada 1783	
Richter, August	Torgau	26/00	A	Canada 1783	
Ricke, Heinrich	Gandersheim	35/10	B		
Ridchefsky, Wilhelm	Goldapp, Prussia	22/00	C	Penobscot 1783	
Riemschneider, Heinr.	Wenzen	29/04	A	Canada 1783	
Riesland, Engelhard	Harzburg	21/00	A	Winterhill 1777	
Rietz, Christian	Gerau, Saxony	57/09	B		
Ringe, Carl	Schaumburg	22/06	C	Canada 1783	
Ringelcke, Christian	Magdeburg	23/08	A	Nobletown 1777	
Ringling, Carl	Braunschweig	25/00	C	Canada 1783	
Rinier, Jacob	from Switzerland	31/10	C	Canada 1783	
Rinnert, Christoph	Knesebeck	30/00	E		
Rintelmann, Heinrich	Wolfenbuettel	21/00	A	Freeman's Farm 1777	
Risch, Franz	Huettenrode	55/00	B		
Rittberg, Wilhem Graf [Count]	Koenigsberg	31/03	A	Canada 1783	
Ritter, Friedrich	Budelstadt	29/07	C	Canada 1783	
Ritter, Hieronymus	Erfurt	42/03	C	Penobscot 1783	
Rocktreschler, Caspar	Kraetz, Vogtland	31/06	C	Canada 1783	
Roderfeld, Conrad	Braunschweig	28/00	A	Canada 1783	
Rodewald, Johann	Braunschweig	25/00	E		
Roebbel, Christian	Gremsen	47/01	A	Quebec 1783	
Roemermann, Heinrich	Badenhausen	26/02	A	Canada 1783	
Roever, Heinrich	Thiede	37/02	C	Canada 1783	
Rohbock, Johann	from Saxony	19/00	A	Virginia 1780	
Rohbock, Christian	Freybessigen, Saxony	19/00	A	Charlestown 1781	
Rohde, Friedrich	Braunschweig	27/00	C	Canada 1783	
Rohmann, Adam	Frellstedt, Wuerttemberg	24/02	C	Canada 1783	
Roloff, Arnd[t]	Watenstedt	26/09	A	Springfield 1777	

Name	Birthplace	Age	Left Service: How Where When		
Rose, Heinrich	Gross Hehlen	43/02	F		
Rosenthal, Christ.	Hornburg	30/01	C	Canada	1783
Roth, Georg	Stuttgart	28/04	C	Canada	1783
Roth, Carl	Keyerde	25/09	A	Soarts Haus [House]	1777
Roth, Edmund	Steinbach	24/00	C	Canada	1783
van [von?] der Rous- sell, Heinrich	Merwellt/Luettich [Liège, Belgium]	22/00	C	Canada	1783
Ruehr, Johann	Lutter a. Barenberge	23/00	E		
Runne, Heinrich	Graewe	41/03	F		
Rupp, Johann	Rothenburg/Wuerz- burg	26/07	A	Kenderhook	1777
Rusack, Andreas	Stiege	40/00	E		
Rust, Georg, Cpl	Goslar	38/10	C	Canada	1783
Ruthe, David	Stroepcke, Branden- burg	36/09	B		
Sabora, Joseph	Turnau, Hungary	40/11	C	Canada	1783
Sackmann, Friedrich	Breustedt	27/06	A	Winterhill	1778
Sackmann, Christoph	Muenchehoff	24/00	A	Winterhill	1778
Sackmann, Heinrich	Osterlinde	30/09	A	Cambridge	1778
Salje, Jacob	Gerendorf/Magdeburg	28/05	A	Cambridge	1778
Salzmann, Johann	Wetzlar	25/00	E		
Sander, Friedrich	Gronau	37/00	A	Winterhill	1778
Sander, Heinrich	Thiede	26/08	C	Canada	1783
Sander, Johann	Braunschweig	22/00	A	Virginia	1779
Sander, Conrad	Hohlenberg	35/04	F		
Sander, Christoph	Ottensleben/Halber- stadt	25/07	C	Canada	1783
Sandhagen, --, (medical corpsman)	Wolfenbuettel	25/07	C	Canada	1783
Sangerhausen, August	Cammerfort	28/06	C	Canada	1783
Santy, Michael	Marticat, Hungary	43/10	A	New Providence	1778
Sarges, Heinrich	Oester/Hoya	30/06	A	Canada	1782
Sasse, Heinrich	Stade	47/08	C	Canada	1783
Sasse, Erdmann	Gross Schoenbergen	29/06	C	Canada	1783
Sattoer, Christoph	Blankenburg	22/07	E		
Sauer, Heinrich, Drm	Braunschweig	32/02	B		
Sauer, Johann	Frellsdorf/Bamberg	24/04	C	Canada	1783
Sauer, Joh. Gottlieb	Chemnitz	27/00	C	Canada	1783
Saupe, Gottlieb	Jena	32/03	C	Canada	1783
Saust, Christian	Wansleben, Branden- burg	37/02	C	Canada	1783
Schacht, Johann, Drm	Braunschweig	24/07	A	Canada	1783

Name	Birthplace	Age	Left Service: How Where When		
			How	Where	When
Schade, Christian	Halberstadt	53/00	F		
Schade, Friedrich	Hessen-Homburg	19/07		Transferred to Hessian regiment Losberg 1782	
Schadt, Julius	Erlingbach/Franken [Franconia]	39/00	E		
Schaeffer, Christoph	Herhausen	38/00	A	Winterhill 1788 [sic; probably 1777]	
Schaeffer, Heinrich	Derenthal	32/00	F		
Schaeffer, Christian	Langenstadt/Schwarz-burg	29/04	C	Canada 1783	
Schaeffer, Andreas	Kies/Wuerzburg	29/00	C	Canada 1783	
Schaeffer, Christoph	Neustadt, Moravia	33/00	C	Canada 1783	
Schaeffer, Joh. Franz	Weilstadt	24/07	C	Canada 1783	
Schammel, Carl	Gummern, Saxony	28/06	C	Canada 1783	
Schaper, Heinrich, Drm	Braunschweig	30/10	A	Canada 1783	
Schaper, Juergen	Hameln	26/04	C	Canada 1783	
Schaper, Heinrich	Alefeld	34/07	A	Simsbury 1778	
Schaphardt, J. Conr.	Soehle/Hildesheim	22/09	A	Canada 1783	
Schaudt, Heinrich	Muttersbach/Wetterau	30/09	C	Canada 1783	
Scheel, Friedrich	Neuruppin	28/00	C	Penobscot 1783	
Schelle, Ludwig	Allersheim	19/00	A	Winterhill 1778	
Schelle, Andreas	Neuhaus	32/09	E		
Schellhammer, Conrad	Tilsit/Litauen [Lithu-ania]	31/08	C	Canada 1783	
Schemers, Georg, Cpl	Amsterdam [Holland]	42/00	A	Winterhill 1778	
Scheppelmann, Christ.	Timmerlah	31/00	E		
Scherkoffsky, Adam	Warschau [Warsaw, Poland]	47/11	C	Canada 1783	
Scherneck, Heinrich	Filbel	33/00	C	Canada 1783	
Scherrer, Joseph	Reiche	33/00	C	Canada 1783	
Scherzeberg, Christ.	Hohlenberg	29/10	F		
Schierding, Christian	Gross Lafferde	21/04	A	Winterhill 1778	
Schiller, Aug. Benj. (medical corpsman)	Koenigsberg	25/05	C	Canada 1783	
Schilling, Carl Christ.	Berlin	23/06	A	Penobscot 1782	
Schirmer, Ernst	Helmstedt	25/08	A	Winterhill 1778	
Schlaffmann, Johann	Guestrow	38/00	E		
Schlamilch, Heinrich	Clausthal	33/00	A	Canada 1783	
Schlechte, Friedrich	Riddagshausen	22/11	A	Osweyo [Oswego?] 1778	
Schlechte, Friedrich	Wolfenbuettel	29/01	B		
Schlechtleitner, Johann	from Tirol [Aus-tria]	37/07	C	Canada 1783	
Schleiffer, Sebastian	Kochum, Bavaria	54/07	C	Canada 1783	

Name	Birthplace	Age	Left Service: How Where When
Schliecker, Andreas	Braunschweig	24/07	C Canada 1783
Schliephake, Heinr.	Wolfenbuettel	47/00	C Canada 1783
Schlirff, Michael	Blankenmuehl, Bavaria	22/06	C Canada 1783
Schlossmacher, Michael	Ludwigsburg	27/00	C Canada 1783
Schlue, Philipp	Wolfenbuettel	48/00	A Winterhill 1778
Schluecker, Georg	Brunsen	31/09	A New Hannover 1778
Schlueter, Andreas	Schwarzfeld	20/00	C Canada 1783
Schmaltz, Andreas	Wieda	31/00	A Shetekok 1777
Schmidt, Diedrich, Drm	Hirschbrook	18/02	A Winterhill 1778
Schmidt, Andreas, Drm	Braunschweig	48/09	B
Schmidt, Johann	Neuhaus	28/06	E
Schmidt, Christoph	Sommerwerder/Brandenburg	36/04	E
Schmidt, Ludwig	Holzminden	25/04	E
Schmidt, Heinrich	Wolfenbuettel	24/02	A Winchester 1781
Schmidt, Christian	Oebisfelde	25/09	A Virginia 1779
Schmidt, Heinrich	Braunschweig	46/07	B
Schmidt, Christian	Calvoerde	30/00	B
Schmidt, Andreas	Hanau	55/01	B
Schmidt, Heinrich	Ollerhausen	18/00	A Winterhill 1778
Schmidt, Christian	Boettgerode	41/00	F
Schmidt, Wilhelm	Negenborn	32/03	F
Schmidt, Friedrich	Braunschweig	20/02	A Winterhill 1777
Schmidt, Michael	Berga/Schwarzburg	28/06	C Canada 1783
Schmidt, Johann	Langbriesel/Mainz	29/05	C Canada 1783
Schmidt, Johann	Frankfurt/Main	26/00	F
Schmidt, Joh. Conrad	Fuemmelse	24/00	A Potomac 1778
Schmidt, Heinrich	Holzminden	32/06	C Canada 1783
Schmidt, Heinrich	Breitenbach, Thuringia	39/01	F
Schmidt, Johann	Heilbronn	25/09	C Canada 1783
Schmidt, August	Leithen/Hannover	38/06	C Canada 1783
Schmidt, Joh. Georg	Altstadt, Brandenburg	44/04	C Canada 1783
Schmidt, Jacob	Breslau	25/09	C Canada 1783
Schmidtmeyer, Wilh.	Nuernberg	47/02	C Canada 1783
Schmiedel, Wilhelm	Magdeburg	22/10	A Canada 1783
Schminck, Johann	Coellnhausen	28/00	E
Schmotter, Joh. Heinr.	Velten/Halberstadt	27/09	C Canada 1783
Schmuecke, Friedrich	Coelln	20/11	A Salisbury 1778
Schnabel, Christoph	Gruenstadt	46/00	E
Schnaepel, Conrad	Wangelnstedt	30/02	A Virginia 1779
Schnee, Anton	Nassau-Dietz	27/07	C Canada 1783
Schneider, Johann, Cpl	Erpach	30/04	C Canada 1783

Name	Birthplace	Age	Left Service: How	Where	When
Schneider, Julius	Zellerfeld	28/10	E		
Schneider, Andreas, Drm	Zellerfeld	34/00	B		
Schneider, Conrad	Lichtenberg	33/08	F		
Schneider, Samuel	Lockwitz, Saxony	36/10	E		
Schneider, Johann	Ascher/Bamberg	23/10	C	Canada 1783	
Schneider, Philipp	Halberstadt	30/08	A	Winterhill 1778	
Schneider, Gottlieb	Ziesar/Magdeburg	26/02	A	Canada 1783	
Schneider, Valentin	Zellerfeld	41/00	C	Canada 1783	
Schneider, Joh. Heinr.	Jeschersdorf/ Franken [Franconia]	28/00	A	Spithead 1779	
Schneider, Christian	Obensleben/Schwarzburg	29/06	A	Canada 1783	
Schnelle, Christian	Schoeppenstedt	39/06	A	Frederickstown 1778	
Schnellmann, Heinr.	Gittelde	26/03	A	Winterhill 1778	
Schnoedler, Johann	Wilhelmstadt	22/06	C	Canada 1783	
Schnurr, Joh. Conrad	Jahnsen	27/07	C	Canada 1783	
Schoenberger, Johann	Gleissenberg/Ansbach	25/04	C	Canada 1783	
Schoenecker, Elias Gottl.	Regensburg	25/07	C	Canada 1783	
Schoening, Georg	Braunschweig	29/00	A	Winterhill 1778	
Schoenitz, Georg	Berlin	18/10	A	Pittstown 1778	
Schondorff, Johann	Halle	33/06	C	Canada 1783	
Schoppe, Anton	Einum	19/00	A	to enemy 1778	
Schorse, Andreas	Braunschweig	19/00	A	Kenderhook 1777	
Schott, Friedrich	Carlsruhe [Karlsruhe]	29/00		Dishonorably discharged 1782	
Schrader, Andreas	Neuwallmoden	51/00	A	Lancaster 1778	
Schrader, Christoph	Gandersheim	33/01	E		
Schrader, Georg	Koenigslutter	32/10	A	Enefield 1778	
Schrader, Jacob	Wedensbuettel	42/10	F		
Schrader, August	Vechelde	25/09	E		
Schrader, Julius	Klein Stoeckheim	29/04	B		
Schrader, Heinrich	Vorsfelde	31/06	A	Canada 1783	
Schrader, Magnus	Fuerstenau/Corvey	20/06	C	Canada 1783	
Schramm, Johann	Woebbeln, Lippe	27/00	A	Winterhill 1777	
Schranckemueller, Michael	Oberhausen/Augsburg	18/00	A	Canada 1778	
Schreck, Christian	Bruegge/Hildesheim	17/00	A	New York 1781	
Schreiber, Johann	Copenhagen [Denmark]	27/00	C	Canada 1783	
Schreiber, August	Braunschweig	24/06	F		
Schreinert, Johann	Ulrichstein	42/01	F		
Schrempf, Andreas	Fulda	24/08	C	Canada 1783	
Schrodt, Franz	Augsburg	28/03	C	Canada 1783	

Name	Birthplace	Age	Left Service: How Where When		
Schroeder, Johann, Drm	Derenthal	22/01	A	Winterhill 1778	
Schroeder, Joachim	Hermannacker, Saxony	18/07	A	Nobletown 1777	
Schroeder, Johann	Nordhausen	31/11	C	Canada 1783	
Schubart, August	Sandersleben/Dessau	32/08	C	Canada 1783	
Schucht, Heinrich	Braunschweig	27/04	F		
Schueler, Joh. Heinr.	Westerbraak	52/08	B		
Schueler, Johann	Bunzlau	26/06	C	Canada 1783	
Schuenemann, Christ.	Essehof	28/04	E		
Schuenemann, Johann	Werne/Eisfeld	22/00	C	Canada 1783	
Schuenemann, Friedrich	Hagen/Hannover	23/06	C	Canada 1783	
Schuetz, Leopold	from Austria	23/00	C	Canada 1783	
Schultze, Heinr., Drm	Hornburg	30/00	A	Virginia 1779	
Schultze, Andreas	Berlin	29/08	C	Canada 1783	
Schultze, Heinrich	Magdeburg	39/00	F		
Schultze, Johann	Denstedt/Magdeburg	36/00	C	Canada 1783	
Schultze, Peter	Frellstedt	40/10	E		
Schultze, Johann	Braunschweig	28/02	B		
Schultze, Heinrich	Stadtoldendorf	33/00	E		
Schultze, Bernhard	Harzburg	46/07	B		
Schultze, Carl	Schlottheim/Schwarz- burg	28/00	C	Canada 1783	
Schultze, Christian	Helmstedt	56/01	B		
Schultze, Heinrich	Braunschweig	32/04	F		
Schultze, Christian	Zobenitz	36/09	F		
Schultze, Gottlieb	Breslau	40/05	C	Canada 1783	
Schultze, Ernst	Tangermuende	32/00	E		
Schultze, Carl	Braunschweig	30/08	A	Freeman's Farm 1777	
Schultze, Johann Gottl.	Luebben/Lausitz	21/06	C	Canada 1783	
Schultze, Johann	Braunschweig	57/00	C	Canada 1783	
Schultze, Friedrich	Simmern	23/05	C	Canada 1783	
Schultze, Joachim	Seehausen	43/11	C	Canada 1783	
Schumann, Joseph	Elberfeld	25/11	C	Canada 1783	
Schumann, Friedrich	from Hannover region	32/05	A	Canada 1783	
Schumann, Peter	Lamspringe	38/03	F		
Schumann, Georg Conr.	Remlingen	27/00	A	Fishkill 1778	
Schumann, Joh. Heinr.	Langelsheim	18/00	A	New Hannover 1778	
Schuntermann, Heinr.	Erkerode	24/00	E		
Schwaab, Stephan	Colmar	42/06	C	Canada 1783	
Schwan, Joh. Heinr.	Uetze/Hannover	24/00	C	Canada 1783	
Schwan, Johann	Bernstadt, Saxony	36/00	C	Canada 1783	
Schwarze, Johann	Wolfenbuettel	31/03	A	Winterhill 1778	
Schwarze, Ludwig	Hanau	19/00	A	Winterhill 1778	
Schwarze, Friedrich	Breslau	55/10	C	Canada 1783	
Schwarzhaupt, Johann	Wendemer, Riedesel [territory]	30/00	D	Boston	

Name	Birthplace	Age	Left Service: How	Where When
Schweimeler, Andreas	Hessen [town of?]	43/07	F	
Schweimeler, Philipp	Hessen [town of?]	40/09	B	
Schwieger, Carl	Fuerstenberg	30/10	F	
Sebbesse, Ernst	Wenzen	39/10	F	
Seeger, Johann	Stralsund	23/02	A	Rutland 1779
Seegers, Andreas	Braunschweig	27/00	E	
Segger, Ernst	Beddingen	26/04	A	Winterhill 1778
Seidenzahl, Johann	Weimar	29/00	C	Canada 1783
Seilecker, Friedrich	Hildesheim	26/00	A	Winterhill 1778
Seiler, Joh. Friedr.	Calvoerde	32/00	A	Frederickstown 1778
Seipel, Heinrich	Essdorf	21/00	E	
Seitz, Jacob	Greilsheim	33/00	C	Canada 1783
Seitz, Johann	Ansbach	21/11	C	Canada 1783
Selchow, Friedr., Drm	Oelsburg	22/00	A	Cambridge 1778
Semler, Johann	Erlangen	29/09	C	Canada 1783
Sempf, Wilh. (muster Roll Clerk)	from Hesse	30/00	A	from prisoner of war camp 1778
Sempf, Lucas	Thiebach, Hesse	55/00	C	Canada 1783
Senckel, August	Braunschweig	25/07	A	New Hartford 1778
Serges, Isaak	Wetzlar	22/00	A	New York 1780
Severin, Johann	Bockenem	25/06	C	Canada 1783
Severt, Johann	Nordhausen	31/01	C	Canada 1783
Sieberling, Carl	Koenigslutter	36/00	E	
Sieburg, Heinrich	Harzburg	39/08	D	Albany
Sieckmann, Christoph	Warstedt	37/10	E	
Siedekum, Conrad	Lutter a. Bbge.	38/05	D	Enefield
Siedentopf, Heinr., Drm	Stadtoldendorf	17/09	A	Cambridge 1777
Siefert, Joh., Drm	Carlshagen, Hesse	20/01	A	Winterhill 1778
Siegert, Johann	Hirschberg	21/00	C	Fort Edward 1777
Sievers, Friedrich	Olenrode	23/00	A	Virginia 1779
Simony, Christian	Cassel [Kassel]	37/08	C	Canada 1783
Simpff, Friedrich	Glentorf	42/00	B	
Sinnemann, Christoph	Holenberg	43/01	B	
Soellig, Ernst	Helmstedt	29/03	C	Canada 1783
Soelter, Heinrich	Helmstedt	41/00	E	
Soldow, Friedrich	Potsdam	31/00	A	St. Anna 1777
Sommer, Wilhelm	Herhausen	33/00	D	Boston
Sommer, Friedrich	Weitstedt	24/11	C	Canada 1783
Sondermann, Conrad	Bevern	24/00	A	New Hannover 1778
Sonnenberg, Heinrich	Semmenstedt	41/04	F	
Sonnenberg, Heinrich	Wolfenbuettel	26/00	A	from prisoner of war camp 1781
Sorge, Christian	Calvoerde	28/00	E	
Spaengeler, Johann	Braunschweig	18/00	A	Springfield 1777

Name	Birthplace	Age	Left Service: How Where When		
Spannuth, Heinrich	Boymenrode	24/00	E		
Specht, Julius, (ensign)	Braunschweig	34/00	C	New York 1783	
Sperling, Levin	Stapelburg/Halber-stadt	28/07	F		
Spitter, Christoph	Bodungen, Schwarz-burg [territory]	22/06	C	Canada 1783	
Sporleder, Johann	Boffzen	42/00	E		
Springemann, Christ.	Jerxheim	41/06	F		
Spuerig, Friedrich	Gandersheim	26/10	A	Oswego 1778	
Stade, Christian	Clausthal	31/00	A	Winterhill 1778	
Stadermann, Anton	Fuerstenau	24/00	A	Winterhill 1778	
Stange, Andreas	Elligerode/Eichsfeld	36/00	B		
Stanze, Christian	Peine	31/01	C	Canada 1783	
Stanze, J. Wilhelm	Braunschweig	23/00	C	Canada 1783	
Staudiegel, Anton	Bamberg	23/08	A	Freeman's Farm 1777	
Stauffenpeil, Adam	Breitenbach/Eichsfeld	31/04	B		
Steckhane, Johann	Nettlingen	28/00	C	Canada 1783	
Steger, Johann	Hausen bei Nuernberg	21/06	C	Canada 1783	
Steghan, Gottlieb	Westerode	21/00	A	Winterhill 1778	
Stein, Theodor (medical corpsman)	Holzminden	32/04	C	Canada 1783	
Stein, Friedrich	Potsdam	23/03	A	Freeman's Farm 1777	
Stein, Philipp	Braunschweig	41/09	F		
Stein, Carl	Wiesbaden	30/06	C	Canada 1783	
Steinbrueck, Heinr. Christ.	Ermanstedt, Thuringia	22/11	A	Canada 1783	
Steinhoff, Johann	Luedingen	34/08	A	Sharon 1778	
Steinmann, Joh. Heinr.	Wolfenbuettel	25/10	C	Canada 1783	
Stendel, Johann	Luechow	25/00	E		
Stenger, Philipp	Mainz	26/03	C	Canada 1783	
Stephan, Ludewig	Ingersleben	33/04	E		
Stieger, Christoph	Schoeningen	44/00	D	Cleverac	
Stirn, Johann	Schwarzenberg	28/07	C	Canada 1783	
Stisser, Heinrich	Braunschweig	21/06	A	Kenderhook 1777	
Stoeckermann, Rudolf	Greene	27/02	A	Potomac 1778	
Stoehr, Johann	Heidelberg	38/00	E		
Stoerell, Carl	Erzhausen	29/04	B		
Stolle, Andreas	Emmersfeld	47/06	E		
Stolte, Heinrich	Dummelbeck	24/06	A	Canada 1783	
Stolze, Johann	Erzhausen/Eichsfeld	23/00	A	Syringham 1777 [Tyringham?]	
Stolzenberg, Fried-rich Christoph	Muehlhausen	20/10	A	Canada 1783	
Straub, Caspar	Muehlhausen	22/06	C	Canada 1783	

Name	Birthplace	Age	Left Service: How	Where	When
Strauss, Johann	Langelsheim	57/07	E		
Strauss, Heinrich	Hamburg	21/05	A	Westfield	1777
Stroding, Johann	Magdeburg	27/10	F		
Stroetz, Friedrich	Tokay, Hungary	38/00	A	Canada	1778
Struve, Christoph	Zellerfeld	28/03	A	Canada	1783
Stuebenitzky, Carl	Leinefelde/Eichsfeld	25/00	A	Canada	1783
Stueber, Christian	Abissingen, Saxony	41/00	A	Canada	1783
Stuerig, Conrad	Coppengrave	39/10	B		
Suess, Johann Paul	Schweinau/Nuernberg	22/06	C	Canada	1783
Suess, Heinrich	Magdeburg	22/05	C	Canada	1783
Suesse, Johann	Lovel	44/00	C	Canada	1783
Summer, Michael	Moenchheim	36/03	C	Canada	1783
Tacke, Johann	Warbsen	23/00	A	from prisoner of war camp	1781
Tacke, Anton	Forst	33/04	F		
Taeger, Andreas	Magdeburg	21/06	C	Canada	1783
Tahde, Heinrich	Braunschweig	17/11	A	Freeman's Farm	1777
Tappe, Heinrich	Bolzen	28/06	C	Canada	1783
Taufall, Christian	Engelade	34/04	A	Winterhill	1778
Tauschmann, Gottfried Ludwig	Weissensee	31/11	C	Canada	1783
Tehtmeyer, Ludwig	Brunckhausen/Corvey	33/04	C	Canada	1783
Temier, Philipp	Bamberg	26/00	E		
Thiede, Heinrich	Gifhorn	57/04	D	Rutland	
Thiedemann, Georg Ludwig	Burg/Magdeburg	22/00	A	Winterhill	1778
Thiele, Friedrich Lorenz, Cpl	Reichhausen, Hannover	35/08	C	Canada	1783
Thiele, Heinrich, Drm	Graevenstein	58/00	B		
Thiele, David	Bernburg	28/00	C	Canada	1783
Thiele, Heinrich	Lichtenberg	36/04	F		
Thiele, Andreas	Hedeper, Brandenburg	38/04	E		
Thiele, Joh. Georg	Weichen, Schwarzburg [territory]	17/00	A	Charleston	1781
Thielebein, Friedrich	Koenigslutter	36/00	C	Canada	1783
Thielemann, Harm	Ahlum	42/00	F		
Thienell, Peter	Zellerfeld	28/09	E		
Thiess, Ferdinand	Herstelle	30/09	A	Lewisbourgh	1779
Thiess, Carl	Schoeningen	39/09	A	Worcester	1778
Thiess, Heinrich	Braunschweig	33/00	F		
Thiess, Johann	Backendorf	24/06	C	Canada	1783
Thofft, Adam	Langfeld/Eichsfeld	25/02	A	Canada	1783
Thomae, Gottlieb	Wolkenuetz, Saxony	27/08	C	Canada	1783
Thomas, -- (auditor)	Wolfenbuettel	31/10	C	Canada	1783

Name	Birthplace	Age	Left Service: How Where When		
Thomas, Jacob	Boernecke	39/04	E		
Thomas, Julius	Braunschweig	20/00	A	Lancaster	1778
Thormann, Andreas	Opperhausen	35/03	E		
Tiebe, Conrad (stable boy for paymaster wagon)	Warnstedt	29/06	A	Reading	1781
Tielecke, Andreas	Altenhausen	33/04	C	Canada	1783
Tietge, Heinrich	Gronau/Hildesheim	25/08	E		
Tiettge, Heinrich	Wolfenbuettel	31/02	F		
Tietz, Ludwig	Braunschweig	30/00	A	Winterhill	1778
Tillert, Christoph (medical corpsman)	Heinrichs, Saxony	26/04	C	Canada	1783
Tippe, Wilhelm	Trautenstein	21/02	A	Syringham 1777 [Tyringham?]	
Tittel, Heinrich	Koennern	27/11	A	Winterhill	1778
Toelle, Johann	Ramingen/Wuerzburg	28/00	C	Canada	1783
Tolle, Juergen	Braunschweig	38/08	F		
Tornier, Carl	Osterwieck	25/00	C	Canada	1783
Tortisch, Thomas	from Croatia	57/07	E		
Tost, Julius	Salzliebenhall	28/00	C	Canada	1783
Tost, Julius	Elligerode	21/09	A	Lancaster	1778
Tost, Christian	Clausthal	29/00	C	Canada	1783
Traumann, Heinrich	Klenzen	24/00	A	Kenderhook	1777
Trautner, Peter	from the Palatinate	26/00	C	Canada	1783
Treues, Johann	Litzingen/Hannover	42/06	B		
Treutz, Caspar	Buschlach, Wuerz-burg [territory]	37/06	C	Canada	1783
de Triff, Friedrich, Cpl	Bayreuth	25/10	C	Canada	1783
de Triff, August	Bayreuth	22/08	C	Canada	1783
Trottmann, Anton	Hadamar	52/06	C	Canada	1783
Truesselmann, Christ.	Baeseckendorf/Eichs-feld	39/00	E		
Turnau, Benedict (medical corpsman)	Rauhaus/Hannover	28/00	C	Canada	1783
Uckermann, Wilhelm	Holzen, Amt Roten-stein	25/04	A	Winterhill	1778
Uhde, Johann	Seboldshausen	28/00	E		
Uhle, Heinrich	Nordsteimke	27/00	E		
Uhlendorf, Friedrich, Drm	Rauschenwasser/Han-nover	17/00	A	Norfolk	1777
Uhr, Georg	Liegnitz	20/08	A	Saratoga	1777
Ullrich, Friedrich	Halberstadt	24/00	A	Winterhill	1778
Ussner, Christian	Darmstadt	30/00	A	New Hannover 1778	

Name	Birthplace	Age	Left Service: How Where When		
Vatterott, Joh. Valentin	Nieder-Urschell/ Eichsfeld	20/09	C	Canada	1783
Veching, Johann	Erfurt	26/10	E		
Vechner, Joseph	Hildesheim	29/11	A	Wilbraham	1778
Verdries, Christoph	Hildesheim	28/08	C	Canada	1783
Vernau, Joh. Christ.	Gotha	23/02	A	Canada	1783
Vetter, Friedrich	Darmstadt	21/03	A	Winterhill	1778
Viano, Andreas	from Savoy [Italy]	29/00	A	Canada	1783
Vogel, Wilhelm	Hohegeiss	42/09	B		
Vogel, Joh. Georg	Rodersberg, Saxony	28/00	A	Winterhill	1778
Vogel, J. Georg	Rotersberg	19/00	A	Canada	1778
Vogel, Stephan	Olensdorf, Bavaria	28/07	C	Canada	1783
Vogeler, Friedrich	Hessen [town of?]	36/07	C	Canada	1783
Vogelsang, Johann	Gustedt/Hildesheim	26/10	A	Winterhill	1777
Vogelsberg, Christoph	Regensdorf, Branden- burg	48/01	C	Canada	1783
Voges, Heinrich	Langelsheim	24/00	A	Virginia	1780
Voges, Christian	Kreiensen	26/00	E		
Voges, Christ. Ernst	Braunschweig	31/00	A	Potomac	1778
Voges, Heinrich	Bohnstedt	27/00	A	Winterhill	1778
Voges, Joh. Heinr.	Greene	25/03	C	Canada	1783
Voigt, Daniel	Hohegeiss	22/00	A	New Hannover	1778
Volck, Heinrich	Hoehne/Hannover	36/00	A	from prisoner of war camp	1777
Vollmann, Sigmund	Wiessenbrunn/Wuerz- burg	33/08	C	Canada	1783
Vollrath, Heinrich, Drm	Rueningen	20/01	A	Sawnytown	1778
Voss, Johann	Gruenenplan	34/10	F		
Voss, Chr. Heinrich	Uelmke/Lueneburg	24/00	A	Kenderhook	1777
Voss, Johann	Erzhausen	30/10	F		
Voss, Christian	Northeim	40/05	C	Canada	1783
Wacker, Johann	Lauterbach	24/03	C	Canada	1783
Wagemann, Conrad	Borntrueck/Paderborn	37/00	A	Winterhill	1778
Wagener, Christian	Calvoerde	30/03	D	Lancaster	
Wagener, Joh. Andreas	Blankenburg	26/09	A	Canada	1783
Wagener, Gottfried	Rothenburg	25/00	E		
Wagener, Ferdinand	Tappenburg	32/00	E		
Wagener, Johann	Naumburg	28/07	B		
Wagener, Joh. Georg	Dorsen, Bavaria	22/09	C	Canada	1783
Wagener, Christ.	Radern, Mecklenburg	35/07	C	Canada	1783
Wagenknecht, Herm.	Darmstadt	48/02		Missing 2 August 1783	
Wahl, Joh. Michael	Breitenbach	24/08	C	Canada	1783
Wahnschape, Christ.	Blankenburg	39/08	F		
Wahnschape, Hr. Andr.	Hoiersdorf	23/02	F		

49

Name	Birthplace	Age	Left Service: How Where When		

Name	Birthplace	Age	How	Where When
Walch, Bernhard	Langemoede/Wuerzburg	25/07	A	Canada 1783
Walter, Friedrich	Oppershausen	32/04	F	
Warnecke, Heinrich	Holzminden	30/08	C	Canada 1783
Warnecke, Johann	Litthausen	27/00	A	Canada 1783
Warnecke, Joh. Ludwig	Helmstedt	41/06	A	Canada 1783
Weber, Heinrich	Braunschweig	42/10	E	
Weber, Johann	Solms-Braunfels	45/06	F	
Weber, Nicolaus	from the Alsace	48/07	E	
Weber, Peter	Heyl	27/00	C	Canada 1783
Weber, Johann	Oettlingen	23/00	C	Canada 1783
Weber, Joh. Georg	Hempenfeld/Nuernberg	29/08	C	Canada 1783
Webse, Philipp	Stade	23/05	A	Winterhill 1778
Wecke, Ludewig	Hagen, Brandenburg	24/00	A	Nobletown 1777
Weddig, Joh. Peter	Garleben	25/05	C	Canada 1783
Wedekind, Heinr., Drm	Kirchbach	24/00	A	Yorktown 1778
Wedekind, Heinrich	Kirchbraak	24/08	A	Soffield 1778
Wedemann, Daniel	Hamburg	22/00	E	
Wegelein, Matth.	Zollingen	23/00	C	Canada 1783
Wegelin, Georg	Ansbach	42/06	C	Canada 1783
Wegener, Carl	Leipzig	30/00	E	
Wegener, Caspar	Tauberzell/Ansbach	28/00	C	Canada 1783
Weger, Martin	Schneeberg	47/08	F	
Wehe, Ernst	Oppershausen	33/05	A	Frederickstown 1778
Wehling, Ernst	Muenster	20/07	A	Canada 1783
Wehmeyer, Christ.	Markoldendorf	19/06	A	Canada 1783
Wehr, Hugo	Bardloff/Eichsfeld	25/00	A	Canada 1783
Wehrmeyer, Christ.	Markoldendorf	19/06	A	Canada 1783
Weidling, Christoph	Lochau	19/03	A	from march column 1778
Weigel, Christoph	Greene	32/10	A	Virginia 1779
Weinkueber, Johann	Brobach/Nuernberg	25/07	C	Canada 1783
Weinreich, Georg	Kreuzberg/Meiningen	34/00	A	Soarts Haus 1777 [Sword's House]
Weiss, Anton	Bayreuth	30/00	E	
Weissenborn, J. Friedr.	Buehringen	25/11	C	Canada 1783
Weissgerber, Ant. Jac.	Westzlar	19/06	A	Kenderhook 1777
Weissleder, Christ.	Stiege	22/03	A	Pieterstown 1778
Weithe, Johann	Rostock	35/05	C	Canada 1783
Welge, Heinrich	Lobmachtersen	23/02	E	
Welling, Christoph	Wolfenbuettel	32/05	A	Winterhill 1778
Wenzel, August	Liebenburg	17/00	A	1777
Weppler, Conrad	Hessen-Homburg	21/01	A	Kenderhook 1777
Werner, Heinrich	Oebisfelde	32/06	A	Winterhill 1778
Werneri, Joh. Christ.	from Italy	42.06	A	Canada 1783
Wesche, Johann	Braunschweig	30/06	A	Canada 1783

German-American Genealogical Research

Monograph No. 2

MERCENARIES FROM ANSBACH AND BAYREUTH, GERMANY,

WHO REMAINED IN AMERICA AFTER THE REVOLUTION

Clifford Neal Smith

List of names taken from Erhard Staedtler, *Die Ansbach-Bay-reuth Truppen in amerikanischen Unabhaenigkeitskrieg, 1777-1783*. Freie Schriftenfolge der Gesellschaft fuer Familien-forschung in Franken, Band 8 (Nuernberg: Kommissionsverlag Die Egge, 1956) by permission of the Gesellschaft fuer Familienforschung in Franken, 85 Nuernberg, Archivstrasse 17. The names have, however, been changed from an alphabetical to a soundexed arrangement. Incidental information regarding individual soldiers has been translated from the German.

MERCENARIES FROM ANSBACH AND BAYREUTH, GERMANY,
WHO REMAINED IN AMERICA AFTER THE REVOLUTION

Clifford Neal Smith

Undoubtedly, the most important work on the Ansbach and Bayreuth mercenaries sent to America in British service during the Revolution is the doctoral dissertation of Dr. Erhard Staedtler, entitled *Die Ansbach-Bayreuther Truppen in Amerikanischen Unabhaengigkeitskrieg, 1777-1783* [The Ansbach-Bayreuth Troops in the American Revolution, 1777-1783].[1] The lists of names which appear therein were transcribed principally from muster rolls in the Public Records Office, London, augmented by additional data from German repositories, particularly the Staatsarchiv Nuernberg.

According to Lowell,[2] until the appearance of Staedler's work the authority on the subject, the following Ansbach-Bayreuth troops were sent to America:

1777	main contingent	1285	
1777	fall contingent	318	1603
1779			157
1780			152
1781			205
1782			236
	Total		2353
Returned to Germany, Fall 1783			1183
Did not return (incl. dead)			1170

The lists used by Staedtler show a higher total number of mercenaries, due apparently to the fact that some troopers were recruited in America.[3] It seems possible, also, that some of the discrepancy may be due to "padding," as it was customary to add supernumerary positions for which the English made payment, but which were not actually filled. The additional funds for these vacant positions accrued to company accounts. Staedtler's figure for soldiers not returning to Europe (desertions, deaths, settlement in Canada) is lower than Lowell's, however. Staedtler computes the following:

	Officers	*Men*	*Total*
Returned to Germany before 1783	–	127	127
Returned to Germany in September, 1783	73	1184	1257
Killed in action, or died, in America	12	389	401
Deserters and settlers in America	3	676	679
Total	88	2376	2464

The Ansbach and Bayreuth units were attached directly to the
British army commanded by generals Howe and Clinton. The Ansbach regiment served at Philadelphia, Newport, Springfield, and Yorktown. The
Bayreuth regiment was at Philadelphia, Newport, and Yorktown. The Ansbach Jaegers (Chasseurs) were attached to the Hessian Jaeger Corps and
fought in nearly every operation of the war.[4] Thus, researchers may
hypothesize that most deserters are likely to have made their ways to
German-speaking areas of Pennsylvania, excepting for the Jaeger deserters,
who may have fled to almost any of the thirteen colonies. A few deserters
are known to have settled in Virginia.

In the list hereinafter the units in which these soldiers served
have been designated as A=Ansbach Regiment, or B=Bayreuth Regiment, or
J=Jaeger Battalion. This is important to the genealogical researcher because it gives a possible dlue as to the soldiers' places of origin.[5]
In practice, the companies were known by the names of their captains,
as follows:

REGIMENT ANSBACH (EYB, VOIT)

Company	*1*	*2*	*3*	*4*	*5*
Jun 1777	Eyb	Reitzenstein	Stain	Ellrodt	Erckert
Dec 1777	"	"	"	Waldenfels	Ellrodt
Jun 1778	Voit	"	"	"	"
Jun 1779	"	"	"	Seitz	"
Dec 1781	"	Seitz	"	Metzsch	"
Jun 1783	"	"	"	"	"

REGIMENT BAYREUTH (VOIT, SEYBOTHEN)

Company	1	2	3	4	5
Jun 1777	Seybothen	Beust	Eyb	Voit	Seitz
Jun 1778	"	"	"	Molithor	"
Jun 1779	"	"	"	Quesnoy	Molithor
Jun 1783	"	"	"	"	"
Sep 1783	Reitzenstein	"	"	"	"

JAEGER (CHASSEUR) BATTALION (CRAMON, REITZENSTEIN)

Company	1	2	3	4	5	6
Jun 1777	Cramon					
Jun 1779	Waldenfels					
Dec 1779	"	Roeder				
Dec 1781	"	"	Reitzen-stein			
Dec 1782	"	"	"	Tritz-schler	Wurm	
Jun 1783	"	"	"	"	Kruse	Koenitz

Staedtler has supplemented his lists with valuable information from several other sources. Used herein are the following abbreviations for these additional manuscript materials:

Abbreviation	Description

AKA = Ansbacher Kriegskaten [Ansbach War Files] in Staatsarchiv Nuernberg.

AMKB = Militaerkirchenbuecher der Militaerpfarrei bei St. Johannis, Ansbach [Military Church Records of the Military Chaplaincy at St. Johannis Church, Ansbach] Microfilm no. 164, to be consulted at the Landeskirchliches Archiv, Nuernberg.

Ans.Ms.hist.487 = a manuscript to be consulted in the Bibliothek des Historisches Verein von Mittelfranken, Ansbach.

Bor = Diary of an unknown soldier. The original of this manuscript is in the Huntington Library, San Marino, California. A transcript was made by Dr. Victor von Borosini in 1929 for the Historisches Verein . . . von Oberfranken zu Bayreuth.

BRM = Bear River Muster Rolls (Halifax, Nova Scotia). Not further described by Staedtler.

Doe = Diary of Johann Conrad Doehla. The original manuscript has been lost, but there have been several published versions. The most readily available of these versions will be found in *Deutsch-Amerikanische Geschichtsblaetter* (Chicago), volume 3 (1917) 107.

DP = Dorchester Papers, Royal Institution, London.

Gilroy = Marion Gilroy, *Loyalists and Land Settlements in Nova Scotia*. Public Archives of Nova Scotia, Publication no. 4. Halifax, 1937.

HAV = Description of this manuscript seems to have been omitted by Staedtler. Perhaps the Gesellschaft fuer Familienforschung in Franken e.V. would be able to identify it. Their address is given below.

Pr = Diary of First Lieutenant Johann Ernst Prechtel. The location of this manuscript is not given by Staedtler but is presumed to be in the Staatsarchiv Nuernberg under call number HStAM II, IV n 2.

The names hereinafter have been presented in soundexed order, because there is considerable evidence that many of the surnames were changed in America to conform to English notions of orthography. Researchers should soundex the American spelling of the surname they are seeking, using the coding in Appendix I hereto, and enter the list under the appropriate soundex number, which will reveal probable variations between the original German and the current American spellings. For example, using the soundex rules in Appendix I, the Americanized name Angelbright would be 7-524, and referral to that soundex number in the list hereinafter discloses the German surname Engelbrecht as a possible equivalent, and Johann Engelbrecht, a soldier of the Bayreuth Regiment, a possible ancestor.

Researchers finding surnames of interest to them should consult the following German regional genealogical society for further aid:

Gesellschaft fuer Familienforschung in Franken e.V.,
D-85 Nuernberg,
Archivstrasse 17,
WEST GERMANY

In a forthcoming number of the *German-American Genealogical Research Monographs*,[6] the Ansbach and Bayreuth muster rolls found in repositories in the United States will be published. Some of these muster rolls bear notations as to where the soldiers deserted, a most valuable supplemental clue for the genealogist.

NOTES

1. Dissertation submitted to the Faculty of Philosophy, Friedrich-Alexander University, Erlangen, Bavaria, in 1955. The dissertation was published by Kommissionsverlag Die Egge, Nuernberg, in 1956 and became volume 8 of the *Freie Schriftenfolge der Gesellschaft fuer Familienforschung in Franken e.V.* I am indebted to Dr. O. Puchner, Oberarchivdirektor and 1. Vorsitzender of the Society, for permission to translate and reproduce relevant portions from this valuable work.

2. Edward J. Lowell, *The Hessians and the Other German Auxiliaries of Great Britain in the Revolutionary War* (1884; reprint ed., New York: Kennikat Press, 1965). *See* Appendix D, p. 300.

3. Staedtler, *op.cit.*, 92-93. There is an unreconciled difference of five men in the number returning to Germany in September 1783.

4. Lowell, *op.cit.*, 298.

5. According to Staedtler, *op.cit.* 91, there appears not to be any extant record of the places of origin or ages of the Ansbach and Bayreuth soldiers, so researchers are left with few clues.

6. Clifford Neal Smith, *Muster Rolls and Prisoner-of-War Lists in American Archival Collections Pertaining to the German Mercenary Troops Who Served with the British Forces during the American Revolution.* German-American Genealogical Research Monograph Number 3, in three parts (DeKalb, Illinois: Westland Publications, 1974).

6

1-100   BUOB, Joseph, Jaeger, J/1. Last mentioned on muster roll of
           Jun 1780.

         POPP, Johann, private, B/4. Deserted 18 Sep 1782.

         POPP, Joseph, private, A/4. Deserted 28 Dec 1782.

1-140   POEBEL, Georg Karl, private, A/5, A/2. Deserted 11 May 1783.
           From Leutershausen; studied in Weikershausen; in Pressburg
           [Bratislava] in 1774; in Erlangen in 1776.

1-155   BUBMANN, Matthias, private, B/2. Absent since Jun 1783. Ac-
           cording to Ansb.Ms.hist.487, he was the son of Johann Chris-
           toph Bubmann of Solnhofen, who was granted support in grain
           by the Ansbach government.

1-200   BECK [Baeck], Johann, 2d Lt., J/1. Deserted Jan 1779.

         BECK, Johann, private, B/2. Deserted 10 Aug 1781.

         BECK, Johann Georg, private, B/4. Deserted 10 May 1783.

         BEETZ, Georg, private, A/3. Last mentioned on muster roll of
           Dec 1782.

         BOCK, Paul, Jaeger, J/2. Deserted 13 Oct 1781.

         BUSCH, Leonhard, private, A/2. Deserted 7 Aug 1781.

         FICK, Johann, grenadier, B/5. No further information.

         FOX. [Might have changed German surname Fuchs to English equi-
           valent. *See* Fuchs, 1-220.]

1-220   FUCHS, Johann, private, B/4. Enlisted with the American troops.

         FUCHS, Johann Kaspar, private, B/4. Deserted 13 May 1783 .

1-234   FICHTEL, Peter, private, B/4. Deserted 10 May 1783

1-235   PECHTNER, Peter, private, A/4, A/1. No further information.

1-240   BUCKEL, Georg Matthias, private, B/1. Deserted 31 Jan 1782.

         BUTZEL, Johann, private, B/2. Last mentioned on muster roll
           of Dec 1782.

         FISEL, Johann Martin, private, B/2. Deserted 27 May 1782.

         FOGEL. [Might have changed the spelling of German surname Vogel
           to preserve original German pronunciation. *See* Vogel 7-240.]

         PUTZEL, Johann, private, B/2. Last mentioned on muster roll of
           Jun 1780.

1-243   PETZOLD, Wilhelm, private, B/4. Deserted 14 May 1783.

1-246   BUCKLER, Konrad, Jaeger, J/2. Last mentioned on muster roll of
         Jun 1781.

1-252   BAUSCHINGER, Heinrich, canoneer, Artillery Detachment. Deserted
         13 May 1783.

         BESENECKER, Johann, private, B/1. With the American troops
         since Jun 1783.

1-256   BACHMEYER, Johann Conrad, private, A/2. Missing since Jun 1783.

1-260   BECKER, Christoph, Jaeger, A/3, J/6. Substitute or replacement
         trooper in 1782; last mentioned on muster roll of Jun 1783.

         BOSER, Johann Jakob, corporal, A/2. Last mentioned on muster
         roll of Dec 1780.

         BOSER, Karl, private, A/1. Last mentioned on muster roll of
         June 1781.

         FISCHER, Franz Thomas, Jaeger, J/3. No further information.

         FISCHER, Johann Christian, private, B/3. Last mentioned on mus-
         ter roll of Jun 1782.

1-266   BESSERER, Johann Salomon, private, B/3. Deserted 3 Feb 1783.

1-320   BATES, BEETZ. [Probably changed to Bates in America to preserve
         original German pronunciation. See Beetz 1-200.

1-326   BUTCHER. [Might have changed German surname Mezger to English
         equivalent. See Mezger 5-260.]

1-340   BATTLE, Leonhard, Jaeger, J/2. Deserted 9 Apr 1783 in Virginia.

1-342   BEUTLICH, Johann, private, A/4. Missing since Jun 1783.

1-346   BUTTLER, Leonhard, Jaeger, J/2. Last mentioned on muster roll of
         Dec 1782.

         FIEDLER, Johann Friedrich, Jaeger, J/2, J/6. Deserted 28 Mar 1783.

1-350   BOETTEN, Konrad, private, A/3. Deserted 31 May 1781.

         BUDIN, Konrad, private, B/2. Deserted 16 Oct 1782.

1-352   POETTING, Friedrich Leonhard, private, B/1. Deserted 1 Jan 1782.

1-354   BITTENHOLZER, Heinrich, private, A/4. Missing since Jun 1783.

1-355   BOTHMANN, Heinrich, Jaeger; servant. Released from active duty
         on 20 Dec 1778.

1-360   PETER, Georg, private, A/4. Missing since Jun 1783.

1-400   BELL, Johann, private, A/3. Last mentioned on muster roll of
         Jun 1783.

         BILLY (a Negro), [Jaeger?] J/2. No further information.

1-420   BELZ, Melchior Christoph, private, A/3. Deserted 24 Feb 1783 in
         Huntington [state not given]; he left property in the value
         of 819 florins in Ansbach.

         BLACK. [Might have changed German surname Schwarz to English equi-
         valent. *See* Schwarz 2-620.]

         BLOOS, Johann Karl Friedrich, Fourier, J/1, J/2. Promoted on
         1 Nov 1779; no further information.

         FALCK, Aberl [Albert?], private, B/2. Deserted 5 Sep 1781.

         FALK, FOLK. [Might have changed spelling of surname Volck to pre-
         serve original German pronunciation. *See* Volck 7-420.]

         PLASS, Johann Wolfgang, private, A/3. No further information.

         POLLACK, Karl Gottlieb, Jaeger, J/1. Released from active duty
         on 1 Feb 1783.

1-426   BLECKER, Heinrich, private, A/4. Deserted 29 May 1778.

1-453   BLENDINGER, Conrad, private, B/1. No further information.

         BLIND, Jakob, private, A/2. Deserted 6 Sep 1781.

         POLLAND, Leonhard, private, B/1. Last mentioned on muster roll of
         Jun 1783[?]; enlisted with the American troops.

1-454   BLUEMLEIN, Johann Michael, private, A/2. Last mentioned on muster
         roll Jun 1780. According to Pr, enlisted with the American
         troops.

         BLUEMLEIN, Karl, Jaeger, J/2. Deserted 10 Aug 1781; from Ans-
         bach; born in 1762.

1-456   BUEHLMEYER, Georg Thomas, private, B/1. Deserted 8 May 1783.

1-460   BILLER, Georg Adam, servant, J/1. Released on 2 Apr 1778. He
         then became a private in B/1. Deserted 1 Dec 1782.

         BLEYER, Peter, private, B/3. Deserted 8 Oct 1781.

         BUEHLER, Joseph, Jaeger. Replacement trooper in 1782. No further
         information.

1-500   BOHANN, Joseph Martin, Jaeger, J/1. Deserted 29 Sep 1778.

         BONN, Heinrich, private, A/1. Deserted 17 Nov 1778.

1-516   BAMBERGER, Franz, private, B/5. With the American troops since
         Jun 1783.

1-520   BUNZ, Johann Georg, Jaeger, J/3. Deserted 11 Nov 1781. From
         Ansbach; born 1757.

1-523   BENNSTAEDT (*or* BONNSTAEDT), Friedrich Wilhelm, Jaeger, J/1.
         Deserted 27 May 1783.

1-526   BAUMGAERTEL, Leonhardt, private, B/2. Deserted 2 Oct 1782.

         BAUMGARTNER, Heinrich, private, A/ 1. Deserted 27 Feb 1782.

         PANZER, Friedrich, private, B/3. Last mentioned on muster
         roll Jun 1783.

1-532   PANDASCH, Konrad, private, B/5. Released from active duty on
         16 Jun 1783. According to Doe, "as a surrenderer he was
         released and went to Philadelphia."

1-534   PFUENDEL, Anton, Jaeger, J/3. No further information.

1-536   BINDER, --, recruit, B/3. Deserted 25 Feb 1778.

1-550   BAUMANN, Christian, corporal, A/5, A/2. Promoted on 3 Oct 1778.
         No further information.

         BAUMANN, Johann Konrad, camp attendant [*valet de tente*], A/3.
         Deserted 28 Aug 1781. According to Bor, he deserted with
         -- Baerngruber, a baggage boy [*Packknecht*] and two horses.
         [Entry for Baerngruber will be found at 1-652 below.]

         BAUMANN, Lorenz, private, A/4. Deserted 13 Aug 1778. Accord-
         ing to Bor, he deserted together with [Johann Georg[Rummel
         and [Johann] Stadler.

         BAUMANN, Peter, piper, A/3. Missing since Jun 1783.

1-552   FENNING. [Might have changed spelling of surname Venning to
         preserve original German pronunciation. *See* Venning 7-552.]

1-563   BUNERTH, Friedrich August, private, B/1. Deserted 12 Oct 1781.

1-600   BAER, Johann, private, B/4. Deserted 2 Aug 1782. According to
         Doe [he deserted] 21 Dec 1782 and enlisted in [American?]
         Armouns [Armonds?] Free Corps.

         BAER, Pancraz, private, B/5. Last mentioned in muster roll of
         Jun 1783.

         BAUER, Friedrich, private, A/2. Replacement trooper in 1781 in
         New York.

         BAUER, Johann, private, A/4. Deserted 11 May 1783.

         BAUER, Johann Georg, grenadier, A/5. Deserted 15 Sep 1782. Ac-
         cording to Pr, with the American troops.

10

1-600   BAUER, Johann Wilhelm, private, A/2. Missing since Jun 1783.

        BAUER, Tobias Konrad, private, B/4. Last mentioned in muster
            roll of Jun 1783. Mentioned in <u>Doe</u>, entry of 29 Jun 1782.

        BEER, Johann Karl Friedrich, Jaeger, A/2. Last mentioned in
            muster roll of Dec 1782.

        BEYER, Heinrich, private, B/3. Deserted 15 Nov 1782.

        BEYER, Paul, private, B/4. Last mentioned on muster roll of
            Dec 1779.

        BOWER. [The German surname Bauer is often Anglicized to Bower.]

        FEHR, Johann Georg, private, B/2, A/1. No further information.

        FEHR, Peter, private, A/4. Deserted 29 Oct 1782.

        FRUEHE, Friedrich, private, A/4. Last mentioned on muster roll
            of Jun 1783.

        FRUEHE, Johann Georg, grenadier, A/5. Missing since Jun 1783.

        PREU, Johann Adam, private, A/3. Last mentioned on muster roll
            of Jun 1783.

1-612   PROBST, Andreas, grenadier, A/5. Deserted 29 Dec 1781.

1-616   FREYBERGER, Johann, private, A/1. Missing since Jun 1783. From
            Ansbach; son of Johann Christian Albrecht Freyberger.

        FRUEHBERGER, Georg, Jaeger. Replacement trooper in 1782. No
            further information.

1-620   BAUERREISS, Johann, private, A/4. Deserted 11 May 1783. From
            M[ark]t Insheim.

        FORCH, Georg, private, B/4. Deserted 13 May 1783.

        FRAAS, Johann Georg, private, B/3. Deserted 18 May 1783.

        FRIES, Michael, private, A/1. Missing since Jun 1783.

        FROSCH, Johann Friedrich, private, A/3. Last mentioned on muster
            roll of Dec 1782.

1-623   PRECHT, Georg, private, A/4. Deserted 27 Dec 1782.

        PRECHTEL, Christoph, medical corpsman [*Feldscher*], B/2. Accord-
            ing to <u>Doe</u>, entry of 3 Jul 1783, "Was given his discharge
            and went to Philadelphia."

1-624   BERGHOLZ, Friedrich, private, A/1. Last mentioned on muster roll
            of Jun 1783.

1-626   BERGER, Johann, grenadier, A/5. Deserted 13 May 1783.

BURCKHARDT, Michael, private, B/4. According to <u>Doe</u>, entry of
   21 Dec 1782 "by Armouns Free Corps" [American or French
   military unit?].

FRICKER, Johann, private, A/4. Deserted 14 Oct 1781.

PRAGER, Christoph, private, A/1. Last mentioned on muster roll
   of Jun 1781.

1-630   BARTH, Adam, conductor [*Condukteur*], Artillery Detachment. Missing since 1783. According to <u>DP</u>, he settled in Nova Scotia;
   one child listed; farmer. Received 100 acres of land.

BARTH, Anton, Jaeger, J/2. Deserted 27 May 1783.

BARTH, Johann Kaspar, Jaeger, J/2. Deserted 25 Apr 1781 in Virginia.

BARTH, Michael, private, B/5. Missing since Jun 1783; with the
   American troops.

BIRD. [Might have changed German surname Vogel to English equivalent. *See* Vogel 7-240.]

BOEHRET, Gottlieb, private, B/4. No further information.

BOEHRET, Johann, private, B/4. According to <u>Doe</u>, entry of 21 Dec
   1782 "by Armouns Free Corps [American or French military
   unit?]."

BURETT, Nikolaus, Jaeger, J/2. Last mentioned on muster roll of
   Dec 1782.

PUERETH, Nikolaus, Jaeger, J/2. [Same as Nikolaus Burett above?]
   Last mentioned on muster roll of Jun 1780.

1-631   FRIEDEBACH, Johann Michael, Jaeger, J/3. Deserted while on patrol
   at Kingsbridge.

1-632   BRAEUTIGAM, Johann, private, B/2. Last mentioned on muster roll
   of Dec 1780.

1-634   BERTHOLD, Johann Georg, Jaeger, J/1. Deserted 18 Aug 1781.

FRIEDLEIN, Konrad, private, A/3. Deserted 8 Oct 1781.

1-635   BRODMERKEL, Friedrich Christoph, private, A/3. Deserted Oct 1782.

1-636   FRIEDRICH, Gottlob, private, A/4. Deserted 29 May 1778.

FREDERICK; FREDERICKS. [Might have changed German surname Friedrich to English equivalent.]

1-640   PRELL, Friedrich, grenadier, B/5. No further information.

1-640   PRELL, Johann, private, B/3. Enlisted with the American troops.

PRELL, Matthias, private, B/5. Deserted 18 Aug 1780. According to <u>Doe</u>, from Thiersheim (Sechsaemter).

PROELL, Nikolaus, private, A/1. Deserted 13 May 1783.

1-645   BAYERLEIN, Andreas, Jaeger, J/2. Replacement trooper 1778. Last mentioned on muster roll of Dec 1779.

1-650   BRAUN, Johann Friedrich, private, A/3. No further information.

BRAUN, Wilhelm, private, A/3. Deserted 24 Jun 1780. According to <u>Bor</u>, he deserted during the retreat from Springfield. Also, according to *Ibid.*, entry of 7 Aug 1780 ". . . he wrote from Philadelphia saying that he had not deserted but had been taken prisoner, but he was not accepted as a prisoner [of war]." Also, according to *Ibid.*, entry of 17 Jan 1781 ". . . Braun returned with his brother Johann Wilhelm as deserters from the Americans." No further information on these men, but they apparently remained in America.

BROWN. [Might have changed from German surname Braun.]

PRAMM, Baptist, Jaeger, J/2. Replacement trooper 1782. No further information.

PRIMM, Paul, private, B/4. Missing since Jun 1783; enlisted with the American troops.

1-652   BERNGRUBER, Sixtus, canoneer, Artillery Detachment. Deserted 29 Aug 1781 with [Johann Konrad] Baumann.

BRINNICK, Christian Andreas, grenadier, A/5. Last mentioned on muster roll of Dec 1780.

FRAENKLER, Gottlob, recruit. Replacement trooper 1782. No further information.

FRANCK, Johann Nikolaus, Jaeger, A/4, J/6. No further information.

FRANCK, Karl, grenadier, A/5. Deserted 11 May 1783.

FRANK, Johann Friedrich, corporal, B/4. Demoted on 2 May 1782 for inciting to mutiny. Deserted 2 Apr 1783.

FRANK, Johann Simon, [private?] B/1. No further information.

PRINCE. [Might have changed German surname Herzog to near English equivalent. *See* Herzog 7-622.]

1-653   BERNETH, Johann, private, B/4. Deserted 2 Jul 1782.

BRAND, Georg Nikolaus, Jaeger, J/1, J/6. Deserted 10 May 1783.

1-654   BAERNLACHER, Georg, private, B/2, B/3. Last mentioned on muster roll of Dec 1780.

13

Soundex
Number

1-656   BAERENREUTHER, Wolff, Jaeger, J/2. Last mentioned on muster
            roll of Dec 1780.

        BERNHARDT, Christoph, grenadier, A/5. Deserted 1 Mar 1778.

        BRUMMER, Johann, private, A/4. Deserted 8 Mar 1778.

        BRUNNER, Georg Simon, private, B/1. Deserted 9 Oct 1781.

        BRUNNER, Johann Baptist, Jaeger, J/3, J/1, J/4. No further
            information.

        FARMER. [Might have translated the German surname Bauer to the
            English equivalent. *See* Bauer 1-600.]

1-656   FERNER, Albrecht, private, B/2. Last mentioned on muster roll
            of Dec 1782.

2-000   SCHUH, Johann, private, B/4. Deserted 1 Jun 1783.

        SHOE. [Might have changed German surname Schuh to English equi-
            valent.]

2-100   KOPF, Johann, private, A/4. Last mentioned on muster roll of
            Jun 1783.

        KOPP, Johann Martin, Jaeger, J/1. Last mentioned on muster roll
            of Jun 1780.

        SCHOEPF, Paul, private, B/2. Deserted 14 Oct 1781 in Virginia.
            Deserted 10 Feb 1783 in Huntington. [No explanation of
            these two desertions; it may have been that he returned
            to his unit after the first desertion and then deserted
            once again, as did several other soldiers.]

        SCHWAAB, Nikolaus, private, B/4. According to <u>Doe</u>, entry of
            29 Jul 1782, "Musketeer Sch[waab] escaped from the poor-
            house hospital but was captured by the field militia [*Feld-
            militz*] and returned on 3 Jun [1782]."

        ZAPF, Johann, private, A/3. Last mentioned on muster roll of
            Jun 1783.

2-116   KIEFHABER, Georg, private, B/4. Last mentioned on muster roll
            of Jun 1782.

2-130   SPAETH, Nikolaus, private, A/3. According to <u>Doe</u>, entry of 12
            Feb 1783, "Private Spaeth returned [from captivity] in
            Virginia and moved into the barracks. He was missing for
            almost a year." According to *Ibid.*, entry of 6 Mar 1783,
            "Private Sp[aeth] again absented himself during the night.
            He is supposed to be married in Virginia and returned to
            the regiment only for the purpose of retrieving his belong-
            ings and baggage."

14

2-140   SCHUEBEL, Johann Adam, private, B/3. Deserted 12 May 1783.

        SEPPEL, Johann, private, A/4. Deserted 13 May 1783.

        ZIPFEL, Georg, private, A/4. Deserted 2 Jun 1778.

2-152   SPENGLER, Nikolaus, Jaeger, J/1, J/2, J/4. Surrenderer [*Kapit-ulant*] until 8 Jan 1788?. Last mentioned on muster roll
        of Jun 1783.

2-155   KAUFMANN, Heinrich, Jaeger, J/2. Deserted 10 Aug 1781 while on
        patrol.

2-160   SAFFER, Georg, private, A/1. Discharged on 30 Jun 1780.

        SCHAEFER, Christian, private, A/3. According to Boe, entries
        of 29 & 30 Jul 1779, "Sentenced to death by hanging for
        desertion but sentence commuted to running a gauntlet of
        200 men on two different days." According to Ans.Ms.hist.
        487, his pregnant wife, Mrs. Eva Margaretha Schaefer, left
        at Ansbach, lives without the least support.

        SCHAEFER, Friedrich Jakob, private, B/2. Deserted on 16 Oct 1782.

        SCHAEFER, Johann, private, B/2. According to AMKB, he married
        Anna Kunigunde [last name not given] who commits adultery
        in Ansbach.

        SCHIPPER, Andreas, Jaeger, J/1, J/4. Deserted 25 Jun 1783.

        SIEBER, Georg Leonhard, private, B/1. Deserted 16 Oct 1782.

2-163   GEBHARDT, Andreas, private, B/1. Deserted 18 Aug 1780. According
        to Doe, he came from Muenchbergisch [territory].

        SHEPHERD. [Might have changed German surname Schaefer to English
        equivalent. *See* Schaefer 2-160.]

        SCHUPPHARD, Gottlob, private, B/2. Last mentioned on muster roll
        of Jun 1783.

        SEFFERT, Johann Adam, grenadier, A/5. Missing since Jun 1783.
        According to Ansb.Ms.hist. 487, he was from Rudolfsberg in
        Crailsheim [territory] and the son of Johann Adam Seffert
        [Senior] born about 1710. [The son was] unmarried.

        SEIFFERT, Georg, private, A/4. Last mentioned on muster roll of
        Jun 1783.

        SEYFERT, Johann Adam, private, B/4. According to Doe, entry of
        13 May 1782, "[Seyfert], who is said to have married an
        American woman, remained away." [This may be the same person
        as Johann Adam Seffert, above.]

Soundex Number

2-163 SEUBERT, Georg, Jaeger, J/2. Deserted 14 Mar 1781 in North Carolina.

2-164 KAEFFERLEIN, Simon, servant, J/2. Last mentioned on muster roll of Dec 1781.

SEIFFERLEIN, Johann Peter, grenadier, A/5. Deserted 27 Jun 1780. According to Bor, "by Philipsburg." [It is not clear what this means, either his birthplace in Germany or place of desertion in America.]

2-200 GOETZ, Johann, Jaeger, A/5. Discharged on 1 Aug 1779.

GOEZ, Johann Martin, grenadier, A/5. Last mentioned on muster roll of Jun 1777.

QUICK. [Might have changed German surname Schnell to English equivalent. *See* Schnell 2-540.]

SCHACK, Peter, Jaeger. Replacement trooper in 1782. No further information.

SEITZ, Adam, Jaeger, J/1. Discharged on 8 Jun 1780.

ZAUSS, Johann Peter, A/2. Deserted 27 Dec 1782.

2-216 CASEBIER. [Might have changed original German surname Kaesebauer to a spelling more easily pronounced by English-speaking persons. *See* Kaesebauer *infra*.]

KAESEBAUER, Christian, private, A/5. Deserted 17 Sep 1781.

KUTZBERGER, Sebastian, private, B/2. Last mentioned on muster roll of Jun 1781.

2-235 CAESTNER, Christoph, Jaeger, J/1. Last mentioned on muster roll of Jun 1780.

KUESTNER, Andreas, private, A/3. No further information.

2-236 GECHTER, Johann Adam, private, B/2. Deserted 29 Sep 1781.

2-240 GASSEL, Johannes Heinrich, private, A/3. Deserted 18 Aug 1779.

2-245 KIESLING, Thomas, private, B/1. Enlisted with the American troops.

2-246 GIESLER, Johann Joseph, Jaeger, J/1, J/4. Last mentioned on muster roll of Dec 1782. According to BRM, settled in Nova Scotia.

2-246 GOSLER, Friedrich, grenadier, A/5. Deserted 8 Jul 1780.

KESSLER, Paulus, Jaeger, J/3, J/1, J/4. Missing since Jun 1783. According to Ansb.Ms.hist. 487, he was the son of Matthaeus Kessler of Kleinlangheim (Castell territory); brother of Johann Kaspar Kessler, not otherwise mentioned, but who returned to Ansbach at the end of hostilities.

2-246 SCHWAEGLER, Johann Matthias, grenadier, A/5. Last mentioned on
muster roll of Jun 1783.

SCHWEGLER, Joseph Peter, private, A/2. Last mentioned on muster
roll of Dec 1782.

ZIEGLER, Johann Georg Heinrich, Jaeger, J/1. Deserted 21 Nov 1778.

2-252 GEISENSIEDER, Johann Martin, private, A/4. Last mentioned on muster roll of Dec 1782. Apparently took an oath of allegiance
[to American government?] at Winchester.

SAZINGER, Christian, private, B/5. Deserted 13 May 1783.

2-255 KATZENWINKEL, Heinrich, private, A/3. Deserted 27 Nov 1782 in
Jerich[o?]. According to Bor, entry of 4 Feb 1780: "Katzenwinkel, who deserted on 10 Mar 1778, returned to his regiment
today. Because of his desertion, he had been dismissed from
service; however, because he has been going under the false
name Ernst von Reitzenstein, Major, he was sentenced to 12
times through the gauntlet." According to Pr: "Dismissed
because he had served with the American army."

2-260 KAYSER, Johann Georg, private, A/2. Deserted 9 May 1783. According to Ansb.Ms.hist. 487, he was the son of Simon Konrad Kayser and Maria Christian, of Wittelsheim/Heidenheim. He left
behind [in Germany] an impoverished, sick mother and three
sisters.

SCHWEIZER, Franz, Jaeger, J/1, J/2. Deserted 26 Dec 1782. According to both Pr and Doe, he enlisted with the American troops.

2-262 SEGERITZ, Michael, Jaeger, J/6. Replacement trooper in 1782.

2-263 SCHWEIGERT, Johann Peter, grenadier, A/5. Missing since Jun 1783.

2-300 SCHOTT, Johann Georg, private, B/4. According to Doe, he deserted
on 3 Apr 1782.

2-315 STEPHAN, Friedrich, private, B/4. Last mentioned on muster roll of
Jun 1782.

2-316 STUEBER, Johann Heinrich, private, B/3. Last mentioned on muster
roll of Jun 1783.

2-320 STOCK, Ludwig, Jaeger, J/3, J/4. Last mentioned on muster roll of
Jun 1783.

2-321 STAUSBERGER, Paul, private, A/4. Deserted 11 May 1783.

2-324 STIEGLER, Johann Kaspar, private, A/3. Last mentioned on muster
roll of Jun 1783.

2-325   STOCKMOHR, --, private, A/2. Deserted 11 Oct 1781.

2-326   SWITZER. [Might have changed German surname Schweizer to Eng-
         lish equivalent. *See* Schweizer 2-260.]

2-334   STADLER, Johann, private, A/4. Deserted 13 Aug 1778. Accord-
         ing to Bor, he deserted with [Johann Georg] Rummel and
         [Lorenz] Baumann. According to HAV, he was born in 1757
         in Ansbach. His height was 5 Schuh 5-1/2 Zoll.

2-340   SCHAEDEL, Johann, private, A/3. Last mentioned on muster roll
         of Jun 1783.

         SCHETTLA, Karl, private, B/1. Enlisted with the American troops
         in 1782.

         SEIDEL, Johann Jakob, private, A/1. Last mentioned on muster
         roll of Dec 1779.

         STAHL, Johann, private, A/2. Last mentioned on muster roll of
         Jun 1783.

         STAHL, Johann Nikolaus, private, A/3. Deserted 18 May 1783.

         STIEHL, Heinrich, private, B/1. Last mentioned on muster roll
         of Jun 1783.

         STOLL, Friedrich, grenadier, A/5. Deserted 20 Feb 1778.

2-341   STUELPNER, Johann, private, A/4. Deserted 6 Jul 1780 in Philips-
         house Barracks.

2-342   STOELZE, Christian, private, B/4. Enlisted with the American
         troops.

2-350   STAIN, Johann Friedrich, private, A/4. Deserted 28 Dec 1782.

2-351   STEINBACH, Johann, private, B/1. Last mentioned on muster roll
         of Dec 1782.

2-352   STENGEL, Konrad, grenadier, A/5. Deserted 16 Oct 1782.

2-353   STEINMETZ, Jobst, private, B/4. Last mentioned on muster roll of
         Jun 1782.

2-355   ZOTTMANN, Heinrich, Jaeger, J/2. Last mentioned on muster roll of
         Dec 1781.

2-356   STEINRICK, Michael, Jaeger, J/2. Replacement trooper in 1782.

2-360   ZEHDER, Johann Georg, Jaeger, J/1. Last mentioned on muster roll
         of Jun 1783.

2-362   STRAUSSBERGER, Paul, private, A/4. Last mentioned on muster roll
         of Dec 1782.

18

2-362   STRICKSTROH, Johann Adam, private, B/4. According to Doe, he
        deserted on 11 May 1783.

2-363   STREIT, Johann Georg, private, B/1. Deserted on 22 May 1783.

2-364   STROEHLEIN, Georg, private, A/4, A/2. Last mentioned on muster
        roll of Dec 1779.

2-400   GOLL, Johann, private, J/3, A/5. Last mentioned on muster roll
        of Dec 1782.

        KAIL, Dominikus, private, B/3. Deserted 20 May 1783.

2-410   KOLB, Johann, private, A/3. Last mentioned on muster roll of
        Jun 1782.

2-413   CALLUPETZKY, Joseph, private, B/5. Deserted 12 Dec 1782.

2-416   ZOLLFRANK, Martin, private, A/4. Deserted 18 Jul 1780 from
        Philippshouse Barracks.

2-420   SCHULZ, Gottlob, private, B/4. Deserted 25 Dec 1782; also de-
        serted 20 Mar 1781.

2-424   SCHLEGEL, Jakob, private, B/5. Last mentioned on muster roll of
        Jun 1783.

2-426   GLASER, Adam, Jaeger, J/3, J/4. Last mentioned on muster roll
        of Dec 1782.

        KLUGHARDT, Martin, private, A/4. Deserted 22 Feb 1778.

        SCHLICKER, Johann, private, A/4. Deserted 10 Jan 1782.

        ZELSER, Georg, private, B/3. Deserted 14 May 1783.

2-431   GOLDBERGER, Matthias, Jaeger, A/4, J/6. Last mentioned on muster
        roll of Jun 1783.

2-432   GOLDEISS, Philipp, private, A/1. Missing since Jun 1783.

        GOLDSCHMIDT, Johann, Jaeger, J/1. Deserted 10 Nov 1778.

        SCHILDKNECHT, Johann, private, A/4. Last mentioned on muster roll
        of Jun 1783. Son of Johann Heinrich Schildknecht from Zirn-
        dorf.

        SCHULTHEISS, Johann, private, B/4. Deserted 14 Sep 1782. Enlisted
        with the American troops.

        ZELTSCH, Nikolaus, private, B/5, A/1. Last mentioned on muster
        roll of Jun 1783.

2-436   SCHLETTERER, Georg, Jaeger, J/5. Replacement trooper 1782.

2-450   KILIAN, Johann Philipp, private, B/2. Last mentioned on muster roll of Dec 1782.

KLEIN, Johann, private, A/4. Missing since Dec 1782.

KLEIN, Johann, private, B/2. Deserted 29 Sep 1781.

KLEIN, Johann Veit, private, A/2. Deserted 30 Oct 1782. According to <u>Bor</u>: "On 29 Sep 1780, while in a working party to Morrisania, he tried to desert; as a consequence, he was today sentenced to ten times running the gauntlet."

KLEIN, Wolfgang, grenadier, A/5. Missing since Jun 1783.

KUHLWEIN, Johann Valentin, Jaeger, J/2, J/1. Deserted on 28 Jun 1783.

2-456   KLEINER, Rupert, Jaeger, J/3, J/4. Last mentioned on muster roll of Jun 1783.

KOHLHAMMER, Peter, private, A/4. Deserted 28 Dec 1782.

SOELLNER, Johann Heinrich, canoneer, Artillery Detachment. Deserted 18 Jan 1780.

ZOELLNER, Georg Peter, private, A/2. Last mentioned on muster roll of Jun 1783.

ZOELLNER, Johann, private, A/4. Last mentioned on muster roll of Jun 1783.

2-460   KELLER, Kaspar, Jaeger, J/3. Discharged on 29 Nov 1782.

KOEHLER, Johann Andreas, Jaeger, J/3. Last mentioned on muster roll of Jun 1783.

SCHALLER, Christian, private, B/2. Last mentioned on muster roll of Jun 1782.

SCHELLER, Michael, grenadier, A/5. No further information.

2-465   KELLERMANN, Jobst, private, A/3. Last mentioned on muster roll of Jun 1783.

2-500   KAM, Johann, private, A/2. Deserted 9 May 1783.

KEIM, Johann Christian, grenadier, A/5. Deserted 16 Jun 1781. Deserted during an attack near Fort Great Bridge in the neighborhood of Portsmouth.

SCHUMM, Georg Adam, grenadier, A/5. Last mentioned on muster roll of Jun 1783.

SCHWIMM, --, recruit, B/4. Deserted on 22 Feb 1778.

20

2-510   KNEIF, Kaspar, private, B/2. Last mentioned on muster roll of
         Jun 1782.

         SCHNEPF, Georg Jakob, Jaeger. Replacement trooper in 1782.

2-512   COMB(S). [Might have changed German surname Kamm to English
         equivalent. *See* Kamm 2-500.]

2-515   KNOPFNADEL, Johann Georg, Jaeger, J/3, J/4. Last mentioned on
         muster roll of Dec 1782.

2-520   KING. [Might have changed German surname Koenig to English
         equivalent.]

         KOENIG, Adam, private, A/3. Last mentioned on muster roll of
         Dec 1782.

         SCHEMIG, Kaspar, private, A/3. Deserted 29 Dec 1782.

2-522   ZWANZIGER, Georg, private, B/3. Last mentioned on muster roll
         of Jun 1782.

2-524   SINSEL, Johann, canoneer, Artillery Detachment. Last mentioned
         on muster roll of Jun 1783.

         ZANGEL, Johann, private, A/5. Deserted 12 May 1783.

         ZENCKEL, Konrad, private, A/4. Last mentioned on muster roll
         of Jun 1783.

2-526   KAEMNITZER, Georg, Jaeger, J/6. Replacement trooper in 1782.
         Deserted 28 Aug 1782 in Halifax.

         SCHENKER, Johann, private, A/2. Missing since Jun 1783.

         SCHOENEKER, Johann, private, A/2. Last mentioned on muster roll
         of Dec 1782. According to Ansb.Ms.hist.487, his mother,
         the widow Appollonia Schoeneker of Wassertruedingen received
         an annual pension paid in grain.

2-530   SCHMID, Karl Friedrich, Jaeger, J/2. Deserted 22 Jul 1781.

2-530   SCHMIDT, Georg, private, B/4. According to <u>Doe</u>, entry of 14
         Oct 1782: "[Schmidt] who was in jail, was bailed out by
         an inhabitant [of Pennsylvania] with whom he found em-
         ployment. His wife has left New York for Philadelphia
         to join him."

         SCHMIDT, Johann Michael, private, A/2. Last mentioned on mus-
         ter roll of Jun 1783. According to <u>Ansb.Ms.hist.487</u>, he
         was the son of Eva Maria Schmidt of Schalkhausen and the
         brother of Andreas Schmidt, private B/1, who returned to
         Europe in 1781. Eva Maria Schmidt had petitioned for an
         annual allotment of bread but this was denied.

         SCHMIDT, Lorenz Friedrich, private, A/3. No further informa-
         tion.

         ZIMMET, Matthias, private, A/1. Last mentioned on muster roll
         of Jun 1783.

2-532   CHEMNITZER. [Might have changed the German surname Kaemnitzer
         to a near English equivalent. *See* Kaemnitzer 2-526.]

2-532   KINDSHOFFER, Jakob, Jaeger, J/2, J/3. Deserted 1 Nov 1782
         while on patrol near Kings Bridge.

         SCHOENTAG, Johann Konrad, private, B/3. Deserted on 13 May 1783.

2-534   GUENTHELMEYER, Michael, private, B/5. Deserted on 12 May 1783.

         SCHINDELBAUER, Georg, drummer, B/1. Brother of Johann who re-
         turned to Germany at the end of the war. According to <u>Doe</u>,
         entry of 14 Oct 1782, he went aboard ship as a seaman.

         SCHINDLER, Johann, private, B/4. For further details, *see*
         Johann Georg ADAM, 7-350, hereinafter.

         SCHINDLER, Johann Adam, private, A/3. Missing since Jun 1783.

2-536   GUENTHER, Michael, Jaeger, J/1. Deserted 11 Nov 1778. According
         to <u>Bor</u>, entry of 13 Jun 1780: "Guenther deserted the Amer-
         ican Light Hussar unit and returned to his Ansbach unit with
         his horse. He was readmitted to his former unit but again
         deserted [to the American side] on 26 Jun 1781 while on an
         expedition in New Jersey."

22

2-536   SCHNEIDER, Johann, private, A/4, A/1. Last mentioned on muster
           roll of Jun 1783.

         SCHNEIDER, Paul, private, A/3. Last mentioned on muster roll
           of Dec 1782.

2-540   GOEMMEL, Karl, Jaeger. Replacement trooper of 1782.

         KNOLL, Adamm, private, B/5. Last mentioned on muster roll of
           Dec 1778.

         SCHNELL, Matthias, private, B/1. Enlisted with the American
           troops.

         SCHOENELL, Johann Balthasar, private, A/1. Deserted 25 Aug 1778.

2-542   SCHMELZER, Georg, private, A/4. Deserted 17 Oct 1781.

         SCHMELZER, Johann Jakob, private, A/2. Deserted 15 Oct 1781.

         SCHMELZER, Johann Leonhard, private. Last mentioned on muster
           roll of Jun 1783.

2-545   KOEHNLEIN, Johann Nikolaus, private, A/4. Last mentioned on
           muster roll of Dec 1782.

         SEMMELMANN, Johann, piper, B/4. Deserted 4 Jan 1782.

         SCHMALENBERG, Peter, Jaeger. Replacement trooper of 1782.

2-546   KEMMLER, Johann Heinrich, private, A/2. Missing since Jun 1783.

         SCHMULLER, Wolf, private, B/2. Deserted 6 Jan 1782.

2-560   KNORR, Johann Michael, Jaeger, J/3, J/4. According to HAV, a
           surrenderer [*Kapitulant*] until 16 Nov 1786. Height: 6
           Schuh.

         SCHNURR, Johann, Jaeger, J/2. Deserted 9 May 1783.

         SCHOEMER, Martin, grenadier, B/5. No further information.

         SCHOENER, Lorenz, private, A/3. Deserted 12 May 1783.

         ZINNER, Matthias, private, B/3. Deserted 22 May 1783.

2-563   GEMMERT, Friedrich Karl, Jaeger, J/2. No further information.

2-600   GAUER, Peter, Jaeger. Replacement trooper in 1782.

GEHWEYER, Leonhard, private, A/4. Deserted 11 May 1783. According to <u>ABA</u>: Gehweyer was a journeyman carpenter employed by the Marquisate Construction Office [*markgraeflichen Bauamt*]. May have been from Feuchtwang. (Note <u>AKA</u> 118: Johann Andreas Gehweyer, born 1765, stonemason; perhaps a brother or relative.)

GEYER, Johann, private, B/3. Deserted 10 Dec 1782.

GRAU, Anton, private, A/3. Missing since Jun 1783.

GRAU, Friedrich, private, Jaeger, J/2. Last mentioned on muster roll of Jun 1781.

SAUER, Christian, Jaeger, J/2. Discharged on 30 Jun 1780.

SAUER, Georg Christian, Jaeger, J/1, J/4. Deserted 2 May 1783. Surrenderer [*Kapitulant*] until 8 Jul 1783.

SCHAUER, Georg Martin, corporal, A/5. Discharged on 1 May 1783. According to <u>Ansb.Ms.hist.487</u>, he came from Oberferrieden; eight other brothers are also in military service, two sisters petition for support to be paid in grain.

SCHORR, Johann Michael, private, A/2. Deserted 9 May 1783. According to <u>HAV</u>, he was from Ehingen/Schwaben [Swabia]; son of Maria Margaretha Schorr.

2-610   GRAF, Georg Michael, Jaeger, J/3. Last mentioned on muster roll of Jun 1783.

GRUB, Jakob, private, B/4. Deserted 8 Sep 1782.

SCHARFF, --, private, A/3. Deserted 16 Feb 1783 at Huntington.

2-616   GRUBER, Kaspar, Jaeger, J/2. Surrendered until 9 Jul 1783. Height: 6 Schuh. Jun 1781 ¶[significance of this date is not given]. According to the town archives of Chester, Nova Scotia, in a petition dated 21 Feb 1793 he describes himself as "late of the Ansbach Yagers, now at Harrietsfield." This town is now a suburb of Halifax.

24

2-620   GAREISS, Johann Georg, private, A/3. Last mentioned on muster
        roll of Jun 1783. Took an oath of allegiance [to the
        United States] at Winchester.

        KARRICH, Johann Kaspar, private, B/3. Deserted 12 May 1783.

        KRAUS, Albrecht, private, B/4. Deserted 20 Jul 1780.

        KRAUSS, Emanuel Friedrich, private, A/2. Last mentioned in
        muster roll of Jun 1783.

        KRAUSS, Johann, private, B/2. Last mentioned in muster roll
        of Jun 1783.

        KRAUSS, Johann Gottlieb, private, B/4. Last mentioned in mus-
        ter roll of Jun 1783.

        KRAUSS, Johann Michael, private, A/2. Deserted 5 Apr 1780.

        KRESS, Johann Michael, private, A/3. Last mentioned in muster
        roll of Dec 1782. According to Ansb.Ms.hist.487, he was
        the son of Barbara Kress of Wuestenau/Crailsheim.

        KRESS, Michael, Jaeger, J/2. Deserted 15 Feb 1778.

        KRUG, Konrad, wagon master, A/1. Last mentioned in muster roll
        of Dec 1782.

        SCHWARTZ, Johann, private, A/2. Last mentioned in muster roll
        of Jun 1783.

        SCHWARZ, Johann, private, B/1. Enlisted with the American troops.

2-621   SCHWARZBAUER, Leonhard, private, B/5. Deserted 2 May 1783.

2-622   GOERSCHKY, Gottlieb, private, B/4. According to Doe, entry of
        24 Nov 1781, he is employed by the French as a wagon driver.

2-623   Christhulf, Georg, private, A/4. Last mentioned in muster roll of
        Jun 1783.

        KOERZDOERFER, Johann, private, B/3. Deserted 13 May 1783.

2-624   GRESEL, Johann Heinrich, private, B/1. Deserted 25 Dec 1782.

Soundex
Number

2-625 GRIEZMACHER, Johann Gottfried, Jaeger, J/2, J/6. Last mentioned
on muster roll of Jun 1783.

GROSSMANN, Johann, private, B/3. Deserted 14 May 1783.

ZSCHARKANY, David, Jaeger. Replacement trooper in 1782.

2-626 CREUTZER, Johann, private, A/3. No further information.

KREUZER, Johann, grenadier, A/5. Last mentioned in muster roll
of Dec 1783?

SCHRICKER, Wolf, private, B/2. Last mentioned in muster roll of
Jun 1782.

2-630 COURDEOU, Baptist, Jaeger, J/6. Replacement trooper in 1782.
Deserted 29 Aug 1782 in Halifax.

GOERT, Johann Stefan, drummer, A/3. Deserted 18 Nov 1781 but
returned on 13 Jun 1782. He again deserted on 28 Sep 1782.
He was from Ansbach and born in 1763. According to Prechtel, page 532, "he entered French service."

SCHARD, Johann, private, A/4. Deserted 8 Mar 1778 at Philadelphia
barracks while on double sentry duty [*Doppelposten*] together
with Cramer. [There were two Cramers with the Ansbach troops
in America, but both returned to Europe after the war and did
not desert. As a consequence, the entry apparently means
that Schard escaped while serving with Cramer on sentry duty.]

SEEHARDT, Georg Friedrich, private, A/3. Last mentioned in muster roll of Jun 1783. He was the son of Hussar corporal
-- Seehardt from Feuchtwangen.

2-635 GAERTNER, Johann Georg Christian, private, B/4. According to Doe,
entry of 1 May 1782: "Private Gaertner returned to us in the
barracks from the country bringing an American woman with him
whom he said he had married." *Ibid.*, entry of 3 Feb 1782:
"Today at noon private Gaertner again deserted with his American woman." According to Pr, under date of July 1782, "He
was taken in the town by an American patrol and as he sought
to escape from them, he was shot in the body."

GARDENAU, Adam, Jaeger, J/2. Deserted 13 Jul 1780.

26

2-636   SCHROEDER, Georg Wilhelm, Jaeger, J/1, J/4. Last mentioned in
         muster roll of Jun 1783.

2-640   CARL, Andreas, private, B/1. No further information.

2-645   GERLINGER, Michael, private, A/4. Deserted 10 May 1783.

2-650   GROOM(S). [Might have translated the German surname Braeutigam
         to the English equivalent Groom, or Grooms. *See* Braeutigam
         1-632.]

         KERN, Jakob, private, B/3. Deserted 22 May 1783.

         KRIMM, Christian, Jaeger, J/1. Deserted 8 May 1783.

2-651   GRUENBECK, Johann Georg, private, B/3. Enlisted in the American
         troops.

2-656   CRONER, David, private, A/4. Missing since Jun 1783.

         GRUNNER, Christoph Friedrich, Jaeger, B/2. Deserted 15 Sep 1782.
         From Ansbach, where he is said to have left property in the
         amount of 600 florins.

         KRAEHMER, Matthias, Jaeger, J/2. Last mentioned in muster roll
         of Jun 1780.

         SCHIRMER, Stefan, private, A/1. Last mentioned in muster roll
         of Jun 1783.

3-140   TEUFEL, Johann, private, B/2, J/3. Last mentioned in muster roll
         of Dec 1782.

3-162   DOBEROSSQUI [Doberossky], Johann, Jaeger, J/1. Last mentioned in
         muster roll of Dec 1781.

3-163   TAUBERT, Christian Friedrich, canoneer, Artillery Detachment.
         Deserted 25 Oct 1782. According to Doe, he enlisted with
         the American troops.

3-200   DIETZ, Johann Gottlieb, private, B/2. Last mentioned in muster
         roll of Dec 1782.

         DOEG, Johann Adam, private, B/1, B/4. Enlisted with the American
         troops.

3-200   DOEG, Johann Georg, private, B/1, B/4. Enlisted in the American
         troops.

         DUKE. [Might have changed German surname Herzog to English equi-
         valent. *See* Herzog 7-622.]

3-245   DOEGELMANN, Peter, private, B/2. Last mentioned in muster roll
         of Jun 1782.

3-246   DAESCHLER, Theophil, Jaeger, J/2. Deserted 28 Apr 1783.

         DOSSLER, Leonhard, private, A/1. Last mentioned in muster roll
         of Jun 1783.

3-260   TAUSCHER, Johann Michael, private, A/3. Last mentioned in muster
         roll of Dec 1779.

3-340   DIETHEL, Johann, Jaeger, J/2. No further information.

         DITTEL, Johann, Jaeger, J/2. Last mentioned in muster roll of
         Dec 1781.

3-345   DIETLEIN, Johann Ludwig, private, A/1. Deserted 5 Mar 1778.

3-362   DIETRICH, Heinrich, private, B/4. Last mentioned in muster roll
         of Jun 1782, according to Doe, entry of 29 Nov 1782.

3-400   DILL, Johann Jakob, private, A/2. Deserted 17 Aug 1778.

         DULLAY(IN), Christiana. *See* NEUPERT, --, 5-163.

3-430   DAUWALD, Johann Daniel, private, B/4. Last mentioned in muster
         roll of Jun 1783.

3-452   DILLING, Konrad, private, B/2. Missing since Dec 1782.

3-460   DILLER, Georg Adam, private, B/1. Last mentioned in muster roll
         of Dec 1779.

         TAYLOR. [Might have changed the German surname Schneider to Eng-
         lish equivalent. *See* Schneider 2-536.]

3-462   TELORAC, Johann Michael, private, A/2. Deserted 18 Aug 1778.

3-500   DUHN, Konrad, private, B/2. Last mentioned in muster roll of
         Jun 1782.

3-510   DYMPE, Bernhard, private, A/5. Deserted 12 May 1783.

3-524   DENGLER, Georg, private, A/4. Last mentioned in muster roll of
          Dec 1782.

          DINKELMEYER, Kaspar, grenadier, A/5. Missing since Jun 1783.

3-530   TWENTY. [Might have changed German surname Zwanziger to near
          English equivalent. *See* Zwanziger 2-522.]

3-560   DEHNER, Johann Georg, Jaeger, J/1. Discharged in Dec 1777.

3-600   DOERR, Jakob, private, A/4. Last mentioned in muster roll of
          Dec 1782.

          TREU, Johann Karl, Jaeger, J/3. Replacement trooper in 1782.
          Last mentioned in muster roll of Jun 1783.

3-612   TRIPS, Johann Peter, Jaeger, J/1. Last mentioned in muster roll
          of Jun 1780.

3-614   DERPLAIM, Nikolaus, Jaeger, J/2. Deserted 27 May 1783.

3-620   DARRACH, Wilhelm, private, A/3. Deserted 22 May 1783.

          DORSCH, Johann Georg, grenadier, A/5. Deserted 9 Oct 1781.

          TUERCK, Johann, wagon master, B. Last mentioned in muster roll
          of Jun 1783.

          TUERCK, Johann Melchior, private, A/3. Last mentioned in mus-
          ter roll of Jun 1781.

3-624   DRESSEL, Konrad, private, B/3. Deserted 9 Jul 1781.

          DRESSEL, Thomas, private, B/5. Deserted 16 Oct 1782. Enlisted
          with the American troops.

3-625   DIRSCHNER, Franz, Jaeger, J/3. No further information.

3-626   TROEGER, Gottlieb, private, A/2. Deserted 30 Dec 1781. Accord-
          ing to Pr, he enlisted with the American Light Horse (Hussars).

3-650   DORN, Georg, private, B/2. Deserted 10 Aug 1781.

3-651   DOERNHOEFER, Johann, private, B/2. Last mentioned in muster roll
          of Dec 1782.

Soundex
Number

3-660   DORER, Johann, private, B/1. Last mentioned in muster roll of
         Jun 1783.

4-100   LOEB, Johann, private, A/3. Last mentioned in muster roll of
         Dec 1782.

4-120   LEYBACH, Konrad, servant, J/1. No further information.

4-140   LIEBEL, Johann, private, A/4. Deserted 10 Sep 1782. According
         to Pr, he enlisted with the American troops. According to
         Stadtarchiv Ansbach AM.1041, his origins in Ansbach were
         unknown. His father was thought to have been "one Reuther
         of this place."

4-200   LEIS, Ignatius, private, B/1. Deserted 11 Oct 1781.

         LEWIS. [Might have changed German surname Ludwig to English equi-
         valent. *See* Ludwig 4-320.]

         LUCK, Johann, private, A/2. Deserted 29 May 1778.

         LUTZ, Johann Andreas, Jaeger & servant. Deserted 22 May 1778.

4-235   LIGHTNER. [Might have changed spelling of German surname Leitner
         to preserve correct pronunciation. *See* Leitner 4-356.]

4-254   LOCHMUELLER, Johann, private, B/4. Missing since Jun 1783.

         LOCHMUELLER, Wolf, private, B/2. Last mentioned in muster roll
         of Jun 1781.

4-255   LESSMANN, Gottlob, Jaeger, J/2, J/4. No further information.

4-256   LECHNER, Joseph, servant, B/4. Missing since Jun 1783.

         LECHNER, Simon, private, B/4. No further information.

         LESNER, Johann Heinrich, private, A/2. No further information.

         LOCHNER, Heinrich, private, A/4. Deserted 28 Dec 1782. Enlisted
         with the American troops.

         LOCHNER, Johann Gregor, Jaeger, A/2, J/1. No further information.

         LOCHNER, Johann Peter, private, B/1. Deserted 25 Sep 1782.

30

*Soundex
Number*

4-320   LUDWIG, Johann Andreas Philipp, Jaeger, J/1. Last mentioned in
         muster roll of Dec 1782.

4-340   LITTLE. [Might have changed the German surname Klein to English
         equivalent. *See* Klein 2-450.]

4-342   LOTHOLZ, Georg, private, A/4. Last mentioned in muster roll of
         Jun 1783.

4-356   LEITNER, Adam, Jaeger, J/2. Deserted 6 Sep 1779.

4-361   LAUTERBACH, Albert, canoneer, B/2, Artillery Detachment. No fur-
         ther information.

         LAUTERBACH, Georg Michael, private, B/1. Deserted 17 Feb 1780.

         LAUTERBACH, Johann, private, B/3. Deserted 13 May 1783.

         LAUTERBACH, Konrad, private, B/5. Deserted 12 May 1783.

         LAUTERBACH, Michael, grenadier, B/5. Deserted 25 Oct 1781.

4-366   LEDERER, Johann, private, B/1. Missing since Jun 1783.

4-520   LANG, Johann Michael, private, B/2. Last mentioned in muster
         roll of Dec 1782.

         LENTZ, Jakob, private, B/2. Deserted 9 May 1783.

4-535   LINDNER, Egydius, private, A/4. Deserted 12 Sep 1782.

4-560   LAMAR, Michael, Jaeger, J/2. Discharged on 1 Jan 1780.

4-565   LAEMMERMANN, Leonhard, Jaeger, J/1. Replacement trooper in 1782.
         No further information.

4-652   LAWRENCE. [Might have changed spelling of German surname Lorenz
         to English equivalent. *See* Lorenz 4-652.]

         LORENZ, Michael, private, B/1. Deserted 13 Aug 1778.

4-656   LAUERMEYER, Johann Georg, Jaeger, A/2, J/6. No further informa-
         tion.

5-000   MAY, Christoph, private, J/6. Deserted 22 Sep 1781.

5-140   NOBLE. [Might have changed German surname Edel to English equi-
         valent. *See* Edel 7-340.]

5-163   NEUBERT, Thomas, private, A/1. Last mentioned in muster roll of
         Jun 1783.

         NEUPERT, --, private, B/4. Enlisted with the American troops.
         According to <u>Doe</u>, entry of 8 Feb 1781, he married Chris-
         tiana Dullayin [the *-in* suffix indicates a female person
         in German; thus the surname is probably Dullay], an Amer-
         ican, from Fleck Bush [Flatbush?] on Long Island.

5-230   MAAGD, Andreas Heinrich, private, B/1. Deserted 13 May 1783.

5-236   NUECHTERLEIN, Johann Michael, private, B/2. Last mentioned in
         muster roll of Dec 1782.

5-240   MEISEL, Peter, Jaeger, J/3, B/3. Deserted 30 Aug 1782.

         MICHEL, Johann, private, B/1. Last mentioned in muster roll of
         Oct 1781.

         NAGEL, Christian, Jaeger, J/2. Replacement trooper in 1778.

         NAGEL, Michael, private, A/3. Last mentioned in muster roll of
         Jun 1783.

         NUETZEL, Johann Karl, Jaeger, A/2, J/4. Last mentioned in mus-
         ter roll of Dec 1782.

5-243   MAGGOLD, Ludwig Friedrich, private, B/2. Last mentioned in mus-
         ter roll of Dec 1782.

5-260   MEZGER, Markus, private, B/2. Last mentioned in muster roll of
         Dec 1782.

         NEUHAUSSER, Johann, camp attendant [*Valet de Tente*], A/4. Last
         mentioned in muster roll of Jun 1783.

5-324   MITCHELL. [Might have changed spelling of German surname Michel
         to English equivalent. *See* Michel 5-240.]

5-360   MEDER, Johann, grenadier, A/5. Deserted 11 May 1783.

5-420   MELZ, Matthias Bernhard, Jaeger, J/1. Enlisted in the American
         troops on 21 Jun 1778.

5-430   de MOLITHE. *See* von MOLITHOR, 5-436.

5-436   von MOLITHOR, Christian Theodor Sigismund, Captain, A/1, B/4, B/5. According to Doe, entry of 21 Jun 1783: "I was detailed to officers' watch, as Grenadier Captain von Molithor and First Lieutenant von Altenstein were under arrest, on the orders of Colonel Seybothen, for having married women, which was against regulations." According to Gilroy, page 11, DP, and BRM, von Molithor was the leader of a group of Ansbach soldiers who settled at Clements Township, Annapolis Royal, Nova Scotia. He received 700 acres of land (2,800 hectares). He changed his name to De Molithe.

5-460   MUELLER, Adam, private, A/?, B/5. No further information.

        MUELLER, Georg Jakob, grenadier, A/5. Deserted 30 Sep 1781.

        MUELLER, Gottlieb, private, A/3. Deserted 12 May 1783.

        MUELLER, Johann Jakob, Jaeger, J/2, J/4. Last mentioned in muster roll of Jun 1783.

        MUELLER, Johann Sebastian, private, A/2. Last mentioned in muster roll of Dec 1782.

        MUELLER, Kaspar, private, A/2. Missing since Jun 1783.

        MUELLER, Michael, Jaeger, J/2. Last mentioned in muster roll of Dec 1782.

        MUELLER, Veit, private, A/4, A/1. Missing since Dec 1781.

        MUELLER, Vitus, private, A/1. Missing since Jun 1782.

5-530   MENDT, Nikolaus, private, A/1. Last mentioned in muster roll of Jun 1783.

5-534   MANTEL, Johann Paul, private, B/1. Enlisted in the American troops.

5-560   NIEMEYER, Heinrich, Jaeger, A/4. A/6. Last mentioned in muster roll of Jun 1783.

5-600   MEYER, Georg, private, A/3. Deserted 13 May 1783.

Soundex
Number

5-600   MEYER, Johann, private, A/2, A/4. Deserted 15 Oct 1781.

        MEYER, Johann, private, A/3. Deserted 22 May 1783.

        MEYER, Johann, drummer, A/3. Deserted 2 Aug 1782.

        MEYER, Johann, grenadier, B/5. Last mentioned in muster roll
            of Dec 1780.

        MEYER, Johann Leonhard, private, A/3. Missing since Jun 1783.

        MEYER, Michael, private, A/4. Last mentioned in muster roll of
            Dec 1783 [?]

        MEYER, Michael, private, B/4. According to Doe, he deserted
            2 May 1782 and left debts.

        MOHR, Paul, private, A/3. According to Ansb.Ms.hist.487, he
            was the son of Johann Georg Mohr, a herder, from Steindl
            near Hilpoltstein (died 1780) and his wife who, after the
            death of her husband, received a pension in the amount of
            10 florins.

        MURR, Lorenz, private, A/3. Missing since Jun 1783.

5-616   MAYERHOEFER, Michael, private, A/4. Deserted 28 Dec 1782.

        MEYERHOFER, Peter, private, B/4. Deserted 13 May 1783. From
            Ansbach.

5-620   MOERSCH, Joseph, Jaeger, J/2. Deserted 27 May 1783.

5-621   MOERSBERGER, Jakob, private, A/4. Last mentioned in muster roll
            of Dec 1782.

5-624   MARSCHALL, Friedrich, Jaeger, J/3, J/4. No further information.

        MERCKEL, Balthasar, private, A/3. Last mentioned in muster roll
            of Dec 1782.

5-626   MARQUARDT, Michael, grenadier, A/5. Deserted 14 Oct 1781. Ac-
            cording to Ansb.Ms.hist.487, he was the son of the master
            blacksmith -- Marquardt of Onolzheim.

34

5-634   MERDELMEYER, Michael, Jaeger, J/2. Last mentioned in muster
       roll of Jun 1781.

5-642   MOERLICH, Karl, servant, A/1. Deserted 27 Dec 1782.

       NOERLICH, Karl, livestock boy [*Steckenknecht*], A/2, A/1, A/4.
       Deserted 27 Dec 1782. According to Pr, he enlisted in
       the American troops. [Probably, Moerlich and Noerlich
       are the same person.]

6-000   RAUH, Matthias, private, A/2. Deserted 17 Aug 1778. Accord-
       ing to HAV, he was from Ansbach; height 5 *Schuh*, 7-3/4
       Zoll. According to AMKB, he was the illegitimate son of
       Johann Georg Rauh; his mother was Anna Maria Weiss.

6-100   RAPP, Friedrich, regimental medic, A/1. According to HAV, and
       Doe: "Remained with his servant in Philadelphia and re-
       sided for a time in Germantown. He is said to have mar-
       ried in America."

       REIF, Johann Nikolaus, drummer, A/5. Last mentioned in muster
       roll of Jun 1783.

6-152   RUPPINGER, Friedrich, Jaeger. Deserted 4 Mar 1778.

6-200   RIES, Adam, private, B/5. Last mentioned in muster roll of Dec
       1782.

       RIES, Andreas, private, B/5. Last mentioned in muster roll of
       Jun 1783.

       RIES, Georg Michael, private, B/1. Enlisted with the American
       troops.

       ROCK, Michael, private, A/2. No further information.

       ROESCH, Michael, private, A/2. Deserted 16 May 1783.

6-240   RIEGEL, Johann, private, B/4. Deserted 13 Jan 1783.

6-243   ROSSELT, Johann Wilhelm, grenadier, A/5. Deserted 25 Oct 1781.

6-246   ROESLER, Johann, private, A/3. Deserted 11 Oct 1781. Accord-
       ing to Doe, he was from Wunsiedel.

6-263   REICHARDT, Georg Nikolaus, drummer, A/3. Enlisted with the American troops.

RUECKERT, Johann Michael, private, A/1. Son of Johann Thomas Rueckert from Doeckingen. His father's brickyard had been deeded to him 11 years before, but is now to be taken over by his brother Andreas. Deserted Jun 1783.

RUECKERT, Johann Simon, private, A/2. Deserted 15 Oct 1781. According to AMKB, his wife, who remained in Ansbach, bore a legitimate [!] child in 1784.

RUECKERT, Peter, grenadier, B/2. Last mentioned in muster roll of Dec 1782.

6-265   ROSSWURM, Matthias, private, A/4. Missing since Jun 1783. However, according to AKA 118, Georg Mathias Russwurm, from Gefrees, was enlisted on 26 Jul 1779 and received 8 *Kroner* bounty. He was discharged on 29 Nov 1783 [presumably in Germany].

6-300   ROTH, Johann Jakob, grenadier, A/5. Last mentioned in muster roll of Jun 1783. From Crailsheim.

6-340   RAITHEL, Johann, private, B/4. According to Doe, entry of 10 May 1782, ". . . he indentured himself for debt. He owed a resident near Frederickstown 64 Spanish dollars for cider, beer, and whiskey which he had sold."

RIEDEL, Johann Adam Friedrich, private, B/4. According to Doe, he deserted on 12 Dec 1781.

RIEDEL, Georg Friedrich, private, B/2. Deserted 14 Oct 1781. According to Doe, "Had wife and child in New York."

ROEDEL, Konrad, private, A/3. Deserted 29 Sep 1782. Enlisted with the American troops.

6-346   RADLER, Johann, private, A/3. Son of Frau -- Radler of Mainbernheim.

6-500   RAHM, Lorenz, private, B/3. Discharged as a surrenderer [*Kapitulant*] on 3 Jul 1783. He went to Philadelphia.

RION, Johann, servant, J/2. Discharged 2 Mar 1781.

36

6-520   REINICKA, Christoph, private, B/3. Deserted 5 Sep 1782.

6-534   REINDEL, Johann Nikolaus, private, B/3. Deserted 13 May 1783.

6-540   RUMMEL, Johann Georg, grenadier, A/5. Deserted 13 Aug 1778.
        According to Bo, he deserted with [Lorenz] Baumann and
        [Johann] Stadler.

6-545   REINLAENDER, Franz, Jaeger, J/3. Replacement trooper in 1782.

6-552   RAHNINGER, Jakob, Jaeger, J/1. Deserted 31 Oct 1779.

6-563   REINHARD, Johann Martin, grenadier, A/5. Deserted 16 Oct 1781

6-625   RUEHRSCHNECK, Johann, private, A/1. Last mentioned in muster
        roll of Jun 1783.

7-100   HOPF, Johann, private, A/4. No further information.

7-120   HEUBECK, Johann Leonhard, Jaeger. Replacement trooper in 1782.

7-130   ABT, Friedrich, Jaeger, J/1. Deserted 23 Sep 1783 from Kings
        barracks on York [Manhattan] Island. In December 1779 he
        had been captured and exchanged in October 1780. Accord-
        ing to Bor, entry of 9 Jun 1779: "He returned, having de-
        serted the enemy. He had been a Light Hussar [with the
        Americans] and came in with his horse and saddle with him."
        According to Doe: ". . . on 1 Oct 1779 while stationed in
        Connecticut he accompanied his captain to buy victuals. He
        was captured by a party of Americans and shortly thereafter
        he resolved to enter rebel service and was enlisted in Wash-
        ington's newly-organized Light Horse (Hussars). Today, he
        was ordered on reconnaissance with others and he escaped
        [back to the Ansbach unit]."

7-140   HUEBEL, Georg, private, A/1. Missing since Jun 1783.

        UEBEL, Christian, private, A/2. Last mentioned in muster roll
        of Jun 1783.

        UEBEL, Georg, drummer, B/3. Enlisted with the American troops.

        UEBEL, Samuel, private, A/3, A/1. Last mentioned in muster roll
        of Dec 1782.

Soundex
Number

7-142   UEBELHACK, Johann Konrad, private, A/3. Deserted on 18 May 1781.

7-143   APPOLD, Andreas, private, B/1. Last mentioned in muster roll of
        Jun 1783.

7-152   HOPPENSTAEDT, Johann Friedrich, Jaeger, J/1. Deserted 27 May
        1783.

7-155   HOFFMANN, Christoph, Jaeger, J/2. No further information.

        HOFFMANN, Johann, private (team driver), B/-. Last mentioned in
        muster roll of Jun 1783.

        HOFFMANN, Johann Georg, private, B/2. Missing since Jun 1783.

        HOFFMANN, Johann Konrad, private, A/3. Last mentioned in muster
        roll of Jun 1783.

        HOFFMANN, Johann Leonhard, Jaeger, J/1. No further information.

        HOFFMANN, Wolff, private, B/2. Deserted Oct 1782.

7-156   HAEFNER, Friedrich, Jaeger, J/3. Deserted 25 Jun 1783.

        HAEFNER, Georg, Jaeger, J/2. Last mentioned in muster roll of
        Jun 1781.

        HAEFNER, Kilian, cannoneer, Artillery Detachment. Deserted 4 Jul
        1780.

        HOFFMEYER, Michael, Jaeger, J/2. No further information.

7-160   HOFER, Ludwig, drummer, A/4. Deserted 2 Jan 1782.

        HOPFER, Simon, private, A/4. Deserted 18 Aug 1781. According to
        Pr, he deserted while guarding the animals.

        WEBER, Georg, private, B/1. Deserted 13 May 1783.

        WEBER, Johann Konrad, private, A/3. Last mentioned in muster roll
        of Jun 1779.

        WEBER, Konrad, grenadier, A/5. Deserted 22 Oct 1781.

        WEBER, Michael, Jaeger, J/2. Surrenderer [*Kapitulant*] until 1 Jul
        1783. Height: 6 *Schuh*.

38

38

7-162   HOHBERGER, Johann Heinrich, private, B/3. Deserted 13 May 1783.

7-164   EBERLEIN, Johann, private, B/2. Deserted 10 Aug 1781.

7-165   OBERMEYER, Franz, Jaeger, J/2. Replacement trooper in 1778.

7-200   HAAG, Georg, private, A/1. Missing since Jun 1783.

HAAG, Johann, officer's servant, J/2. Last mentioned in muster roll in Dec 1781.

HAAS, Anton, Jaeger, J/2. Deserted 21 Jun 1781 in New Jersey.

HAAS, Johann Georg, private, B/4. Deserted 2 Apr 1782.

HOSCH, Christoph, private, A/3. Last mentioned in muster roll of Dec 1782.

WAESCH, Michael, private, A/1. Deserted 27 Dec 1782.

WEISS, Konrad, private, A/4. Deserted 1 Jan 1782. Enlisted in the American Light Horse (Hussars).

7-210   JAKOBY, Lorenz, grenadier, B/5. Deserted 7 Oct 1781.

7-230   VOIGT, Georg, private, B/2. Deserted 14 Oct 1781.

WUEST, Georg, private, A/4. Last mentioned in muster roll of Jun 1783.

ASTMANN, Jakob, Jaeger, A/4, J/6. According to Gilroy, page 7, he received 150 acres of land in Clements Township, Annapolis County, Nova Scotia, in 1784. He had a wife and two children.

7-235   WESTZSTEIN, Johann Andreas, Jaeger, J/1. Recruited 27 Jan 1779. No further information.

7-236   OSTERMEYER, Johann Philipp, private, B/3. Deserted 22 May 1783.

OSTERTAG, Johan Michael, private, A/2. Deserted 11 Oct 1781.

7-240   EUSELE, Joseph, private, B/4. According to Doe, entry of 31 Jul 1783: "Today, he took his leave and stayed in New York as a surrenderer [*Kapitulant*]."

7-240   HOEGEL, Johann, Jaeger. Replacement trooper in 1782.

       OCKEL, Heinrich, grenadier, A/5. Deserted 22 Oct 1781. According to <u>Stadtarchiv Ansb.AM 1041</u>, he came from Ansbach and was born in 1763.

       VOGEL, Gilbert, Jaeger, J/2. Deserted 27 May 1783.

       VOGEL, Michael, private, A/3. Deserted 6 Aug 1781.

       VOGEL, Wolfgang, private, B/4. According to <u>Doe</u>, he deserted on 3 Apr 1782.

       WEIGEL, Adam, Jaeger, J/2. Deserted 22 Jul 1781 in Virginia.

7-241   HASSELBACHER, Peter, private, A/4. Missing since Jun 1783.

7-245   WEGELEIN, Johann Paul, private, A/3. Last mentioned in muster roll of Jun 1783.

7-246   HUCKLER, Johann Ludwig, Jaeger, J/2. Last mentioned in muster roll of Dec 1781.

7-250   JOACHIM, Erhard, Jaeger, J/1. Deserted 16 Feb 1778.

7-251   ESENBECK, Christoph Wilhelm, corporal, J/1, J/2. According to <u>HAV</u>, he came from Schoenberg. He deserted with new uniform and wages received. "Since he has much property to be inherited at home, it is impossible to understand why he does not return."

7-252   HEISINGER, Johann, private, A/4. Last mentioned in muster roll of Dec 1782.

7-254   HECKENMUELLER, Konrad, private, B/3. Deserted 12 May 1783.

7-255   HEISCHMANN, Johann Nikolaus, private, A/3. Deserted 12 May 1783.

       WIZMANN, Konrad, private, B/2. Last mentioned in muster roll of Dec 1782.

7-256   WAEGNER, Prokop, horn player, J/2. Deserted 16 Aug 1779.

       WAGNER, Johann Christoph, chaplain, B/-. According to <u>Doe</u>, entry of 15 Jun 1783: "Chaplain Wagner . . . remained in Frederickstown; a congregation has been promised him in Maryland and he wishes to marry. We no longer have a chaplain for either regiment." According to Pr, 18 Jul 1783: "Chaplain Wagner was granted his discharge and intends to accompany the settlers [*English Gesinnte*] to Nova Scotia." According to Gilroy, p. 24, he was granted 400 acres of land in Clements Township, Annapolis Royal, Nova Scotia. According to DP, he had four children. According to BRM, Wagner probably returned to Germany later in life. There is further information on his life in Staedtler, p. 73 *et seq*.

7-256   WAGNER, Johann Heinrich, horn player, J/2. Deserted 16 Aug 1779. [This might be the same person as Prokop Waegner above.]

7-260   HAGER, Heinrich, Jaeger. Replacement trooper in 1782.

HAEGER, Georg, Jaeger. Replacement trooper in 1782.

JAEGER, Johann Leonhardt, Jaeger, J/1. Deserted 29 Dec 1777.

7-262   ESCHERICH, Johann Georg, cannoneer, A/3. Deserted 11 Oct 1781.

7-263   ECKART, Johann Michael, private, B/3. Deserted 24 Dec 1782. From Ansbach.

HECKERT, Johann Gottlieb, private, B/3. Last mentioned in muster roll of Jun 1783.

7-264   ECKERLEIN, Paul, private, A/2, A/5. Last mentioned in muster roll of Oct 1781.

7-265   EICHHORN, Wolf Andreas, Jaeger, J/1. Deserted 6 Sep 1781 while on an expedition to New London.

7-300   HEAD. [Might have changed German surname Kopf to English equivalent. *See* Kopf 2-100.]

OED, Johann Michael, private, A/2. Deserted 7 Aug 1781.

OTT, Friedrich, drummer, A/1. Deserted 16 Oct 1782.

OTT, Michael Friedrich Ludwig, private. Deserted 14 Sep 1782. From Ansbach; enlisted with the American troops.

7-320   JUDAS, Veit, Jaeger, J/2. Deserted 24 Sep 1781.

7-323   HATTSTEDT, Georg Heinrich, Jaeger, J/1. Last mentioned in muster roll of Jun 1780.

Soundex
Number

7-324   WETSCHEL, Christian, private, A/3. Last mentioned in muster roll
           of Jun 1783.

7-340   EDEL, Johann Konrad, musician, J/4. Replacement trooper in 1782.

           HUTTEL, Theophil, Jaeger, J/2. Last mentioned in muster roll of
           Dec 1781. From Selb.

7-350   ADAM, Johann Georg, private, B/4. Deserted 22 May 1783. Accord-
           ing to Doe: "Today, two privates Schindler I and Adam of
           Quesnoy [company?] loitered behind the marching troops near
           Washington Tavern. They took Lieutenant von Cyriacy's new
           uniform and baggage, as well as the equipment of officer
           Knoll and others, which were in the wagon which they were
           driving."

7-352   HEYDINGSFELDER, Johann Konrad, private, B/4. No further informa-
           tion.

7-356   HEYDENREICH, Johann, private, B/2. Last mentioned in muster roll
           of Dec 1782.

7-360   HEYDER, Wilhelm, private, B/5. Deserted 15 May 1783. Father was
           Michael Heider [so spelled]; no property; mother supported
           by public charity.

           WIEDER, Joseph, private, A/1. No further information.

7-361   HADOERFER, Johann Michael, grenadier, A/5. Deserted 28 Apr 1782.

           ODOERFER, Wolfgang, private, A/5. Deserted 12 Oct 1782. Accord-
           ing to Stadtarchiv Ansbach AM 1041, ". . . he had spent all
           his estate and, therefore, had to enter military service.
           He has a wife, a 15-year-old son, and a 12-year-old daughter
           who are in very straitened circumstances."

7-400   HILL. [Might have translated the German surname Hoegel into a
           near English equivalent. See Hoegel 7-240.]

           HOEHL, Melchior, grenadier, B/5. Last mentioned in the muster
           roll of Jun 1783.

           HOEHL, Johann Georg, private, A/3. No further information.

           HOLY, Lorenz, Jaeger. Replacement trooper in 1782.

42

7-400   OEL, Valentin, private, A/5. Son of Adam Oehl [so spelled],
           citizen of Ochsenfurt. Soldier since 1780.

         WILL, Matthias, private, B/5. Enlisted with the American troops.

7-410   WOLF, Johann Adam, private, B/4. According to <u>Doe</u>, deserted on
           2 Apr 1783.

         WOLFF, Adam, Jaeger, J/3, J/2, J/4. Last mentioned in muster
           roll of Jun 1783.

         WOLFF, Friedrich, Jaeger, J/1. Deserted 16 Mar 1777.

7-416   HILPERT, Theodor, Jaeger, J/1. No further information.

         WOLFRUM, Johann Adam, corporal, B/4. No further information.

7-420   ELIAS, Mathias, private, B/3. Deserted 14 Oct 1781.

         VOLCK, Friedrich Ernst, private, A/4. Son of Georg Volck from
           Creglingen. Last mentioned in muster roll of Jun 1783.

7-421   ULSHOEFER, Johann Georg, private, B/3. Deserted 18 Aug 1779.
           Son of the citizen [*Ratsbuerger*] of Creglingen, clerk
           -- Ulshoefer.

7-425   HOLZHEIMER, Georg, private, B/1. Missing since Jun 1783.

         HOLZINGER, Georg Simon, B/1. No further information.

         ILGEN, Ludwig Albrecht Wilhelm, Jaeger, J/1. Deserted 9 Aug 1779.

7-426   WALKER, Friedrich, Jaeger, J/2. Deserted 2 Nov 1779.

7-430   WILD, Lorenz, livestock attendant, Artillery Detachment. Accord-
           ing to <u>DP</u>, his profession was blacksmith; he had one child.

         WELT, Blasius, Jaeger. Replacement trooper in 1782.

7-436   WALTHER, Caspar, private, B/2. Last mentioned in muster roll of
           Jun 1782.

         WALTHER, Christoph, private, A/1. Last mentioned in muster roll
           of Jun 1783.

7-452   WALLING, Simon, private, A/3. Last mentioned in muster roll of
           Jun 1783.

7-456   HELMERT, Johann Gerlach, private, A/2. Last mentioned in muster roll of Dec 1782.

WILLMEHR, Nikolaus, private, A/1. Last mentioned in muster roll of Jun 1783.

7-460   HALLER, Kaspar, private, A/4. Deserted 12 May 1783.

HELLER, Johann Anton, Jaeger, B/5, J/1. Last mentioned in muster roll of Jun 1783.

HELLER, Konrad, private, A/4. Last mentioned in muster roll of Jun 1783.

7-462   HELLERICH, Johann, private, B/3. Deserted 20 Jul 1780.

7-500   HAHN, Christoph, horn player, J/3. Deserted 23 Sep 1782.

HAHN, Johann, private, B/1. No further information.

HAHN, Johann, private, B/2. Last mentioned in muster roll of Dec 1782.

HEIM, Johann, private, A/1. Last mentioned in muster roll of Jun 1783.

HYENE, Johann, Jaeger, J/2. Replacement trooper in 1782.

JOHN, Thomas, servant, J/1. Last mentioned in muster roll of Jun 1783.

7-514   HAENFLING, Erhard, livestock attendant, Artillery Detachment. Deserted 2 Jun 1778.

7-516   HOHENBERGER, Georg, grenadier, B/5. Deserted 6 Jul 1780.

7-520   HENZE, Heinrich August, Jaeger, J/2. Last mentioned in muster roll of Jun 1781.

7-524   AMSCHLER, Erhard, private, B/2. Deserted 29 Sep 1781. Same date mentioned in Doe.

ENGELBRECHT, Johann, private, B/1. Deserted 13 May 1783.

ENGELHARD, Johann Konrad, private, B/3. Last mentioned in muster roll of Jun 1782.

44

7-524   HENZOLD, Michael, private, A/4. No further information.

       WINCKLER, Johann Anton, private, A/2. Last mentioned in muster
           roll of Jun 1783.

       WINCKLER, Johann Christian, private, B/1. Last mentioned in mus-
           ter roll of Dec 1782.

7-525   ENSENBERGER, Johann Friedrich, Jaeger, J/4, J/6. Replacement
           trooper in 1782. According to Gilroy, p. 12, he received
           150 acres of land in Clements Township, Lunenburg County,
           Nova Scotia, in 1784. According to DP, he was a shoemaker
           and had one child.

7-526   HUNGER, Peter, private, A/3. Deserted 19 Aug 1779; also deserted
           2 May 1782. [No further information given; it is possible
           that he deserted in 1779, returned to his former regiment,
           and again deserted in 1782. There are a number of such
           cases noted in this list.]

7-530   HUND, Georg, private, A/1. Last mentioned in muster roll of Dec
           1782.

       HUNDT, Georg, private, A/1. Last mentioned in muster roll of Dec
           1782. [Probably the same person as Georg Hund above.]

       WEYANDT, Andreas, private, A/3. Last mentioned in muster roll of
           Jun 1783. According to AKA 118, however, he was a surrenderer
           [*Kapitulant*] for a four-year period. He came from Fuerth and
           was a subject of the Cathedral Estate [*Domherrisch*]. He was
           25 years old (born 1759) and his heigh was 5 *Schuh* 9 *Zoll*.
           He was enlisted on 21 Oct 1774 and received a bounty of 30
           Kroner. On 18 Jul 1786 [?] he is shown as an invalid.

7-532   ANDIG, Christoph, private, B/3. Deserted on 8 Oct 1781. According
           to Doe, date of desertion was 18 Oct 1781.

7-534   WENDEL, Heinrich Thomas, Jaeger, J/3. No further information.

7-535   ANTHONY (a Negro), officer's servant, J/2. Last mentioned in mus-
           ter roll of Dec 1781.

7-536   HUNTER. [Might have changed German surname Jaeger to English equi-
           valent. *See* Jaeger 7-260.]

Soundex
Number

7-536   WUNDERLICH, Lorenz, private, A/3. Last mentioned in muster roll
             of Jun 1783.

             WUNDERLICH, Peter, Jaeger, J/2. Discharged 31 Mar 1780.

7-545   HEINLEIN, Johann, private, A/4. Last mentioned in muster roll
             of Dec 1779.

7-546   WIMMLER, Christoph, private, A/3. Last mentioned in muster roll
             of Jun 1783.

7-550   WEYMANN, Johann, Jaeger, J/1. Discharged on 20 Oct 1777.

7-552   HENNINGER, Johann, drummer, B/2. Last mentioned in muster roll
             of Jun 1782.

             VENNING, Johann Jakob, Jaeger, J/5. Replacement trooper in 1782.

             WANNENMACHER, Sophonias, private, A/3. Deserted 16 Oct 1782.
             Enlisted with the American troops. He was from Ansbach and
             the son of Paul Wannenmacher. He had one brother and two
             sisters. He was a butcher by trade.

7-560   HAMMER, Michael, Jaeger, J/2. Deserted 17 Oct 1779.

7-562   HEINRIZ, Johann, Jaeger, J/1, J/2. Last mentioned in muster roll
             of Dec 1780.

7-564   EMMERLING, Johann Friedrich, piper, B/5. Deserted 31 Dec 1783.

7-600   HAUER, Matthias, Jaeger, J/2. Deserted 9 May 1783.

             WEERY (a Negro), J/2. Deserted 2 Jul 1781.

             WEHR, Johann Paul, private, B/3. Deserted 8 Jul 1781.

7-621   HOERSCHBERGER, Jakob, private, A/4. Deserted 5 May 1783.

             WURZBACH, Johann Andreas, drummer, A/2. Deserted 14 Jan 1782 at
             Winchester. According to Pr, "He came back as a recruiter
             for the American troops to the [German prisoner of war camp]
             at Frederickstown."

7-622   HERZOG, Georg, private, A/1. Missing since Jun 1783.

7-634   HAERTLEIN, Georg, Jaeger, J/2. Deserted 27 May 1783.

        HARTLEIN, Leonhard, private, A/3. Deserted 30 Sep 1781.

        HERTLEIN, Jobst, private, A/3. Deserted 28 Dec 1782. Enlisted with the American troops.

        OERTEL, Johann Albrecht, private, B/3. Deserted 15 May 1783.

7-635   HARTMANN, Daniel, private, A/4, J/3. Last mentioned in muster roll of Dec 1782.

        HARTMANN, Heinrich, private, A/1. Deserted 29 May 1783.

        HARTUNG, Heinrich, private, A/4. Missing since Jun 1783.

        JORDAN, Nikodemus, Jaeger, J/1. Enlisted on 2 Jan 1781.

7-636   HERTERICH, Johann Konrad, private, B/3. Born 12 Dec 1752 at Laubersreuth/Muenchberg [territory], son of Leonhard Herterich and Margarethe Walther of Ploessen. Johann Konrad married Eleanor Schenck, a soldier's widow. He was discharged from Marquisate [Ansbach] service on 1 Aug 1783 in New York. According to Gilroy, p. 14, he was granted 100 acres of land in Clements Township, Annapolis Royal, Nova Scotia. According to DP, he was a farmer. According to BRM, he died on 25 Jan 1839 in Nova Scotia. A modern descendant is Max Sutherland of Annapolis Royal, Nova Scotia.

7-642   HARLES, Georg, private, B/1. Last mentioned in muster roll of Jun 1783.

        HARLES, Johann, private, B/4. Last mentioned in muster roll of Dec 1782.

7-643   AROLD, Georg, private, A/4. Missing since Jun 1783.

        HEROLD, Johann, grenadier, A/5. Deserted 29 Apr 1782. Enlisted in the American Light Horse (Hussars).

7-645   ERLWEIN, Johann, private, A/2. Deserted 18 Aug 1779.

7-651   HORNEBER, Andreas, Jaeger, B/4, J/4. According to Gilroy, p. 15, and DP, he received a grant of 100 acres of land in Clements Township, Annapolis County, Nova Scotia, in 1784. He was a farmer and miller; he had one child.

7-652   ERNST, Johann, private, A/3. Last mentioned in muster roll of
          Jun 1783.

          HAERMS, Jakob, Jaeger, J/1. Deserted 27 May 1783.

          HERING, Johann Peter Christian, Jaeger. Replacement trooper in
            1783.

          HEERING, Bartholomaei, corporal, B/5. No further information.

7-653   ARND, Daniel, private, A/2. Missing since Jun 1783. He apparently took oath of allegiance [to the United States] in Winchester. According to AMKB, he married Maria Margaretha [surname not given] on 1 Mar 1773; she remained in Germany and died 13 Jan 1784 in Ansbach.

7-654   ARNOLD, Sigismund Friedrich, regimental medic in the Jaeger Regiment. He settled in Nova Scotia, according to DP. According to Ans.Ms.hist.487, his wife Mrs. Margaretha Sibilla Arnold, who remained in Ansbach, received an annual grain pension. When it became known that her husband did not intend to return to Germany, her right to this pension ceased and she was given a payment in cash by the MzB [governmental ministry]. According to AMKB, a daughter Maria Margaretha was born on 18 Feb 1777.

7-655   HERMANN, Bernhard, Jaeger, J/2. Deserted 9 Aug 1779.

          HERMANN, Konrad, private, A/3. Deserted 1t Sep 1782. Enlisted with the American troops.

7-656   ERMERT, Georg, private, A/1. Deserted 25 Aug 1778.

          WERNER, Christian, private, A/4. Last mentioned in muster roll of Dec 1782.

          WERNER, Georg, servant, J/1. Discharged on 19 Jun 1783. He became a citizen and municipal drummer in Philadelphia.

7-663   ERHARDT, Michael, grenadier, A/5. Deserted 7 Jul 1780.

48

APPENDIX I

SOUNDEX CODING GUIDE FOR GERMAN SURNAMES

National Archives Soundex Rules (Modified)*

Code Class	Key Letters and Equivalents
1	b, p, f, v**
2	c, s, k, g, j, q, x, z [also tz*]
3	d, t
4	l
5	m, n
6	r
7	See rule 1 below

Rule 1: The letters a, e, i, o, u, y, w, and h are not coded, when within a surname, but are given code class 7 when the initial letter of a surname; this latter being at variance with the National Archives rule.

Rule 2: The first letter of a surname is not coded in National Archives rules but is in these modified rules. For example, the surname Carl is coded as C-640 in National Archives rule, but is 2-640 in these modified rules.

Rule 3: Every soundex number must contain three digits. A name yielding no code numbers, as Lee, would thus be L-000 in National Archives rules or 4-000 in the modified rules. A surname yielding one code number would have two zeros added, example Kuhne, coded K-500 (or 2-500 in modified rules). A surname yielding two code numbers would have one zero added, example Ebell, coded E-140 (or 7-140 in modified rules). Not more than three digits are to be used, so Ebelson would be coded E-142, rather than E-1425 (or 7-142 in modified rules).

Rule 4: When two key letters or equivalents appear together, or one key letter immediately follows or precedes an equivalent, the two are coded as one letter, by a single number, as follows: Kelly is coded as K-400 (or 2-400 in modified rules); Buerck is coded B-620 (or 1-620 in modified rules); Lloyd is coded L-300 (or 4-300 in modified rules); Schaefer is coded S-160 (or 2-160 in modified rules).

Rule 5: Such prefixes to surnames as von, van, di, de, le, D', de la, or du are sometimes disregarded in alphabetizing and in coding.

Additional Measures for German Surnames Only

Despite the great power of the National Archives soundex rules, further steps can be taken to enhance their usefulness in tracing German surnames. The following are suggested:

Step 1: After having coded the German surname under normal soundex rules above, compare the coding with all other initial letters of the same code class:

> Example 1:   Crumbine   C-651   (2-651)
>   Grumbine   G-651   (2-651)
>   Krumbein   K-651   (2-651)

C, G, and K, being of the same code class 2 in the soundex rules above, leads to the conclusion that the three surnames are variations of a common root. Since Krumbein is the original German surname (it means "crooked leg"), it is clear that Crumbine and Grumbine are American variations unlikely to appear in German emigration and vital records.

> Example 2:   Awalt   A-430   (7-430)
>   Ewald   E-430   (7-430)

A and E, being of the same code class 7, makes the two surnames equivalent. German speakers will quickly point out that the immigrant probably sought to preserve the German pronunciation of his surnames by changing it to Awalt from its original German spelling of Ewald.

Step 2: A few letters of the alphabet are pronounced differently in German and English, thus causing orthographic changes when they are written by English speakers. These possibilities are not fully dealt with by the National Archives soundex rules, as they now stand:

Ger- man	Eng- lish	
W	V	German W is prounced like English V. The German surname West might become Vest in English. (In the instant list, V and W surnames have been soundexed in class 7.)
J	Y	German J is pronounced like English Y. The German surname Jaeger, for example, is often written as Yeager in America, thus preserving the original German pronunciation. (German surnames beginning with J have been soundexed in class 7 in the instant list.)
G	Y	German G has frequently been softened to Y in Pennsylvania German dialect (Palatine dialects). Goder is said to have become Yoder; Goetter became Yetter.

50

Step 3:   Finally--and quite apart from soundex considerations--researchers
          will want to consider the possibility of complete name transla-
          tions. This occurs, in particular, when the German surname de-
          notes a trade, a quality, a color, or a day of the week. Here
          are some examples:

In Germany	In America	In Germany	In America
Zimmermann	Carpenter	Schreiner	Joiner
Jaeger	Hunter	Schneider	Taylor
Schaefer	Shepherd	Suess	Sweet
Vogel	Bird	Fuchs	Fox
Koenig	King	Freitag	Friday
Gerber	Tanner	Schwartz	Black
Weiss	White	Roth	Redd

There is, of course, no sure way to determine when a direct translation has taken place. There are some clues, however:

(1)   When a German *given* name accompanies an English-sounding surname, one may suspect such translation of the surname. For example, Johannes Farmer was probably Johannes Bauer; Franz Josef
(or Francis Joseph) Carpenter was doubtless Franz Josef Zimmermann;
George Caesar may have been Georg Kaiser (or Keiser, Keyser).

(2)   When an English surname oddly appears in a group of German surnames, here also a translation may be suspected.

(3)   When a translatable English surname cannot be traced before the
first world war, one should look for its German equivalent. Anti-
German feelings were high during the period and some German-Americans
found it advantageous to change their surnames.

---

*German TZ--when appearing together only--has been coded as class 2; German
J has been coded as a vowel (class 7). These are modifications of standard
National Archives soundex rules meant only to juxtapose certain German surnames
which otherwise would be in two different classes.

**Since German W is the equivalent of English V, the few German surnames in
this list beginning with V have been placed in Class 7.

INDEX

Brunner, Johann Baptist, 1-656
Bubmann, Matthias, 1-155
Buckel, Georg Matthias, 1-240
Buckler, Konrad, 1-246
Budin, Konrad, 1-350
Buehler, Joseph, 1-460
Buehlmeyer, Georg Thomas, 1-456
Bunerth, Friedrich August, 1-563
Bunz, Johann Georg, 1-520
Buob, Joseph, 1-100
Burckhardt, Michael, 1-626
Burett, Nikolaus, 1-630
Burett. *See also* Boehret
Busch, Leonhard, 1-200
Butcher. *Translation of* Mezger
Buttler, Leonhard, 1-346
Butzel, Johann, 1-240

Caestner, Christoph, 2-235
Callupetzky, Joseph, 2-413
Carl, Andreas, 2-640
Casebier. *See* Kaesebauer
Chemnitzer. *See* Kaemnitzer
Creutzer, Johann, 2-626
Christhulf, Georg, 2-623
Comb(s). *Translation of* Kam(m)
Count. *Translation of* Graf
Courdeou, Baptist, 2-630
Croner, David, 2-656

Daeschler, Theophil, 3-246
Darrach, Wilhelm, 3-620
Dauwald, Johann Daniel, 3-430
Dehner, Johann Georg, 3-560
Dengler, Georg, 3-524
Derplaim, Nikolaus, 3-614
Deshler. *See* Daeschler
Devil. *Translation of* Teufel
Diethel, Johann, 3-340
Diethel. *See also* Dittel
Dietlein, Johann Ludwig, 3-345
Dietrich, Heinrich, 3-362
Dietz, Johann Gottlieb, 3-200
Dill, Johann Jakob, 3-400
Diller, Georg Adam, 3-460
Dilling, Konrad, 3-452
Dinkelmeyer, Kaspar, 3-524
Dirschner, Franz, 3-625

Dittel, Johann, 3-340
Dittel. *See also* Diethel
Doberossqui [Doberossky], Johann, 3-163
Doeg, Johann Adam, 3-200
Doeg, Johann Georg, 3-200
Doegelmann, Peter, 3-245
Doernhoefer, Johann, 3-651
Doerr, Jakob, 3-600
Dorer, Johann, 3-660
Dorn, Georg, 3-650
Dorsch, Johann Georg, 3-620
Dossler, Leonhard, 3-246
Dressel, Konrad, 3-624
Dressel, Thomas, 3-624
Duhn, Konrad, 3-500
Duke. *Translation of* Herzog
Dullay(in), Christiana, 3-400
Dympe, Bernhard, 3-510

Easterday. *Translation of* Ostertag
Eberlein, Johann, 7-164
Eckart, Johann Michael, 7-263
Eckerlein, Paul, 7-264
Edel, Johann Konrad, 7-340
Eichhorn, Wolf Andreas, 7-265
Elias, Matthias, 7-420
Emmerling, Johann Friedrich, 7-564
Engelbrecht, Johann, 7-524
Engelhardt, Johann Konrad, 7-524
Ensenberger, Johann Friedrich, 7-525
Erhardt, Michael, 7-663
Erlwein, Johann, 7-645
Ermert, Georg, 7-656
Ernst, Johann, 7-652
Escherich, Johann Georg, 7-262
Esenbeck, Christoph Wilhelm, 7-251
Eusele, Joseph, 7-240

Falck, Aberl, 1-420
Falk. *See also* Volck
Farmer. *Translation of* Bauer
Fehr, Johann Georg, 1-600
Fehr, Peter, 1-600
Fenning. *See* Venning
Ferner, Albrecht, 1-656

Fichtel, Peter, 1-234
Fick, Johann, 1-200
Fiedler, Johann Friedrich, 1-346
Fischer, Franz Thomas, 1-260
Fischer, Johann Christian, 1-260
Fisel, Johann Martin, 1-240
Fogel. *See* Vogel
Folk. *See* Volck
Forch, Georg, 1-620
Fox. *Translation of* Fuchs
Fraas, Johann Georg, 1-620
Fraenkler, Gottlob, 1-652
Franck, Johann Nikolaus, 1-652
Franck, Karl, 1-652
Frank, Johann Friedrich, 1-652
Frank, Johann Simon, 1-652
Frederick(s). *See* Friedrich
Freyberger, Johann, 1-616
Fricker, Johann, 1-626
Friedebach, Johann Michael, 1-631
Friedlein, Konrad, 1-634
Friedrich, Gottlob, 1-636
Fries, Michael, 1-620
Frosch, Johann Friedrich, 1-620
Fruehberger, Georg, 1-616
Fruehe, Friedrich, 1-600
Fruehe, Johann Georg, 1-600
Fuchs, Johann, 1-220
Fuchs, Johann Kaspar, 1-220

Gaertner, Johann Georg Christian,
   2-635
Gardenau, Adam, 2-635
Gareiss, Johann Georg, 2-620
Gassel, Johann Heinrich, 2-240
Gauer, Peter, 2-600
Gebhardt, Andreas, 2-163
Gechter, Johann Adam, 2-236
Gehweyer, Leonhard, 2-600
Geisensieder, Johann Martin, 2-252
Gemmert, Friedrich Karl, 2-563
Gerlinger, Michael, 2-645
Geyer, Johann, 2-600
Giesler, Johann Joseph, 2-246
Glaser, Adam, 2-426
Goemmel, Karl, 2-540
Goerschky, Gottlieb, 2-622
Goert, Johann Stefan, 2-630
Goetz, Johann, 2-200

Goez, Johann Martin, 2-200
Goldberger, Matthias, 2-431
Goldeiss, Philipp, 2-432
Goll, Johann, 2-400
Gosler, Friedrich, 2-246
Graf, Georg Michael, 2-610
Grau, Anton, 2-600
Grau, Friedrich, 2-600
Gray. *Translation of* Grau
Greenbeck. *See* Gruenbeck
Gresel, Johann Heinrich, 2-624
Griezmacher, Johann Gottfried,
   2-625
Gritsmaker. *See* Griezmacher
Groom(s). *Translation of*
   Braeutigam
Grossmann, Johann, 2-625
Grub, Jakob, 2-610
Gruber, Kaspar, 2-616
Gruenbeck, Johann Georg, 2-651
Grunner, Christoph Friedrich,
   2-656
Guenthelmeyer, Michael, 2-534
Guenther, Michael, 2-536

Haag, Georg, 7-200
Haag, Johann, 7-200
Haas, Anton, 7-200
Haas, Johann, 7-200
Hadoerfer, Johann Michael, 7-361
Haefner, Friedrich, 7-156
Haefner, Georg, 7-156
Haefner, Kilian, 7-156
Haeger, Georg, 7-260
Haenfling, Erhard, 7-514
Haerms, Jakob, 7-652
Haertlein, Georg, 7-634
Haertlein. *See also* Hartlein, Hert-
   lein
Hager, Heinrich, 7-260
Hager. *See also* Haeger
Hahn, Christoph, 7-500
Hahn, Johann, 7-500
Haller, Kaspar, 7-460
Haller. *See also* Heller
Hammer, Michael, 7-560
Harles, Georg, 7-642
Harles, Johann, 7-642
Hartlein, Leonhard, 7-634

Hartlein. *See also* Haertlein, Hertlein

Hartmann, Daniel, 7-635

Hartmann, Heinrich, 7-635

Hartung, Heinrich, 7-635

Hasselbacher, Peter, 7-241

Hattstedt, Georg Heinrich, 7-323

Hauer, Matthias, 7-600

Head. *Translation of* Kopf

Heckert, Johann Gottlieb, 7-263

Heckenmueller, Konrad, 7-254

Heering, Bartholomaei, 7-652

Heering. *See also* Hering

Hefner. *See* Haefner

Heilig. *German translation of* Holy

Heim, Johann, 7-500

Heinlein, Johann, 7-545

Heinriz, Johann, 7-562

Heischmann, Johann Nikolaus, 7-255

Heisinger, Johann, 7-252

Heller, Konrad, 7-460

Heller, Johann Anton, 7-460

Heller. *See also* Haller

Hellerich, Johann, 7-462

Helmert, Johann Gerlach, 7-456

Henninger, Johann, 7-552

Henze, Heinrich August, 7-520

Henzold, Michael, 7-524

Hering, Johann Peter Christian, 7-652

Hering. *See also* Heering

Hermann, Bernhard, 7-655

Hermann, Konrad, 7-655

Herold, Johann, 7-643

Hershberger. *See* Hoerschberger

Herterich, Johann Konrad, 7-636

Hertlein, Jobst, 7-634

Hertlein. *See also* Haertlein, Hartlein

Herzog, Georg, 7-622

Heubeck, Johann Leonhard, 7-120

Heydenreich, Johann, 7-356

Heyder, Wilhelm, 7-360

Heydingsfelder, Johann Konrad, 7-352

Hill. *Translation of* Hoegel

Hilpert, Theodor, 7-416

Hoegel, Johann, 7-240

Hoehl, Melchior, 7-400

Hoehl, Johann Georg, 7-400

Hoerschberger, Jakob, 7-621

Hofer, Ludwig, 7-160

Hoffmeyer, Michel, 7-156

Hoffmann, Christoph, 7-155

Hoffmann, Johann, 7-155

Hoffmann, Johann Georg, 7-155

Hoffmann, Johann Konrad, 7-155

Hoffmann, Johann Leonhard, 7-155

Hoffmann, Wolff, 7-155

Hohberger, Johann Heinrich, 7-162

Hohenberger, Georg, 7-516

Holzheimer, Georg, 7-425

Holy, Lorenz, 7-400

Holzinger, Georg Simon, 7-425

Hopf, Johann, 7-100

Hopfer, Simon, 7-160

Hoppenstaedt, Johann Friedrich, 7-152

Horneber, Andreas, 7-651

Hosch, Christoph, 7-200

Huckler, Johann Ludwig, 7-246

Huebel, Georg, 7-140

Hund, Georg, 7-530

Hundt, Georg, 7-530

Hunger, Peter, 7-526

Hunter. *Translation of* Jaeger

Huttel, Theophil, 7-340

Hyene, Johann, 7-500

Ilgen, Ludwig Albrecht Wilhelm, 7-425

Jaeger, Johann Leonhardt, 7-260

Jakoby, Lorenz, 7-210

Joachim, Erhard, 7-250

John, Thomas, 7-500

Jordan, Nikodemus, 7-635

Judas, Veit, 7-320

Kaefferlein, Simon, 2-164

Kaemnitzer, Georg, 2-526

Kaesebauer, Christian, 2-216

Kaestner. *See* Caestner

Kail, Dominikus, 2-400

Kam(m), Johann, 2-500

Karl. *See* Carl

Karrich, Johann Kaspar, 2-620

Ries, Andreas, 6-200
Ries, Georg Michael, 6-200
Rock, Michael, 6-200
Roedel, Konrad, 6-340
Roesch, Michael, 6-200
Roesler, Johann, 6-246
Rosselt, Johann Wilhelm, 6-243
Rosswurm, Matthias, 6-265
Roth, Johann Jakob, 6-300
Rueckert, Johann Michael, 6-263
Rueckert, Johann Simon, 6-263
Rueckert, Peter, 6-263
Ruehrschneck, Johann, 6-625
Rummel, Johann Georg, 6-540
Ruppinger, Friedrich, 6-152
Ryan. *See* Rion

Saffer, Georg, 2-160
Sauer, Christian, 2-600
Sauer, Georg Christian, 2-600
Sazinger, Christian, 2-252
Schack, Peter, 2-200
Schaedel, Johann, 2-340
Schaefer, Christian, 2-160
Schaefer, Friedrich Jakob, 2-160
Schaefer, Johann, 2-160
Schaller, Christian, 2-460
Schard, Johann, 2-630
Scharff, --, 2-610
Schauer, Georg Martin, 2-600
Scheller, Michael, 2-460
Schemig, Kaspar, 2-520
Schenker, Johann, 2-526
Schettla, Karl, 2-340
Schildknecht, Johann, 2-432
Schindelbauer, Georg, 2-534
Schindler, Johann, 2-534
Schindler, Johann Adam, 2-534
Schipper, Andreas, 2-160
Schirmer, Stefan, 2-656
Schlegel, Jakob, 2-424
Schletterer, Georg, 2-436
Schlicker, Johann, 2-426
Schmalenberg, Peter, 2-545
Schmelzer, Georg, 2-542
Schmelzer, Johann Jakob, 2-542
Schmelzer, Johann Leonhard, 2-542
Schmid, Karl Friedrich, 2-530

Schmidt, Georg, 2-530
Schmidt, Johann Michael, 2-530
Schmidt, Lorenz Friedrich,
  2-530
Schmuller, Wolf, 2-546
Schneider, Johann, 2-536
Schneider, Paul, 2-536
Schnell, Matthias, 2-540
Schnepf, Georg Jakob, 2-510
Schnurr, Johann, 2-560
Schoemer, Martin, 2-560
Schoeneker, Johann, 2-526
Schoenell, Johann Balthasar,
  2-540
Schoener, Lorenz, 2-560
Schoentag, Johann Konrad, 2-532
Schoepf, Paul, 2-100
Schorr, Johann Michael, 2-600
Schott, Johann Georg, 2-263
Schricker, Wolf, 2-626
Schroeder, Georg Wilhelm, 2-636
Schuebel, Johann Adam, 2-140
Schuh, Johann, 2-000
Schultheiss, Johann, 2-432
Schulz, Gottlob, 2-420
Schumm, Georg Adam, 2-500
Schwaab, Nikolaus, 2-100
Schwaegler, Johann Matthias,
  2-246
Schwaegler. *See also* Schwegler
Schwartz, Johann, 2-620
Schwarz, Johann, 2-620
Schwarzbauer, Leonhard, 2-621
Schwegler, Joseph Peter, 2-246
Schwegler. *See also* Schwaegler
Schweigert, Johann Peter, 2-263
Schweizer, Franz, 2-260
Schwimm, --, 2-500
Seehardt, Georg Friedrich, 2-630
Seffert, Johann Adam, 2-163
Seffert. *See also* Seiffert, Sey-
  fert
Segeritz, Michael, 2-262
Seidel, Johann Jakob, 2-340
Seifferlein, Johann Peter, 2-164
Seiffert, Georg, 2-163
Seiffert. *See also* Seffert, Sey-
  fert

Weigel, Adam, 7-240
Weiss, Konrad, 7-200
Welt, Blasius, 7-430
Wendel, Heinrich Tomas, 7-534
Werner, Christian, 7-656
Werner, Georg, 7-656
Westzstein, Johann Andreas, 7-235
Wetschel, Christian, 7-324
Weyandt, Andreas, 7-530
Weymann, Johann, 7-550
White. *See* Weiss
Wieder, Joseph, 7-360
Wild, Lorenz, 7-430
Will, Matthias, 7-400
Willmehr, Nikolaus, 7-456
Wimmler, Christoph, 7-546
Winckler, Johann Anton, 7-524
Winckler, Johann Christian, 7-524
Wise. *See* Weiss
Wiseman. *See* Wizmann
Wizmann, Konrad, 7-255
Wolf, Johann Adam, 7-410
Wolff, Adam, 7-410
Wolff, Friedrich, 7-410

Wolfrum, Johann Adam, 7-416
Wuest, Georg, 7-230
Wunderlich, Lorenz, 7-536
Wunderlich, Peter, 7-536
Wurzbach, Johann Andreas, 7-621

Zangel, Johann, 2-524
Zapf, Johann, 2-100
Zauss, Johann Peter, 2-200
Zehder, Johann Georg, 2-360
Zelser, Georg, 2-426
Zeltsch, Nikolaus, 2-432
Zenckel, Konrad, 2-524
Ziegler, Johann Georg Heinrich,
  2-246
Zimmet, Matthias, 2-530
Zinner, Matthias, 2-560
Zipfel, Georg, 2-140
Zoellner, Georg Peter, 2-456
Zoellner. *See also* Soellner
Zollfrank, Martin, 2-416
Zottmann, Heinrich, 2-355
Zscharkany, David, 2-625
Zwanziger, Georg, 2-522

German-American Genealogical Research
Monograph Number 5

MERCENARIES FROM HESSEN-HANAU WHO REMAINED IN CANADA AND THE UNITED STATES AFTER THE AMERICAN REVOLUTION

Clifford Neal Smith

1976

INTRODUCTION

Not a great deal is known about the activities of mercenaries
from Hessen-Hanau who were members of the British forces in North America
during the American Revolution. Generally speaking, the contingent was
associated with the troops from Braunschweig (Brunswick),[1] rather than
with the contingent from Hessen-Kassel (Electoral Hessen). The reason
for this seems to have been that the rulers of Hessen-Hanau and Hessen-
Kassel, though son and father, were not friendly toward one another, and
it would not have been easy for the officers of the Hessen-Hanau contingent (none of whom ranked higher than colonel) to have been subordinated
to the higher ranking officers from Hessen-Kassel.

The ruling prince of Hessen-Hanau sent 2,038 troopers to America
under various treaties with Great Britain; some 50 recruits were sent in
April 1781 and an additional 334 in April 1782. Of the total 2,422 who
served in America, some 981 did not return to Europe after the Revolution.[2] This figure includes the dead, the deserters in the American
states, and settlers who remained in Canada after 1783.

A considerable part of the contingent from Hessen-Hanau was captured during the Saratoga battles along with the Brunswickers in October
1777. The Hanau artillery unit had been active on Lake Champlain during
the campaign of 1776; some of the Hanau Jaegerkorps (Chasseurs) took
part in St. Leger's expedition; a portion of the Prince Friedrich Regiment remained at Ticonderoga during the Saratoga campaign.

Hessen-Hanau troopers captured at Saratoga were marched under
American custody to the so-called Winter Barracks near Cambridge, Massachusetts; the march from Saratoga lasted from 17 October to 7 November
1777. In November of the following year these prisoners of war were

obliged to leave the neighborhood of Boston, as it was thought they might be liberated by the British, and to begin a long march to southern Virginia, where they arrived at Charlottesville in January 1779. All along the route through the states of New York, New Jersey, Pennsylvania, and Maryland, there were opportunities to escape, and there is ample evidence that many of them did. It seems likely that these escapee-deserters struck out for German-speaking settlements in New York state and Pennsylvania, where they would be less likely to be noticed. At Charlottesville there were also opportunities for escape, no doubt to the settlements of their countrymen in the Blue Ridge Mountains and to Rowan, Cabarrus, and Mecklenburg counties in North Carolina.

Researchers are especially enjoined to compare the information contained in this monograph with that which appears in the British and American muster rolls and prisoner-of-war lists published in the three parts of *German-American Genealogical Research Monograph No. 3.*[3] The monographs complement each other, often providing information on an individual trooper not reported back to Hanau.

Abbreviations used herein are as follows: B = bombardier; C = canoneer; D = drummer; Gr = grenadier; M = musketeer; P = private.

1. Edward J. Lowell, *The Hessians and the Other German Auxiliaries of Great Britain in the Revolutionary War* (New York: 1884; reprint ed., Port Washington, N.Y.: Kennikat Press, 1965), p. 298.

2. Ibid., p. 299.

3. Clifford Neal Smith, *Muster Rolls and Prisoner-of-War Lists in American Archival Collections Pertaining to the German Mercenary Troops Who Served with the British Forces During the American Revolution.* German-American Genealogical Research Monograph No. 3 (in three parts). DeKalb, Illinois: Westland Publications, 1974-1976.

Serial No.: 1   Language: German   Number of entries in MS: 42

Source: Staatsarchiv, Place: --   Number of pages in MS: 2
  Marburg, Bestand
  4h:415:46:p. 25   Date: 1780? 1783?

Name of Unit: Hessen-Hanau Artillery Corps

MS Heading: Dismissal list of deserters and missing soldiers from the
        princely Hessen-Hanau Artillery Corps, from [date of] de-
        parture from Hanau on 15 May 1776

Name	Birthplace	Age	Remarks
1. Handel, Joh[ann]	Wiesenfeld? in Würzburg Territory	21	Deserted 8 Oct 1777; recaptured
2. Koerber, Henr[ich]	Eckenheim?	25	Deserted 20 Oct 1777
3. Hahn, Conrad	Marjoss	25	Deserted 20 Oct 1777
4. Rapp, Peter	Doerklinge? in the Pfalz	34	Deserted 21 Oct 1777
5. Hofmann, Andr[eas]	Isny, Imperial Free City	33	Deserted 23 Oct 1777
6. Fautstroh, Henr[ich]	Rodheim?	29	Deserted 24 Oct 1777; recaptured and sent to Canada
7. Kreuzer, Sebastian	Olmütz, Moravia	46	Deserted 26 Oct 1777
8. Weber, Christian	Weinselheim? in Hessen	18	Deserted 26 Oct 1777
9. Stenger, Adam	Bernbach	20	Deserted 1 Mar 1778 with his equipment and entered enemy [American] service; recaptured 3 Oct 1778
10. Unger, Eberhard, Surgeon	Karlsruhe	35	Deserted 20 Oct 1777
11. Brod, Henrich, Master blacksmith	Ostheim	46	Deserted 18 Oct 1777
12. Losberger, Joh[ann], Wagon master	Alsfeld bei Heilbronn	28	Deserted 18 Oct 1777
13. Siebert, Georg, Artillery attendant	Kahlgrund? in Waldeck Territory	36	Deserted 6 Oct 1777

	Name	Birth-place	Age	Remarks
14.	Bock, Wilhelm, Artillery attendant	Niedererlebach [Niedererlen-bach?]	38	Deserted 10 Oct 1777
15.	Heep, Georg	Rothenburg in Hessen	22	Deserted 1 Nov 1777
16.	Lochmann, Balthasar	Eichen	27	Deserted 1 Nov 1777
17.	Lantz, Henrich	Alt-Hanau	33	Deserted 3 Apr 1778 with all equipment and entered enemy [American] service; recaptured
18.	Haupt, Mathias	Strasburg	20	Deserted from Winter-hill 15 May 1778 and entered enemy [American] service at Boston
19.	Quelmann? Peter, Artillery attendant	Neu-Hanau	38	Deserted 17 May 1778 and entered enemy [American] service at Boston
20.	Felsenheim, Joseph, Artillery attendant	Kitzingen in Würzburg Territory	31	Deserted 26 Jul 1778
21.	Bauer, Peter	Gelnhausen	32?	Deserted 12 Nov 1778
22.	Bandel, Joh[ann] Georg	Burghaslach in Würzbur Territory	29?	Deserted 24 Nov 1778
23.	Billout, Jacob, Drummer	Neu-Hanau	18	Deserted 30 Nov 1778; recaptured and sent to Canada
24.	Wegmann, Peter	Eydengesäs	26	Deserted 8 Dec 1778
25.	Hofmann, Balth[asar]	Wachenbüchen?	20	Deserted 8 Dec 1778
26.	Metzler, Peter	Langstadt	27	Deserted 10 Dec 1778
27.	Hamann, Conr[ad]	Langstadt	24	Deserted 10 Dec 1778
28.	Sensel, Nicol[as], Junior	Bieber	25	Deserted 10 Dec 1778; recaptured and sent to Canada
29.	Becker, Conrad	Enzheim	32	Deserted 26 Dec 1778

Serial No.: 1 (continued)

	Name	Birth-place	Age	Remarks
30.	Stock, Johannes	Bieber	20	Deserted 26 Dec 1778
31.	Mörschel, Joh[ann] Bombardier	Eichen	32	Deserted 16 Apr 1779
32.	Schröder, Johannes	Hochstadt	23	Deserted 2 Jan 1779
33.	Lempert, Friedr[ich]	Gedern in Stollberg Territory	21	Deserted 2 Jan 1779
34.	Sensel, Peter, Senior? Junior?	Bieber	27	Deserted 7 Jan 1779
35.	Schwaab, Joh[ann] Georg	Kircheimbohland [Kirchheim-Bolanden]	21	Deserted 1 Mar 1779
36.	Hausmann, --, Bombardier	Neu-Hanau	-	Deserted 1 Jun 1780
37.	Zorbach, --, Senior	[not given]	-	Deserted 20 Jun 1780
38.	Walther, --	[not given]	-	Deserted 20 Jan 1780
39.	Rüffer, Fridr[ich]	[not given]	-	Deserted 15 Sep 1780
40.	Dacke, Conr[ad] Hein[rich]	[not given]	-	Deserted 25 Oct 1780
41.	Kleimbel, Georg	[not given]	-	Deserted 25 Oct 1780
42.	Müller, Andreas	[not given]	-	Deserted 25 Oct 1780

Serial No.: 2   Language: German   Number of entries in MS: 70

Source: Staatsarchiv Place: Hanau?   Number of pages in MS: 3
   Marburg, Bestand
   4h:415:46:p. 26   Date: 31 Mar 1777

Name of Unit: Hessen-Hanau Jaeger [Chasseur] Corps

MS Heading: Dismissal list of discharged and missing soldiers, deserters,
                and those [who have] surrendered, from the Princely Hessen-
                Hanau Jaeger [Chasseur] Corps, from [date of] departure from
                Hanau to 31 March 1777

Dorso: None

Serial No.: 2 (continued)

	Name	Birth-place	Age	Company	Remarks
1.	Pierri, Joseph, Cpl	Mainz	21	Castendyck	Taken away on 8 Mar 1777 in Mainz
2.	Schmitt, Jacob	Ehlfeld? Mainz. [Territory]	16	Castendyck	Taken away on 8 Mar 1777 in Mainz
3.	Ruppert, Peter	Mainz	18	Castendyck	Taken away on 8 Mar 1777 in Mainz
4.	Backes, Wilhelm	Limburg in Trier. [Territory]	18	Staff	Deserted 3 Apr 1777 near Koblenz
5.	Völcker, Anthon	Coblenz	18	Staff	Deserted 3 Apr 1777 near Koblenz
6.	Wüst, Johannes	Preunigs-heim?	31	v. Francken	Deserted 5 Apr 1777 at Koblenz
7.	Landwehr, Jacob	Rabschwier, Alsace	36	v. Wittgen-stein	Driven away 5 Aug 1777
8.	Külp, Carl	Weinheim, Pfalz	19	v. Francken	Driven away to La Chine 5 Aug 1777
9.	Stein, Jost	Hochstadt	36	Castendyck	Missing from Fort Stan-wix 6 Aug 1777
10.	Strott, Johannes	Sannertz, Fulda. [Territory]	27	Castendyck	Missing from Fort Stan-wix 6 Aug 1777
11.	Kessler, Joseph	Fischbach, Alsace	20	Castendyck	Missing during retreat 22 Aug 1777
12.	Freyburger, Alexand[er]	-aasel?	48	Castendyck	Missing during retreat 22 Aug 1777
13.	Ebert, Johannes	Birkenhain, Pfalz	34	Castendyck	Missing during retreat 22 Aug 1777
14.	Jaeger, Fried-r[ich]	Reinwind?	34	Staff	Dismissed at La Prairie 22 Sep 1777
15.	Crass, Carl	Neustadt	28	v. Wittgen-stein	Missing during the march on 24 Sep 1777
16.	Ammon, Gottfried	Frankfurt	18	v. Wittgen-stein	Missing during the march on 25 Sep 1777
17.	Mayr, Joseph, 1st Lt	Frankfurt	18	v. Wittgen-stein	Discharged 26 Sep 1777

	Name	Birth-place	Age	Company	Remarks
18.	Müller, Fried-rich	Hanau	16	v. Francken	Missing from guard duty 4 Oct 1777; according to information received became prisoner of war
19.	Major, Georg	Gross-Starben? Karben?	20	v. Francken	Missing from guard duty 4 Oct 1777; according to information received became prisoner of war
20.	Wuth, Carl	Dietz	18	v. Francken	Missing from guard duty 4 Oct 1777; according to information received became prisoner of war
21.	Ebersbach, Peter	Weidershain, Pfalz	17	v. Francken	Missing from picket duty 5 Oct 1777
22.	Obrick, Mathias	Verole, France	30	Staff?	Driven out because of rebellious incitement
23.	Amann, Martin	Tyrol	17	v. Francken	Deserted 12 Oct 1777
24.	Thöne, Hen-[rich]	–	–	Staff?	Deserted 24 Oct 1777
25.	Friderici, Sal-omon	Niewisch, Saxony	27	v. Wittgen-stein	Deserted 24 Oct 1777 while on picket duty
26.	Fuchs? Jacob, Cpl	Niewisch, Saxony	27	Castendyck	Captured [or caught] by the Army and discharged by the Corps
27.	Hirschberger, Friedr[ich]	Magensenn Hannover [Territory]	24	Staff?	Discharged 10 Nov 1777 and entered service with LtCol v. Creutz-berg; now on duty with the Corps
28.	Kuckumus, --, Cpl	Magensenn, Hannover [Territory]	24	v. Francken	Captured [or caught] by the Army and discharged by the Corps
29.	Spahn, Adam	Breitenbach	21	Castendyck	Driven out 12 Jan 1778 because of several thefts

Serial No. 2 (continued)

	Name	Birth-place	Age	Company	Remarks
30.	Kitzstein, Leonhard	Auszach	17	v. Francken	Transferred 1 May 1778 to Captain v. Francken as servant; now with the Corps again
31.	Atlohn, Joh[ann]	Hanau	17	v. Francken	Transferred 1 May 1778 to Lt Krafft as servant
32.	Krafft, Nic[olas]	Grasdorf? in Weilburg [Territory]	49	v. Wittgenstein	Driven away 1 May 1778 because of thefts and robbery at Montreal
33.	Grossmann, Georg	Dittenberg, Darmstadt [Territory]	22	Staff?	Deserted 22 May 1778
34.	Raimond, Peter	Paris	30	Castendyck	Deserted 25 Oct 1778
35.	Bruckhof, Georg	Grossenlinden, Darmstadt [Territory]	44	v. Francken	Driven out 25 Feb 1779 because of theft
36.	Penz, Martin	Lange, Darmstadt Territory	30	v. Francken	Driven out 25 Feb 1779 because of theft
37.	Lindner, Joseph	Bamberg [Territory?]	34	v. Wittgenstein	Discharged 15 Jun 1779
38.	Hufschmidt, Jacob	Strasburg	27	v. Wittgenstein	Deserted with equipment 26 Aug 1779
39.	Lentner, Jacob	Schlüsselfeld, Würzburg [Territory]	26	Staff?	Transferred to LtCol v. Creuzburg as servant
40.	Montreal, Joachim	Trier [Territory]	20	v. Wittgenstein	Transferred to Major v. Francken as servant
41.	Gergens, Anthon	Aschafenb[ur]g?	18	v. Wittgenstein	Transferred to Lt Scheurer as servant
42.	Bauer, Jacob	Hüttingen	20	v. Wittgenstein	Transferred to Lt von den Velden as servant
43.	Seibert, Balthasar	Ulmstadt, Pfalz	16	Castendyck	Transferred to Captain v. Leth as servant
44.	Ochs, George	Neu-Hanau	20	Castendyck	Sent back to Hanau as invalid 26 Oct 1779 due to lost arm

Serial No. 2 (continued)

	Name	Birth-place	Age	Company	Remarks
45.	Jordan, Anthon	Neu-Hanau	29	Castendyck	Sent back to Hanau as invalid 26 Oct 1779 due to lost foot?
46.	Weinlein, Joh-[ann] Adam	Bayreuth [Territory]	35	Staff?	Sent back to Hanau as invalid 26 Oct 1779 due to lost hands

Serial No. 3   Language: German   Number of entries in MS: 1

Appended to serial no.2 above.

Name of Unit: Hessen-Hanau Regiment Erbprinz [Crown Prince], First Battalion

MS Heading: List of prisoners of war in America from the first battalion of the Hessen-Hanau Regiment Erbprinz

	Name	Birth-place	Age	Company	Remarks
1.	Finck, Carl, Fourier	Steinau	–	–	–

Serial No. 4   Language: German   Number of entries in MS: 26

Appended to serial no. 2 above.

Name of Unit: Hessen-Hanau Artillery

MS Heading: List of the prisoners of war in America from the Artillery

	Name	Birth-place	Age	Company	Remarks
1.	List, Wilh[elm], Bombardier	Harres-hausen	–	–	–
2.	Hock, Conr[ad], Bombardier	Seckbach	–	–	–
3.	Dickhaut, Hen-r[ich], Bombardier	Dudenhofen	–	–	–
4.	Müller, Henr[ich] Canonier	Breitenbach	–	–	–
5.	Lichmann, Peter, Canonier	Bockenheim	–	–	–

Serial No. 4 (continued)

	Name	Birth-place	Age	Company	Remarks
6.	Elsässer, Lud-w[ig], Canonier	Schlüchtern	-	-	-
7.	Kappes, Peter, Canonier	Seckbach	-	-	-
8.	Pflug, Joh[ann] Canonier	Seckbach	-	-	-
9.	Harnischfeger, Christoph, Can-onier	Seidenrod	-	-	-
10.	Viltz, Thomas, Canonier	Enckheim	-	-	-
11.	Hartmann, Paul, Canonier	Harreshausen	-	-	-
12.	Paul, Mich[el], CAnonier	Hohenzell	-	-	-
13.	Zischler, Georg, Canonier	Ergersheim, Ansbach [Territory]	-	-	-
14.	Müller, Joh[ann], Canonier	Marköbel	-	-	-
15.	Willmann? Michel, Canonier	Langstadt	-	-	-
16.	Weil, Thomas, Canonier	Enckheim	-	-	-
17.	Urbach, Henr[ich] CAnonier	Schlüchtern	-	-	-
18.	Vorbach, Joh[ann] Canonier	Rodheim	-	-	-
19.	Petzinger? [Pelz-inger?] Joh[ann] Canonier	Dudenhofen	-	-	-
20.	Frischkorn, Joh-[ann] Canonier	Hinter-steinau	-	-	-
21.	Funck, Peter, Canonier	Dudenhofen	-	-	-
22.	Erdmann, August, Canonier	Niederdor-felden	-	-	-

	Name	Birth-place	Age	Company	Remarks
23.	Hickmann? [Heck-mann?] Michel, Canonier	Eichen	-	-	-
24.	Eckhard, Georg, Canonier	Eichen	-	-	-
25.	Vogt, Peter, Canonier	Coburg	-	-	-
26.	Roth, Thomas, Canonier	Herbolts-heim, Würzburg [Territory]	-	-	-

Serial No. 5   Language: German   *Number of entries in MS:* 303?

Source: Marburg Staats-Place: Not given   *Number of pages in MS:* 4
Archiv, Bestand
4h:415:46:p. 45-46   Date: Not stated

Name of Unit: Hessen-Hanau Infantry Regiment Erbprinz [Crown Prince]

MS Heading: List of the present men in Virginia from the battalions of the Hessen-Hanau Infantry Regiment Erbprinz, by companies

Dorso: Recapitulation: 13 officers, 20-non-commissioned officers, 16 military band members, 254 soldiers

Grenadier Company

	Name	Rank	Birth-place
1.	v. Germann, Aug[ust]	Capt	Cassel [Kassel]
2.	v. Trott, Fridr[ich]	1st Lt	Schwarzenhassel/Hessen
3.	v. Richtersleben, Wilh[elm]	2d Lt	Cassel [Kassel]
4.	Krill, Joh[ann]	1st Sgt	Rosdorf
5.	Donné, Johannes	Sgt	Hanau
6.	Klingel, Phil[ip]	Cpl	Bergen
7.	Albrecht, Jac[ob]	Drummer	Cassel [Kassel]
8.	Gerlach, Phil[ip]	Gr	Schlüchtern
9.	Dietrich, Joh[ann]	Gr	Ginnheim
10.	Hofmann, Henr[ich]	Gr	Windecken
11.	Sedler, Conr[ad]	Gr	Enckheim

Serial No. 5 (continued)

		Rank	Birth-place
12.	Schlinglof [Schlingluff], Georg	Gr	Hintersteinau
13.	Mühl, Georg	Gr	Rödgen
14.	Rüfer, Nicol[as]	Gr	Wallrod
15.	Cramer, Joh[ann]	Gr	Schlüchtern
16.	Walter, Conr[ad]	Gr	Dudenhofen
17.	Birgler, Nicol[as]	Gr	Bockenheim
18.	Fritz, Mich[el]	Gr	Bischofsheim
19.	Engel, Henr[ich]	Gr	Hanau
20.	Gärtner, Jost	Gr	Marköbel
21.	Baer, Henr[ich]	Gr	Marköbel
22.	Leick, Phil[ip]	Gr	Schlüchtern
23.	Kalbfleisch, Joh[ann]	Gr	Cleestadt
24.	Rüfer, Joh[ann]	Gr	Ahlersbach
25.	Vetter, Lorenz	Gr	Niederdorfelden
26.	Knot, Conr[ad]	Gr	Lützelhausen
27.	Sterlepper, Anth[on]	Gr	Eckenheim
28.	Klingel, Bernhard	Gr	Bergen
29.	Hofmann, Joh[ann]	Gr	Altenhaslau
30.	Lehr, Peter	Gr	Rosdorf
31.	Hahn, Isaac	Gr	Bockenheim
32.	Seibert, Henr[ich]	Gr	Dudenhofen
33.	Leimbach, Joh[ann]	Gr	Ostheim
34.	Köhler, Math[ias]	Gr	Lanzingen
35.	Müller, Nicol[as]	Gr	Steinau
36.	Hachenberger, Jost	Gr	Schwalheim
37.	Immig, Daniel	Gr	Hanau

Serial No. 6   *Heading as in Serial No. 5*

Leib [Bodyguard] Company

1.	v. Eschwege, Christian	1st Lt	Reichensachsen/Hessen
2.	v. Weyhen [Weyhers?] Wilh[elm]	2d Lt	Gersfeld/Fulda Territory

Serial No. 6 *(continued)*

	Name	Rank	Birth-place
3.	Heerwagen, Fridr[ich]	2d Lt	Hanau
4.	Vaupel, Samuel	1st Sgt	Reichenbach
5.	Lenz, Henr[ich]	Fourier	Bieber
6.	Böckel, Fridr[ich]	Captain des Armes	Gronau
7.	Weber, Peter	Cpl	Babenhausen
8.	Gottschalck, Wilh[elm]	Orderly	Solingen
9.	Klee, Leonhard	Regimental Drummer	Hanau
10.	Raab, Johannes	Clarinet	Kirchheim
11.	Müller, Adam	Clarinet	Steinau
12.	André, Joh[ann]	Clarinet	Cassel [Kassel]
13.	Justorf, Fridr[ich]	Clarinet	Halberstadt
14.	Emmert, Leopold	Clarinet	Mosbach
15.	Justorf, Wilh[elm]	Clarinet	Dietz
16.	Giese, Wilhelm	Drummer	Cassel [Kassel]
17.	Gewald, Jac[ob]	Drummer	Hanau
18.	Kitz, Georg	Drummer	Holzhausen
19.	Heinzinger, Phil[ip]	M	Rumpenheim
20.	Walt [Walz?] Phil[ip]	M	Marköbel
21.	Zimmermann, Joh[ann]	M	Bergen
22.	Koch, Johannes	M	Heuchelheim
23.	Wiskemann, Christoph	M	Hanau
24.	Pfaf[f], Jacob	M	Fechenheim
25.	Orth, Conrad	M	Marköbel
26.	Fischer, Henrich	M	Babenhausen
27.	Krieg, Conrad	M	Altenhausen
28.	Rüfer, Daniel	M	Hintersteinau
29.	Traut, Conrad	M	Kilianstedten
30.	Stein, Frid[rich]	M	Hochstadt
31.	Finzel, Conr[ad]	M	Nieder-Eschbach
32.	Mahr, Georg	M	Dudenhofen

		Rank	Birth-place
33.	Henzel, Joh[ann]	M	Bergheim
34.	Sickenberger, Wilh[elm]	M	Dörnigheim
35.	Mörler, Conr[ad]	M	Nauheim
36.	Remy, Michel	M	Wolflingen
37.	Mahr, Phil[ip]	M	Dudenhofen
38.	Lotz, Wilh[elm]	M	Grossenhausen
39.	Hallatschka, Joh[ann]	M	Hanau
40.	Grimm, Wilh[elm]	M	Bergen
41.	Kaempf, Caspar	M	Steinau
42.	Lack, Johannes	M	Dorheim
43.	Böckel, Philip	M	Gronau
44.	Aufleiter, Georg	M	Köppern/Homburg Territory
45.	Rauch, Joachim	M	Babenhausen
46.	Weitzel, Johannes	M	Hohenzell
47.	Hüfner, Urbanus	M	Steinau
48.	Maul, Caspar	M	Steinau
49.	Kraft, Andr[eas]	M	Breidenbach
50.	Bohländer, Adam	M	Schlüchtern
51.	Kohlepp, Caspar	M	Hohenzell
52.	Unger, Carl	M	Windecken
53.	Schädel, Georg	M	Ober-Eschbach
54.	Lehnung, Henr[ich]	M	Fechenheim
55.	Burckhard, Theod[or]	M	Bergen
56.	Selzer, Joh[annes]	M	Cleestadt
57.	Lenz, Carl	M	Hanau
58.	Sommerlade, Conr[ad]	M	Dornigheim
59.	Stein, Peter	M	Wachenbuchen
60.	Ziegler, Georg	M	Marios [Marjoss]
61.	Bode, Peter	M	Hanau
62.	Pohl, Nicol[as]	M	Fechenheim
63.	Kayser, Frid[rich]	M	Fechenheim

Captain Scheel's Company

		Rank	Birth-place
1.	Scheel, Aug[ust]	Captain	Hanau
2.	v. Geyling, Wilh[elm]	1st Lt	Hanau
3.	Kitz, Augustin	1st Sgt	Ober-Eschbach
4.	Stoppel, Nicol[as]	Sgt	Niederzell
5.	Kayser, Henr[ich]	Captain des Armes	Fechenheim
6.	Leonhard, Christian	Drummer	Hanau
7.	Müller, Henr[ich]	M	Ginnheim
8.	Emmerich, Joh[ann]	M	Rodheim
9.	Treiter, Henr[ich]	M	Ostheim
10.	Hallatschka, Phil[ip]	M	Hanau
11.	Schäfer, Johannes	M	Nauheim
12.	Schmid, Christian	M	Langstadt
13.	Bender, Sigmund	M	Bockenheim
14.	Baer, Joh[ann]	M	Eichen
15.	Hofmann, Peter	M	Köppern, Homburg Territory
16.	Breitenbach, Wilh[elm]	M	Bockenheim
17.	Hamann, Peter	M	Langstadt
18.	Becker, Conr[ad]	M	Rödgen
19.	Traut, Phil[ip]	M	Windecken
20.	Bensing, Georg	M	Niederzell
21.	Unger, Andr[eas]	M	Ostheim
22.	Zipf, Adam	M	Schlüchtern
23.	Göbel, Paul	M	Rodenbach
24.	Ruppel, Conr[ad]	M	Mittelbuchen
25.	Bauscher, Valent[in]	M	Windecken
26.	Obrich, Joh[ann]	M	Rodheim
27.	Bechtold, Georg	M	Brachköbel
28.	Börner, Caspar	M	Niederzell

Serial No. 7 (continued)

		Rank	Birth-place
29.	Roth, Ludwig	M	Langstadt
30.	Trabant, Conrad	M	Steinau
31.	Henzel, Henr[ich]	M	Rodheim
32.	Färber, Fridr[ich]	M	Windecken
33.	Seiler, Joh[ann]	M	Eydengesäs [Eidengesäss]
34.	Mörschel, Wilh[elm]	M	Eichen
35.	Rüb, Caspar	M	Hohenzell
36.	Müller, Balthasar	M	Babenhausen
37.	Mertz, Henr[ich]	M	Eichen
38.	Gutermuth, Joh[ann]	M	Schlüchtern
39.	Bausum, Lorenz	M	Rodheim
40.	Kreim, Christoph	M	Babenhausen
41.	Rullmann, Georg	M	Rodheim
42.	Hachenberger, Georg	M	Schwalheim
43.	Bauscher, Joh[ann]	M	Bischofsheim
44.	Weyd, Joh[ann]	M	Holzhausen
45.	Meuer, Martin	M	Tauernheim
46.	Deckert, Theodor	M	Kesselstadt
47.	Schlauch, Paul	M	Marios [Marjoss]
48.	Ifland, Henr[ich]	M	Hutten
49.	Schad, Thomas	M	Windecken
50.	Werheim, Lorenz	M	Rodheim

Serial No. 8

First Vacant Company

		Rank	Birthplace
		Heading as in Serial No. 5	
1.	v. Buttlar, Wilh[elm] Sbs? [Sebastian?]	Captain	Friemen/Hessen
2.	Weitzel, Valent[in]	Ensign	Schlüchtern
3.	Eiffert, Georg	1st Sgt	Babenhausen
4.	Denhard, Christoph	1st Sgt	Homburg
5.	Baist, Nicol[as]	1st Sgt	Schlüchtern

		Rank	Birthplace
6.	Eckel, Caspar	Captain des Armes	Kesselstadt
7.	Schmid, Joh[ann]	Cpl	Rumpenheim
8.	Gnüge, Frid[rich]	Orderly	Hanau
9.	Reichmann, Mich[el]	Drummer	Asmutshausen
10.	Bommersheim, Henr[ich]	M	Dorheim
11.	Kressel, Nicol[as]	M	Babenhausen
12.	Stamm, Georg	M	Windecken
13.	Müller, Christian	M	Nauheim
14.	Lehr, Moritz	M	Rodenbach
15.	Klüe, Georg	M	Reinhards
16.	Gruner, Conr[ad]	M	Nieder-Issigheim
17.	Bruckmann, Christian	M	Rodheim
18.	Westphal, Gottfr[ied]	M	Windecken
19.	Boos, Carl	M	Hanau
20.	Fack, Carl	M	Rodenbach
21.	Manckel, Joh[ann]	M	Wachenbuchen
22.	Zipf, Henr[ich]	M	Schlüchtern
23.	Klees, Georg	M	Eckenheim
24.	Dönges, Christoph	M	Mittelbuchen
25.	Schmidt, Joh[ann]	M	Nauheim
26.	Kitz, Caspar	M	Nieder-Eschbach
27.	Heil, Daniel	M	Eschersheim
28.	Spahn, Henr[ich]	M	Dudenhofen
29.	Becker, Wilh[elm]	M	Bergen
30.	Müller, Joh[ann]	M	Vilbel [Bad Vilbel]
31.	Wächtershäuser, Joh[ann]	M	Ober-Eschbach
32.	Barthold, Mich[el]	M	Windecken
33.	Lins, Joh[ann]	M	Trasenberg
34.	Liller, Henr[ich]	M	Dudenhofen
35.	Hess, Caspar	M	Bischofsheim
36.	Henzel, Conrad	M	Schwalheim

Serial No. 8 (continued)

		Rank	Birthplace
37.	Löwenstein, Conr[ad]	M	Nauheim
38.	Frischkorn, Fridr[ich]	M	Schlüchtern
39.	Fix, Peter	M	Hanau
40.	Bartmann, Joh[ann]	M	Windecken
41.	Hensler, Adam	M	Schlüchtern
42.	Manckel, Martin	M	Bieber
43.	Arnold, Wilh[elm]	M	Gieslitz
44.	Fehl, Joh[ann]	M	Wallrod
45.	Aumann, Henr[ich]	M	Babenhausen
46.	Schäfer, Christian	M	Nauheim
47.	Schäfer, Martin	M	Schlüchtern
48.	Müller, Johann	M	Schlüchtern

Serial No. 9

Second Vacant Company

Heading as in Serial No. 5

		Rank	Birthplace
1.	v. Bischhausen, Fridr[ich]	2d Lt	Hanau
2.	Bäumert, Georg	Ensign	Hanau
3.	Scheer, Henr[ich]	1st Sgt	Marburg
4.	Lapp, Adam	Fourier	Hanau
5.	Beck, Phil[ip]	Captain des Armes	Babenhausen
6.	Schubert, Fridr[ich]	Drummer	Hanau
7.	Kayser, Adam	M	Ginnheim
8.	Mebus, Peter	M	Rodheim
9.	Leybold, Joh[ann]	M	Nieder-Eschbach
10.	Müller, Wilh[elm]	M	Babenhausen
11.	Heyd, Joh[ann]	M	Marios [Marjoss]
12.	Schäfer, Caspar	M	Hintersteinau
13.	Gauel, Conrad	M	Steinau
14.	Holl, Melchior	M	Rodheim
15.	Jahn, Fridr[ich]	M	Gumfritz
16.	Justemer, Joh[ann]	M	Rodheim

	Rank	Birthplace
17. Klinckerfus, Gottl[ob] [or Gottlieb]	M	Nauheim
18. Hallatschka, Peter	M	Hanau
19. Neider, Henr[ich]	M	Altenhaslau
20. Hartmann, Peter	M	Hanau
21. Traband, Joh[ann]	M	Steinau
22. Reuschebach, Carl	M	Bockenheim
23. Förter, Caspar	M	Ostheim
24. Schäfer, Michel	M	Rodheim
25. Kratz, Conr[ad]	M	Seckbach
26. Heyer, Conr[ad]	M	Eschersheim
27. Pfeffer, Henr[ich]	M	Dorheim
28. Schepp, Conr[ad]	M	Rodenbach
29. Winckler, Phil[ip]	M	Nieder-Eschbach
30. Bitter, Stephan	M	Wallrod
31. Müller, Leonhard	M	Steinau
32. Cress, Henr[ich]	M	Wallrod
33. Sterlepper, Phil[ip]	M	Eckenheim
34. Held, Henr[ich]	M	Selters
35. Lohmüller, Nicol[as]	M	Steinau
36. Holzheimer, Jonas	M	Bischofsheim
37. Hamburger, Phil[ip]	M	Berckersheim
38. Kenner, Peter	M	Bieber
39. Lotz, Georg	M	Ostheim
40. Koch, Joh[ann]	M	Hintersteinau
41. Hinckel, Phil[ip]	M	Rüdigheim
42. Mager, Georg	M	Dudenhofen
43. Emmerich, Phil[ip]	M	Mittelbuchen
44. Herchenröder, Joh[ann]	M	Steinau
45. Jost, Joh[ann]	M	Cleestadt
46. Mörschel, Phil[ip]	M	Eichen
47. Leybold, Nicol[as]	M	Niederzell

Serial No. 9 *(continued)*

		Rank	Birthplace
48.	Strohl, Christoph	M	Rumpenheim
49.	Müller, Caspar	M	Marköbel
50.	Cress, Caspar	M	Marköbel
51.	Weyter, Joh[ann]	M	Windecken
52.	Müller, Phil[ip]	M	Gelnhaar
53.	Wicht, Carl	M	Hanau

Serial No. 10

Lieutenant Colonel Lentz' Company

Heading as in Serial No. 5

		Rank	Birthplace
1.	Lenz [or Lentz], Christoph	LtCol	Frankfurt[/Main?]
2.	Staaf [Staal?] Henr[ich]	1st Sgt	Cressenbach
3.	Becker, Ludw[ig]	Sgt	Dudenhofen
4.	Rauch, Ludwig	Drummer	Langstadt
5.	Heck, Martin	Drummer	Fechenheim
6.	Jahn, Nicol[as]	M	Breitenbach
7.	Bach, Conrad	M	Rodenbach
8.	Knobloch, Carl	M	Steinau
9.	Schott, Carl	M	Steinau
10.	Schenck, Joh[ann]	M	Hintersteinau
11.	Krieg, Henr[ich]	M	Niederdorfelden
12.	Hafner, Pancratz	M	Schlüchtern
13.	Schmidt, Nicol[as]	M	Bellings
14.	Uhrlettig, Henrich	M	Bergen
15.	Müller, Conrad	M	Steinau
16.	Roth, Conrad,	M	Langstadt
17.	Westphal, Henr[ich]	M	Windecken
18.	Baer, Henr[ich]	M	Marköbel
19.	Bender, Phil[ip]	M	Windecken
20.	Wieteram, Christoph	M	Eisenberg/Sachsen Territory [Saxony]

		Rank	Birthplace
21.	Resch, Henr[ich]	M	Dudenhofen
22.	Bremer, Conrad	M	Ober-Issigheim
23.	Müller, Phil[ip]	M	Steinau
24.	Schilling, Henr[ich]	M	Niederdorfelden
25.	Resch, Nicol[as]	M	Dudenhofen
26.	Petri, Phil[ip]	M	Schlüchtern
27.	Beck, Johann	M	Gelnhaar
28.	Schwab, Peter	M	Preungesheim
29.	Eipp, Caspar	M	Steinbach
30.	Mencke, Conr[ad]	M	Ginnheim
31.	Selb, Wendel	M	Dudenhofen
32.	Zinckhan, Joh[ann]	M	Trasenberg
33.	Faber, Henr[ich]	M	Nieder-Issigheim
34.	Peter, Thomas	M	Eschersheim
35.	Schröder, Peter	M	Hochstadt
36.	Weigand, Joh[ann]	M	Kempfenbrunn
37.	Baumann, Phil[ip]	M	Ostheim
38.	Best, Walter	M	Ober-Eschbach
39.	Stickel, Henrich	M	Grossenhausen
40.	Korn, Georg	M	Ahl/Fulda Territory
41.	Schilling, Henr[ich]	M	Dorheim
42.	Weigand, Peter	M	Marköbel
43.	Schmidt, Gerhard	M	Kirndorf
44.	Meerbott, Joh[ann]	M	Hochstadt
45.	Zorbach, Carl	M	Preungesheim
46.	See, Johannes	M	Bischofsheim
47.	Meyer, Fridr[ich]	M	Göppingen
48.	Hetterich, Peter	M	Marköbel
49.	Schwab, Adam	M	Rödgen
50.	Horn, Nicol[as]	M	Nauheim
51.	Sohl, Fridr[ich]	M	Hanau

Serial No. 10   *(continued)*

		Rank	Birthplace
52.	Weil, Hartmann	M	Hungen
53.	Gürtler, Christoph	M	Nauheim

Serial No. 11   *Language:* German   *Number of serial entries in MS:* 271

Source: Marburg Staatsarchiv, *Place:* not given
  Bestand 4h:415:46: pp. 46-
  47   *Date:* not given   *Number of pages in MS:* 2

Name of Unit: Hessen-Hanau Infantry Regiment Erbprinz [Crown Prince]

MS Heading: List of the men present in Canada from the Battalion of the
         Hessen-Hanau Infantry Regiment Erbprinz, by companies

Dorso: Recapitulation: 4 officers, 19 non-commissioned officers, 4 order-
      lies, 6 musicians, 238 soldiers

Grenadier Company		Rank	Birthplace
1.	Seiffert, Georg	2d Lt	Eschersheim
2.	Henzel, Henr[ich]	Fourier	Rodheim
3.	Müller, Gottl[ob][or Gottlieb]	Cpl	Halle
4.	Walter [Walzer?] Georg	Cpl	Gronau
5.	Werner, Mich[el]	Cpl	Eichen
6.	Freund, Henr[ich]	Private 1st Class	Bieber
7.	Weiss, Georg	Orderly	Rastadt
8.	Drill, Conrad	Drummer	Langen/Darmstadt Territory
9.	Auer, Philipp	Gr	Dudenhofen
10.	Cress, Caspar	Gr	Wallrod
11.	Hommel, Nicol[as]	Gr	Wallrod
12.	Berger, Joh[ann]	Gr	Gudensberg/Hessen
13.	Lauckhart, Nicol[as]	Gr	Fechenheim
14.	Bender, Henr[ich]	Gr	Marköbel
15.	Krautwurst, Joh[ann]	Gr	Babenhausen
16.	Brust, Thomas	Gr	Ostheim

		Rank	Birthplace
17.	Wagner, Henr[ich]	Gr	Daubringen/Darmstadt Territory
18.	Freund, Adam	Gr	Bieber
19.	Leonhard, Joh[ann]	Gr	Strasburg
20.	Mahr, Andr[eas]	Gr	Dudenhofen
21.	Etzig, Michel	Gr	Rodenbach
22.	Höger, Henr[ich]	Gr	Erfurth
23.	Lindner, Joh[ann]	Gr	Boppenhausen/Fulda Territory
24.	Dümler, Conr[ad]	Gr	Wassermungenau/Ansbach Territory
25.	Däfner, Georg	Gr	Marios [Marjoss]
26.	Gärtner, Georg	Gr	Marköbel
27.	Genaud, Jac[ob]	Gr	Neu-Isenburg
28.	Kropp, Jac[ob]	Gr	Bieber
29.	Stock, Andr[eas]	Gr	Flörsbach
30.	Globedanz, Gottl[ob][or Gottlieb]	Gr	Burck/Brandenburg Territory
31.	Hachenberger, Wilh[elm]	Gr	Rödgen
32.	Wagner, Phil[ip]	Gr	Hochstadt
33.	Grünewald, Caspar	Gr	Babenhausen
34.	Eichler, Gottfr[ied]	Gr	Dorheim
35.	Puth, Peter	Gr	Bergen
36.	Liebegott, Henr[ich]	Gr	Bleichenbach
37.	Wien, Philip	Gr	Rodheim
38.	Gescheidle, Joh[ann]	Gr	Rothenburg am Neckar
39.	Beratt, Henr[ich]	Gr	Hausen/Mainz Territory
40.	Kirsch, Ludwig	Gr	Frankfurt/Oder
41.	Müller, Michel	Gr	Volmerts/Degenfeld Territory
42.	Butz, Joseph	Gr	Roswangen/Ritterschaftl. Territory
43.	Werner, Jacob	Gr	Ammersbach/Würzburg Territory

Serial No. 11 (continued)

		Rank	Birthplace
44.	Maisch, Joach[im]	Gr	Rommingen/Würzburg Territory
45.	Rau, Conr[ad]	Gr	Bernheim/Frankfurt Territory
46.	Zlabinger, Bernh[ard]	Gr	Kloster Zwetel/Lower Austria [Zwettl an d. Rodl?]
47.	Krämer, Henr[ich]	Gr	Frankfurt

Serial No. 12   *Heading as in Serial No. 11*

Leib [Bodyguard] Company

		Rank	Birthplace
1.	Heisterreich, Ludw[ig]	Sgt	Tabiau/Prussia
2.	Haumann, Jac[ob]	Free Cpl	Hanau
3.	Bellinger, Joh[ann]	Cpl	Steinau
4.	Ewald, Peter	Private 1st Class	Bergen
5.	Seebach, Conrad	Drummer	Schlüchtern
6.	Lind, Johannes	M	Hochstadt
7.	Kohlepp, Georg	M	Marios [Marjoss]
8.	Schauberger, Joh[ann]	M	Seidenrod
9.	Ruhl, Phil[ip]	M	Seckbach
10.	Bewalle, Joh[ann]	M	Löwen/Brabant [Louvain, Belgium]
11.	Eidebenz, Henr[ich]	M	Babenhausen
12.	Lapp, Joh[ann]	M	Useborn/Stollberg Territory
13.	Bickes, Conr[ad]	M	Nieder-Eschbach
14.	Fleischmann, Jacob	M	Gersheim/Württemberg Territory
15.	David, Henr[ich]	M	Ettighofen
16.	Merckel, Reinhard	M	Giesen
17.	Welter, Caspar	M	Rodheim

		Rank	Birthplace
18.	Glas, Jonas	M	Selters
19.	Däfner, Joh[ann]	M	Marios [Marjoss]
20.	Bieling, Andr[eas]	M	Eisfeld/Sachsen [Saxony]
21.	Tack, Jac[ob]	M	Rodenbach
22.	Christ, Fridr[ich]	M	Ober-Issigheim
23.	Deschemer, Georg	M	Rottingen/Bayern [Bavaria]
24.	Zeh, Caspar	M	Neu-Hanau
25.	Marofsky, Anth[on]	M	Breiten/Hannover Territory
26.	Eiffert, Jac[ob]	M	Babenhausen
27.	Bechtel, Casp[ar]	M	Steinbach
28.	Engelhard, Wilhelm	M	Berckersheim
29.	Schmid, Nicol[as]	M	Trasenberg
30.	Henrich, Christoph	M	Steinbach
31.	Hermann, Paul	M	Birck/Bayern [Bavaria]
32.	Cress, Johannes	M	Breitenbach
33.	Schauer, Gottl[ob?][or Gottlieb]	M	Siehl/Sachsen [Saxony]
34.	Müllner, Fridr[ich]	M	Mölln/Lauenburg Territory
35.	Zehner, Adolph	M	Altengronau
36.	Schäfer, Jac[ob]	M	Neu-Hanau
37.	Diehl, Christoph	M	Lanzingen
38.	Fengel, Peter	M	Dudenhofen
39.	Kling, Jac[ob], Senior	M	Haitz/Würzburg Territory
40.	Hessler, Fridr[ich], Junior	M	Schlüchtern
41.	Kling, Theodor, Junior	M	Hasselstein/Fulda Territory
42.	Filsinger, Joh[ann]	M	Eckenheim
43.	Hessler, Christoph	M	Frankfurt
44.	Spanier, Anselm	M	Oberschimeltewog?/Pfalz [Palatinate]
45.	Kühn, Christoph	M	Frankfurt

Serial No. 13

Heading as in Serial No. 11

Captain Scheel's Company	Rank	Birthplace
1. Metzler, Adam	Sgt	Langstadt
2. Vaupel, Georg	Fourier	Reichensachsen/Hessen
3. Orth, Johannes	Cpl	Schlüchtern
4. Becker, --	Cpl	Dudenhofen
5. Unger, Nicol[as]	Private 1st Class	Ostheim
6. Schitter, Wilh[elm]	Orderly	Lingen/Prussian Territory
7. Neunobel, --	Drummer	Seckbach
8. Gimbel, Johannes	M	Bergheim
9. Walter? [Walcer?] Daniel	M	Gronau
10. Schwab, Henr[ich]	M	Gambach/Braunfels Territory
11. Kraft, Henr[ich]	M	Selters
12. Velten, Adam	M	Bleichenbach
13. Bauscher, Valent[in]	M	Windecken
14. Heil, Phil[ip]	M	Preungesheim
15. Müller, Johannes	M	Rendeln
16. Simon, Conr[ad]	M	Seidenrod
17. Braumann, Joh[ann]	M	Preungesheim
18. Hofmann, Joh[ann]	M	Flörsbach
19. Traband, Joh[ann]	M	Cressenbach
20. Ohl, Joh[ann]	M	Kilianstedten
21. Dümler, Christoph	M	Wassermungenau/Ansbach Territory
22. Schmidt, Georg	M	Altenhaslau
23. Roth, Phil[ip]	M	Langstadt
24. Brust, Phil[ip]	M	Langstadt
25. Stein, Georg	M	Dorheim
26. Schäfer, Balth[asar]	M	Niederdorfelden
27. Lotz, Joh[ann]	M	Wallrod
28. Knapp, Anth[on]	M	Aschaffenburg

		Rank	*Birthplace*
29.	Weber, Caspar	M	Obernsee/Gadrisch? Territory
30.	Leick, Adam	M	Greweiler/Pfalz [Palatine Territory]
31.	Franisko, Christoph	M	Mannheim
32.	Gans, Christoph	M	Versbach/Würzburg Territory
33.	Schad, Caspar	M	Oberlauringen/Franconian Territory
34.	Nauheimer, Georg	M	Nauheim/Darmstadt [Territory]
35.	Capitzky, Benjam[in]	M	Gesnitz/Dessau Territory
36.	Gerhard, Phil[ip]	M	Littersbach/Zweibrücken [Territory]
37.	Schmidt, Henr[ich]	M	Hildburg/Hildburg Territory
38.	Borbach, Joh[ann]	M	Hüttengesäss/Schönburg [Territory]
39.	Heicke, Ludw[ig]	M	Schöningen/Braunschweig [Brunswick Territory]
40.	Hofmann, Franz	M	Zwickau/German Bohemia
41.	Reichenbach, Ludw[ig]	M	Breslau
42.	Wilhelm, Joh[ann]	M	Hildpoltstein/Pfalz [Palatine Territory]
43.	Rullmann, Joh[ann]	M	Nidda/Darmstadt [Territory]
44.	Kessler, Michel	M	Rottenstadt/Schwaben [Swabian Territory]
45.	Gunckel, Joh[ann]	M	Schimeltewog/Pfalz [Palatine Territory]

Serial No. 14

Heading as in Serial No. 11

First Vacant Company	Rank	Birthplace
1. v. Hohorst, --	2d Lt	Hoya/Hannover [Territory]
2. Kohlepp, Adam	Cpl	Bellings
3. Amend, Adam	Private 1st Class	Steinau
4. Otto, Samuel	Drummer	Niemburg/Hannover [Territory]
5. Metzler, Sebastian	M	Langstadt
6. Förter, Conrad	M	Ostheim
7. Möller, Martin	M	Marios [Marjoss]
8. Alter, Fridr[ich]	M	Geislitz
9. Conrad, Georg	M	Dudenhofen
10. Traut, Phil[ip]	M	Bruchköbel
11. Schmidt, Johannes	M	Oberbreitenbach/Darmstadt [Territory]
12. Kunes, Stephen	M	Marköbel
13. Beck, Georg	M	Gelnhaar
14. Nübel, Henr[ich]	M	Lingfeld/Pfalz [Palatine Territory]
15. Hinckel, Conrad	M	Massenheim
16. Schönburger, Peter	M	Marköbel
17. Menck, Phil[ip]	M	Neu-Hanau
18. Werner, Nicol[as]	M	Enckheim
19. Weipert, Cyriac[us]	M	Mörstadt/Würzburg [Territory]
20. Kessler, Lorenz	M	Lohrhaupten
21. Kämmerer, Wendel	M	Harreshausen
22. Krieg, Leonhard	M	Rothenburg an der Tauber [Rothenburg ob d. T.]
23. Klöber, Caspar	M	Schlüchtern
24. Dörr, Nicol[as]	M	Eichen
25. Oehl, Henr[ich]	M	Braune/Hessen

Serial No. 14 (continued)

		Rank	Birthplace
26.	Cress, Nicol[as]	M	Rumpenheim
27.	Will, Johannes	M	Rodheim
28.	Engel, Peter	M	Dörnigheim
29.	Diehl, Henr[ich]	M	Bergen
30.	Parisch, Jonathan	M	Breslau
31.	Löter, Georg	M	Scheffersheim/Würz-burg [Territory]
32.	Weber, Andr[eas]	M	Frankfurt
33.	Beil, Johannes	M	Metz
34.	Mehrling, Phil[ip]	M	Ostheim
35.	Schmoll, Christoph	M	Beilstein/Würzburg [Territory]
36.	Stier, Gottlieb	M	Leipzig
37.	Kerzner, Joh[ann]	M	Würzburg
38.	Zinck, Joh[ann]	M	Schweinfurth
39.	Brill, Peter	M	Wenern/Nassau Terri-tory
40.	Hiller, Michel	M	Weilsachsen/Würzburg [Territory]
41.	Schnetter, Nicol[as]	M	Donnersdorf/Würzburg [Territory]
42.	Schneider, Henr[ich]	M	Obererlebach/Ingelheim [Territory]
43.	Schumpf, Christoph	M	Enckkirch/Zweibrücken [Territory]

Serial No. 15

Heading as in Serial No. 11

Second Vacant Company

		Rank	Birthplace
1.	v. Schöll, --	Captain	Frankfurt
2.	Schraidt, Phil[ip]	Sgt	Rodheim
3.	Buss, Jonas	Free Cpl	Ostheim
4.	Urbig, Valent[in]	Cpl	Nieder-Eschbach

Serial No. 15   (continued)

		Rank	Birthplace
5.	Michel, Henr[ich]	Cpl	Gelnhaar
6.	Bobat, Carl	Orderly	Bremen
7.	Schröder, Joh[ann]	Drummer	Bieber
8.	Bingel, Joh[ann]	M	Marköbel
9.	Klärle, Jac[ob]	M	Steinau
10.	Müller, Christoph	M	Babenhausen
11.	Storch, Melchior	M	Reinhards
12.	Dietrich, Christian	M	Babenhausen
13.	Bott, Joh[ann]	M	Steinau
14.	Fritzel, Dionys[ius]	M	Ober-Eschbach
15.	Diehl, Nicol[as]	M	Babenhausen
16.	Klotzbach, Martin	M	Hanau
17.	Menzer, Joseph	M	Coburg
18.	Döll, Jacob	M	Burggräfenrode
19.	Wolf, Christoph	M	Nauheim
20.	Hofmann, Kraft	M	Mainbernheim/Ansbach [Territory]
21.	Wenzel, Jac[ob]	M	Ihnede/Laubach [Territory]
22.	Bender, Georg	M	Ginnheim
23.	Hens, Andreas	M	Mosborn
24.	Lotz, Caspar	M	Marios [Marjoss]
25.	Schneider, Thomas	M	Neusäs
26.	Hachenberg, Christoph	M	Schwalheim
27.	Muth, Henr[ich]	M	Babenheim
28.	Brescher, Daniel	M	Hanau
29.	Ifland, Joh[ann]	M	Hutten, Amt Frankenstein
30.	Hamann, Jac[ob]	M	Langstadt
31.	Müs, Wilh[elm]	M	Brügge in Flandern [Belgium]
32.	Paro, Joh[ann]	M	Hercheheim/Darmstadt [Territory]
33.	Georgi, Frid[rich]	M	Dresden

Serial No. 15 (continued)

		Rank	Birthplace
34.	Emmerich, Conr[ad]	M	Frankfurt
35.	Müller, Joach[im]	M	Breitenbach
36.	Barth, Joh[ann]	M	Heubach/Pfalz [Palatine Territory]
37.	Hencke, Henr[ich]	M	Hildesheim
38.	Rottner, Georg	M	Nürnberg
39.	Rödiger, Nicol[as]	M	Würzburg
40.	Kraus, Georg	M	Aschaffenburg
41.	Vicario, Joh[ann]	M	Udine in Italien [Italy]
42.	Asmus, Michel	M	Frankfurt
43.	Weimar, Adam	M	Lützelhausen
44.	Stoll, Henr[ich]	M	Praunheim
45.	Feul, Henr[ich]	M	Droppershausen/Waldeck
46.	Heck, Caspar	M	Asbach/Hessen

Serial No. 16

Heading as in Serial No. 11

Lieutenant Colonel Lenz' Company

		Rank	Birthplace
1.	Kempfer, --	Ensign	Hanau
2.	Kirchhof, Ad[am]	Captain des Armes	Bellings
3.	Spohn, Ferdinand	Cpl	Justingen/Würzburg [Territory]
4.	Rohre, Leopold	Cpl	Militz, Bohemia
5.	Klemm, Christian	Orderly	Plauen/Voigtland
6.	Carl, Fridr[ich]	Drummer	Braunschweig
7.	Hemmerle, Thateus [Thadeus?]	M	Altmünster/Schwäbisch. [Swabian Territory]
8.	Kunckel, Henr[ich]	M	Flörsbach
9.	Rüpp, Henr[ich]	M	Marios [Marjoss]
10.	Voltz, Henr[ich]	M	Enckheim

		Rank	Birthplace
11.	Klee, Nicol[as]	M	Schlüchtern
12.	Zehner, Peter	M	Marios [Marjoss]
13.	Wehrling, Joh[ann]	M	Grimberg/Darmstadt [Territory]
14.	Uffelmann, Nicol[as]	M	Hohenzell
15.	Vogelsberger, Georg	M	Bergen
16.	Lotz, Joh[ann]	M	Wallrod
17.	Hammann, Nicol[as]	M	Dudenhofen
18.	Voltz, Conr[ad]	M	Langstadt
19.	Göbel, Fridrich	M	Hanau
20.	Mahla, Peter	M	Harreshausen
21.	Geschke, Michel	M	Berlin
22.	Hartmann, Peter	M	Harreshausen
23.	Pulver, Henr[ich]	M	Ginnheim
24.	Rüb, Adam	M	Seidenrod
25.	Diefenbach, Wilh[elm]	M	Nassau Dietz [see under Dietz/Nassau]
26.	Klentsch, Balthas[ar]	M	Zweybrück [Zweibrücken?]
27.	Fix, Valent[in]	M	Cleestadt
28.	Borckmann, Lorenz	M	Bieber
29.	Kayser, Nicol[as]	M	Rumpenheim
30.	Franz, Jac[ob]	M	Windecken
31.	Geschwind, Joh[ann]	M	Rodenbach
32.	Holl, Phil[ip]	M	Neu-Hanau
33.	Felger, Henr[ich]	M	Beilstein/Würzburg [Territory]
34.	Sauerwein, Christoph	M	Langstadt
35.	Rasch, Henr[ich]	M	Frankfurt
36.	Kappes, Engelb[ert]	M	Bischofsheim
37.	Breckel, Nicol[as]	M	Coburg
38.	Fetzer, Franz	M	Weingarten/Schwäbisch. [Swabian Territory]
39.	Hofmann, Gottfr[ied]	M	Frauenstadt, Poland

Serial No. 16   (continued)

		Rank	Birthplace
40.	Latuwa? [Laluwa?] Phil[ip]	M	Neu-Hanau
41.	Porth, Joh[ann]	M	Eckenheim
42.	Kretzler, Fridr[ich]	M	Heilbronn
43.	Hopfenrath, Fridr[ich]	M	Leipzig
44.	Diehl, Martin	M	Langstadt
45.	Buss, Joh[ann]	M	Leider/Mainz Territory

Serial No. 17

Source: Marburg Staatsarchiv, Bestand 4h:415:46: p. 47

Language: German

Place: not given

Date: not given

Number of serial entries in MS: 11 (appended to Serial No. 11-16)

Number of pages in MS: 1

Name of Unit: Hessen-Hanau Infantry Regiment Erbprinz [Crown Prince]

MS Heading: List of the men present in New York from the battalion of the Hessen-Hanau Infantry Regiment Erbprinz

Dorso: *Recapitulation: 1 officer, 4 non-commissioned officers, 6 soldiers*

		Company	Rank	Birthplace
1.	v. Lindau, --	LtCol*	Lt	Vommen/Hessen
2.	Knittel, Georg	2d Vacant	Sgt	Herzbach
3.	Koch, Andr[eas]	LtCol*	Fourier	Bergen
4.	v. Pape, Franz	LtCol*	Free Cpl	Warstein/Westphalia
5.	Fuhr, Henr[ich]	Scheel	Free Cpl	Darmstadt
6.	Weingärtner, Frid[rich]	Leib**	M	Neu-Hanau
7.	Becker, Henr[ich]	Grenadier	Gr	Fechenheim
8.	Treulieb, Wilh[elm]	1st Vacant	M	Rudigheim
9.	Traut, Phil[ip]	1st Vacant	M	Bruchköbel
10.	Bender, Conr[ad]	1st Vacant	M	Eschersheim
11.	Werheim, Conr[ad]	1st Vacant	M	Rodheim

*LtCol Lenz's Company.   **Leib [Bodyguard] Company.

Serial No. 18   Language: German   Number of serial entries
                                                in MS: 21

Source: Marburg Staatsar-   Place: not given
  chiv, Bestand 4h:415:46:
  p. 49   Date: not given   Number of pages in MS: 1

Name of Unit: Hessen-Hanau Artillery

MS Heading: List of the troops present in Virginia from the Hessen-Hanau
             Artillery
Dorso: Recapitulation: In Virginia, 1 officer, 4 bombardiers, 1 band
        member, 12 canoneers, 3 artillery train. Total 21.

		Company	Rank	Birthplace
1.	Dufais, Wilh[elm]	Artillery	1st Lt	Hanau
2.	Wall, Conr[ad]	Artillery	Bombardier	Rodheim
3.	Hof, Joh[ann]	Artillery	B	Allendorf
4.	Müller, Joh[ann]	Artillery	B	Seckback
5.	Encke, Jac[ob]	Artillery	B	Bieber
6.	Hofmann, Georg	Artillery	Drummer	Hanau
7.	Lohra, Georg	Artillery	C	Hanau
8.	Loos, Balthas[ar]	Artillery	C	Nieder-Eschbach
9.	Urbach, Joh[ann], Sr.	Artillery	C	Schlüchtern
10.	Selzer, Georg	Artillery	C	Rodheim
11.	Lochmann, Wilh[elm]	Artillery	C	Marköbel
12.	Heyd, Georg	Artillery	C	Wallrod
13.	Leonhard, Jac[ob]	Artillery	C	Cleestadt
14.	Bender, Math[ias]	Artillery	C	Bockenheim
15.	Zorbach, Georg, Jr.	Artillery	C	Eckenheim
16.	Koch, Christian	Artillery	C	Nieder-Eschbach
17.	Simon, Mich[el]	Artillery	C	Gräbendorf
18.	Gehring, Dan[iel]	Artillery	C	Dörnigheim
19.	Zicklam, Georg	Artillery	Wagonmaster	Holzhausen in Hessen
20.	Spah, Casp[ar]	Artillery	Journeyman Wagoner	Breitenbach
21.	Stahrenfänger, Joh-[ann]	Artillery	Artillery Boy	Lützelhausen

Serial No. 19   *Language:* German   *Number of serial entries*
                                            in MS: 42

Source: Marburg Staatsar-   *Place:* not given
   chiv, Bestand 4h:415:46:
   p. 49   *Date:* not given   *Number of pages in MS:* 1

Name of Unit: Hessen-Hanau Artillery

MS Heading: List of the troops present in Canada from the Illustrious
              Hessen-Hanau Artillery

Dorso: Recapitulation: 3 bombardiers and noncomissioned officers, 2
         band members, 35 canoneers, 2 artillery train. Total 42.

		Company	*Rank*	*Birthplace*
1.	Mörschel, Joh[ann]	Artillery	B	Eichen
2.	Hestermann, Frid[rich]	Artillery	B	Hanau
3.	Keller, Hen[rich]	Artillery	Cpl	Hanau
4.	Kayser, Joh[ann]	Artillery	Drummer	Fechenheim
5.	Billow, Jac[ob]	Artillery	Drummer	Hanau
6.	Faulstroh, Henr[ich]	Artillery	C	Rodheim
7.	Schibber, Georg	Artillery	C	Ober-Dulpen in Würz-burg. Territory
8.	Nantz, Henr[ich]	Artillery	C	Hanau
9.	Appel, Christoph	Artillery	C	Cassel [Kassel]
10.	Remshard, Joh[ann]	Artillery	C	Langenau, Ulm Ter-ritory
11.	Kappes, Adam, Junior	Artillery	C	Siel, Solmisch Ter-ritory
12.	Orpel, Arnold	Artillery	C	Schaller, Meerholz. Territory
13.	Stenger, Adam	Artillery	C	Bernbach
14.	Pahr, Georg	Artillery	C	Niederwildung, Wall-dorf. Territory
15.	Fridrich, Joh[ann]	Artillery	C	Bernsfeld, Darmstädt. Territory
16.	Senzel, Nicol[as] Jr.	Artillery	C	Bieber
17.	Henning, Daniel	Artillery	C	Wertha
18.	Knorr, Conrad	Artillery	C	Ober-Eschbach
19.	Huber, Jacob	Artillery	C	Sebach in der Schweiz [Switzerland]

		Company	Rank	Birthplace
20.	Klein, Phil[ipp]	Artillery	C	Tolitten, Darmstädt. Territory
21.	Meyer, Leonhard	Artillery	C	Lindflor
22.	Kühn, Conrad	Artillery	C	Kirchbach, Darmstädt. Territory
23.	Scheuerlein, Leonh[ard]	Artillery	C	Weinheim, Pfälz. Territory
24.	Grubenstein, Phil-[ipp]	Artillery	C	Wertha
25.	Bleich, Elias	Artillery	C	Forsheim, Bamberg.? Territory
26.	Fleckstein, Rudolph	Artillery	C	Recon, Preussisch. Territory
27.	Handel, Joh[ann]	Artillery	C	Wiesefeld, Würzburg.? Territory
28.	Schäfer, Gregorius	Artillery	C	Ahl, Fulda. Territory
29.	Volmert, Nicol[as]	Artillery	C	Eslem, Würzburg. Territory
30.	Reift, Vitus	Artillery	C	Altenburg, Würzburg. Territory
31.	Scheid, Martin	Artillery	C	Sandhausen, Pfälz. Territory
32.	Stroh, Martin	Artillery	C	Windecken
33.	Trabant, Joh[ann]	Artillery	C	Gelnhausen
34.	Fischer, Bernh[ard]	Artillery	C	Breitenbach
35.	Hildner, Fridr[ich]	Artillery	C	Worms
36.	Desselberger, Fridr[ich]	Artillery	C	Schlettau, Schlesien?
37.	Bauer, Leonh[ard]	Artillery	C	Oberkalbach
38.	Schmid, Georg	Artillery	C	Ebersburg, Sächs. Territory [Saxony]
39.	Jahn, Johannes	Artillery	C	Umbach, Fulda. Territory
40.	Carl, Adam	Artillery	C	Wetzlar
41.	Kayser, --	Artillery	Oberknecht [head boy]	Hanau
42.	Stelter, --	Artillery	Artillery boy	Münden

Serial No. 20   *Language:* German   *Number of serial entries*
                                              in MS: 8

Source: Marburg Staatsar-   *Place:* not given
    chiv, Bestand 4h:415:46:
    p. 49   *Date:* not given   *Number of pages in MS:* 1

Name of Unit: Hessen-Hanau Artillery

MS Heading: List of the troops present in New York from the Illustrious
               Hessen-Hanau Artillery

Dorso: Recapitulation: 2 officers, 2 canoneers, 4 artillery train. Total
          8.

		Company	*Rank*	*Birthplace*
1.	Paeusch, Georg	Artillery	Major	Hirschfeld
2.	Bach, Michel	Artillery	2d Lt	Windecken
3.	Bangert, Conr[ad]	Artillery	C	Lohrhaupten
4.	Körber, Caspar	Artillery	C	Wachenbuchen
5.	Eichelmann, Bernh[ard]	Artillery	Master saddler	Batavia
6.	Müller, Nicol[as]	Artillery	journeyman blacksmith	Fechenheim
7.	Schmid, Mich[el]	Artillery	artillery boy	Gontermengen
8.	Kühorn, Johannes	Artillery	artillery boy	Glisselbach, Mainz. Territory

Serial No. 21   *Language:* German   *Number of serial entries*
                                              in MS: 5

Source: Marburg Staatsar-   *Place:* not given
    chiv, Bestand 4h:415:46,
    p. 50   *Date:* not given   *Number of pages in MS:* 1

Name of Unit: Hessen-Hanau Mittelstab

MS Heading: List of the *Mittelstab* [intermediate staff] in Virginia

Dorso: None

		Rank	*Birthplace*
1.	Sartorius, C? A.	Quartermaster, Reserve Lieutenant	Hanau
2.	Heim, Ph[illip?]	Riflemaker	Weimar

		Rank	Birthplace
3.	Urbach, Adam	Provost	Schlüchtern
4.	Schmidt, Joh[ann]	*Stecken-junge*	Hanau

In New York:

| 5. | Heidelbach, Just[us] | Regimental orderly | Alsfeld |

Serial No. 22   *Language:* German   *Number of serial entries in MS:* 178

Source: Marburg Staatsar- *Place:* not given
   chiv, Bestand 4h:415:46,
   pp. 53-56   *MS Date:* not given   *Number of pages in MS:* 4

Name of Unit: Hessen-Hanau Infantry Regiment Erbprinz [Crown Prince or Hereditary Prince]

MS Heading: Deletion list [from the active service] of the missing and deserters from the Hessen-Hanau Infantry Regiment Erbprinz [Crown or Hereditary Prince], since departure [of the unit] from the garrison at Hanau on 15 March 1776

1. Kraft, Justus
   Age: 32
   Birthplace: Bleichenbach
   Company: Grenadier

Missing on 16 Aug 1777 near Benningthown [Bennington]; carried as present on the muster roll [since his name is underlined, it may be assued that he was returned to his unit].

2. Zehner, Adolph
   Age: 18
   Birthplace: Altengronau
   Company: Leib [Bodyguard]

Missing while in the commando near Freeman's Farm on 26 Sep 1777; recaptured and sent to Canada.

3. Anschütz, Paul
   Age: 29
   Birthplace: Benshausen in Saxony
   Company: Major v. Passern

Missing on 26 Sep 1777 from the general watch across the waters from Freeman's Farm; carried as having been sent to Canada [name is underscored, so it may be assumed he was recaptured].

4. Firres, Conrad
   Age: 29
   Birthplace: Weichersbach, Amt Schwarzenfeld
   Company: LtCol Lenz

Deserted on 5 Oct 1777 from Freeman's Farm.

5. Kirchner, Adam
   Age: 21
   Birthplace: Tielefeld,
      Thuringia
   Company: Major v. Passern

   Missing on 7 Oct 1777 near the affair
   at Freeman's Farm. He died.

6. Tempel, Georg
   Age: 28
   Birthplace: Spitzaltheim?
   Company: Leib [Bodyguard]

   Missing on 9 Oct 1777 during the retreat from Freeman's Farm.

7. Boutton, Phil[ipp], Drummer
   Age: 18
   Birthplace: Alt-Hanau
   Company: Grenadier

   Missing on 10 Oct 1777 during the retreat from Freeman's Farm.

8. Hüfner, Henrich
   Age: 20
   Birthplace: Hintersteinau
   Company: v. Gall

   Missing on 20 Oct 1777 at Newstadt
   [so spelled]; recaptured and sent to
   Canada.

9. Uhl, Adam
   Age: 20
   Birthplace: Semmenheim in
      Darmstädt. Territory
   Company: Lentz

   Missing on 20 Oct 1777 during the
   march from Newstadt [so spelled] to
   Kenderoga [Ticonderoga].

10. Starck, Caspar, Drummer
    Age: 18
    Birthplace: Nieder-
       dorfelden
    Company: v. Gall

    Deserted on 23 Oct 1777 at Kenderoga
    [Ticonderoga].

11. Müller, Peter
    Age: 28
    Birthplace: Nauheim
    Company: Major v. Passern

    Deserted on 23 Oct 1777 at Kenderoga
    [Ticonderoga].

12. Steinmetz, Johannes
    Age: 28
    Birthplace: Niedereschbach
    Company: Major v. Passern

    Deserted on 23 Oct 1777 at Kenderoga
    [Ticonderoga].

13. Zelly, Johannes
    Age: 24
    Birthplace: Nauheim
    Company: Major v. Passern

    Deserted on 23 Oct 1777 at Kenderoga
    [Ticonderoga].

14. Winter, Michael
    Age: 22
    Birthplace: Babenhausen
    Company: Grenadier

    Deserted on 24 Oct 1777 near Kenderoga
    [Ticonderoga].

15. Keppenhan, Christoph
    Age: 22
    Birthplace: Nehmersdorf
        in Thuringia
    Company: Grenadier

Deserted on 24 Oct 1777 near Kenderoga [Ticonderoga].

16. Krencke, Gottlieb
    Age: 23
    Birthplace: Nieder-
        trabern in Saxony
    Company: Major v. Passern

Deserted on 24 Oct 1777 near Kenderoga [Ticonderoga].

17. Ifland, Johannes
    Age: 22
    Birthplace: Hutten, Amt
        Brandenstein
    Company: Major v. Passern

Deserted on 25 Oct 1777 at Kenderoga [Ticonderoga]; recaptured and sent to Canada.

18. Schüler, Johannes
    Age: 29
    Birthplace: Niedereschbach
    Company: Scheel

Deserted on 24 Oct 1777 at Kenderoga [Ticonderoga].

19. Knoch, Ehrenfried
    Age: 24
    Birthplace: Frankfurt
    Company: Scheel

Deserted on 24 Oct 1777 at Kenderoga [Ticonderoga].

20. Fus, Johannes
    Age: 19
    Birthplace: Altengronau
    Company: v. Gall

Missing on 24 Oct 1777 on march to Nobeltown [so spelled].

21. Diehl, Andreas
    Age: 20
    Birthplace: Langstadt
    Company: v. Gall

Missing on 24 Oct 1777 on march to Nobeltown [so spelled].

22. Genaud, Isaac
    Age: 22
    Birthplace: Ysenburg
    Company: Grenadier

Deserted on 25 Oct 1777 on march from Nobeltown [so spelled] to Barrington; recaptured and sent to Canada.

23. Weitzell, Nicolaus
    Age: 25
    Birthplace: Hohenzell
    Company: Grenadier

Deserted on 25 Oct 1777 on march from Nobeltown [so spelled] to Barrington; recaptured and sent to Canada.

24. Müller, Peter
    Age: 24
    Birthplace: Nauheim
    Company: Grenadier

Deserted on 25 Oct 1777 during march from Nobeltown [so spelled] to Barrington.

25. Bohm, Nicolaus
    Age: 24
    Birthplace: Feilroth? in
        Degenfeld. Territory
    Company: Scheel

Deserted on 25 Oct 1777 during march from Nobeltown [so spelled] to Barrington.

26. Ifland, Henrich
    Age: 17
    Birthplace: Hutten, Amt
        Frankenstein
    Company: Scheel

Deserted on 25 Oct 1777 during march from Nobeltown [so spelled] to Barrington; recaptured on 3 Jul 1778.

27. Rosenberger, Joh[ann]
    Age: 26
    Birthplace: Niederzell
    Company: Leib [Bodyguard]

Missing on 25 Oct 1777 during march from Nobeltown [so spelled] to Barrington.

28. Linz, Friedr[ich]
    Age: 23
    Birthplace: Ahlersbach?
    Company: v. Gall

Missing on 25 Oct 1777 during march from Nobeltown [so spelled] to Barrington.

29. Velten, Augustin
    Age: 19
    Birthplace: Bleichenbach
    Company: v. Gall

Missing on 25 Oct 1777 during march from Nobeltown [so spelled] to Barrington; recaptured and sent to Canada.

30. Kraemer, Lorenz
    Age: 20
    Birthplace: Echenheim? in
        der Pfalz [Palatinate]
    Company: Lenz

Missing on 25 Oct 1777 during march from Nobeltown [so spelled] to Barrington.

31. Rau, Johannes
    Age: 23
    Birthplace: Marjoss
    Company: Lenz

Missing on 25 Oct 1777 during march from Nobeltown [so spelled] to Barrington.

32. Spielmann, Conrad
    Age: 28
    Birthplace: Seidenroth
    Company: v. Passern

Missing on 25 Oct 1777 during march from Nobeltown [so spelled] to Barrington.

33. Wolf, Martin
    Age: 27
    Birthplace: Nauheim
    Company: v. Passern

Missing on 26 Oct 1777 at Barrington

34. Göbel, Georg
    Age: 19
    Birthplace: Alt-Hanau
    Company: Lenz

Missing on 26 Oct 1777 during march from Barrington to Greenwod [illegible; appears to have been recaptured].

35. Herber, Michael
    Age: 20
    Birthplace: Stutz-
      hausen? in Saxony
    Company: Leib [Bodyguard]

Deserted on 26 Oct [1777] at Barrington.

36. Freyensener, Georg
    Age: 19
    Birthplace: Alt-Hanau
    Company: v. Gall

Missing on 26 Oct 1777 from Greenwod
[so spelled]; recaptured and sent to
Canada.

37. Scheltenberger, Friedrich,
    Free Corporal
    Age: 20
    Birthplace: Alt-Hanau
    Company: Lenz

Missing on 27 Oct 1777 from Greenwod
[so spelled].

38. Reppert, Georg
    Age: 42
    Birthplace: Glauendahl? in
      nassau. Saarbrück[en]
    Company: Lenz

Missing on 27 Oct 1777 from Greenwood.

39. Meyer, Henrich
    Age: 21
    Birthplace: Dauernheim
    Company: v. Passern

Missing on 27 Oct 1777 from Greenwood.

40. Spengler, Georg
    Age: 24
    Birthplace: Wiesbaden
    Company: Leib [Bodyguard]

Deserted from prisoner-of-war camp at
Winterhill [near Cambridge, Massachu-
setts] on 11 Nov 1777.

41. Knaus, Balthasar
    Age: 22
    Birthplace: Dinsheim? in
      Degenfeld. Territory
    Company: Scheel

Deserted from prisoner-of-war camp at
Winterhill [near Cambridge, Massachu-
setts] on 20 Nov 1777.

42. Schmitt, Melchior
    Age: 21
    Birthplace: Bellings
    Company: Leib [Bodyguard]

Deserted on 10 Dec 1777 from Winterhill [prisoner-of-war camp at Cambridge, Massachusetts].

43. Alter, Friedrich
    Age: 28
    Birthplace: Geislitz?
    Company: v. Gall

Deserted on 10 March 1778 from Winterhill [prisoner-of-war camp at Cambridge, Massachusetts]; recaptured and
sent to Canada.

44. Schneider, Thomas
    Age: 27
    Birthplace: Neufäss?
    Company: v. Passern

Deserted on 10 Mar 1778 from Winterhill [prisoner-of-war camp at Cambridge, Massachusetts]; recaptured
and sent to Canada.

45. Bender, Henr[ich]
    Age: 23
    Birthplace: Marköbel
    Company: Grenadier

    Deserted on 3 Apr 1778 from the barracks at Winterhill [at Cambridge, Massachusetts]; recaptured and sent to Canada.

46. Hermann, Johannes
    Age: 23
    Birthplace: Ofenbach
    Company: Leib [Bodyguard]

    Deserted on 3 Apr 1778 from the barracks at Winterhill [at Cambridge, Massachusetts].

47. Käster, Johannes
    Age: 26
    Birthplace: Eikenheim?
    Company: v. Gall

    Deserted on 3 Apr 1778 from the barracks at Winterhill [at Cambridge, Massachusetts].

48. Schmid, Caspar
    Age: 31
    Birthplace: Marköbel
    Company: v. Passern

    Deserted on 3 Apr 1778 from the barracks at Winterhill [at Cambridge, Massachusetts].

49. Bieling, Andreas
    Age: 31
    Birthplace: Eisfeld, in
       Saxony
    Company: Leib [Bodyguard]

    Deserted on 11 May 1778 from Winterhill [Cambridge, Massachusetts]; returned and sent to Canada on 29 Oct [1778?].

50. Klee, Nicolaus
    Age: 24
    Birthplace: Schlüchtern
    Company: Lenz

    Deserted on 11 May 1778 from Winterhill [Cambridge, Massachusetts]; returned and sent to Canada on 29 Oct [1778?].

51. Werling, Johannes
    Age: 25
    Birthplace: Grünberg in
       Darmstadt. Territory
    Company: Lenz

    Deserted on 11 May 1778 from Winterhill [Cambridge, Massachusetts]; recaptured.

52. Brodbeck, Michael
    Age: 63
    Birthplace: Glatendorf?
       near Stuttgart
    Company: Scheel

    Deserted from Winterhill [Cambridge, Massachusetts] on 25 May 1778.

53. Urbig, Valentin, Corporal
    Age: 26
    Birthplace: Nieder-Eschbach
    Company: v. Passern

    Deserted from Winterhill [Cambridge, Massachusetts] on 26 May 1778; returned and sent to Canada on 29 Oct [1778?].

54. Holl, Philipp
    Age: 19
    Birthplace: Neu-Hanau
    Company: Lenz

    Deserted from Winterhill [Cambridge, Massachusetts] on 30 May 1778; recaptured and sent to Canada.

55. Buss, Georg Jonas, Free
    Corporal
    Age: 21
    Birthplace: Ostheim
    Company: v. Passern

    Deserted on 31 May 1778 from Winter-
    hill [Cambridge, Massachusetts] while
    on watch with the German Corps; re-
    turned and sent to Canada.

56. Gruber, Johannes
    Age: 20
    Birthplace: Reichenburg,
      Switzerland
    Company: Leib [Bodyguard]

    Deserted on 14 Jun 1778 from Winter-
    hill [Cambridge, Massachusetts].

57. Gruber, Xaverius
    Age: 20
    Birthplace: Reichenburg,
      Switzerland
    Company: Leib [Bodyguard]

    Deserted on 14 Jun 1778 from Winter-
    hill [Cambridge, Massachusetts].

58. Lindebauer, Joh[ann]
    Age: 24
    Birthplace: Alt-Hanau
    Company: v. Gall

    Deserted on 31 Aug 1778 from Winter-
    hill [Cambridge, Massachusetts].

59. Jacobi, Tobias
    Age: 30
    Birthplace: Nauheim
    Company: Lenz

    Deserted on 28 Oct 1778 from Winter-
    hill [Cambridge, Massachusetts].

60. Siebert, Heinrich Adolph,
    Second Lieutentant
    Age: 23
    Birthplace: Niederaubel,
      Hessen
    Company: Scheel

    Deserted on 6 Jul 1778 from Winter-
    hill [Cambridge, Massachusetts].

61. Schnur, Joh[ann]
    Age: 27
    Birthplace: Dudenhausen
    Company: Grenadier

    Deserted on 19 Sep 1778 at Nortwelsch
    [so spelled].

62. Funck, Georg
    Age: 22
    Birthplace: Spitzaltheim
    Company: Grenadier

    Deserted on 19 Sep 1778 at Nortwelsch
    [so spelled].

63. Stein, Conrad
    Age: 22
    Birthplace: Freiensinn
      [Freiensee?] Darmstädt.
      Territory
    Company: v. Gall

    Deserted on 2 Nov 1778 from Winterhill
    [Cambridge, Massachusetts].

64. Krutsch, Henr[ich]
    Age: 22
    Birthplace: Marjoss
    Company: Vacant

    Deserted on 5 Nov 1778 from Winterhill [Cambridge, Massachusetts].

65. Bernges, Fridr[ich]
    Age: 22
    Birthplace: Bleichenbach
    Company: Scheel

    Deserted on 10 Nov 1778 from Winterhill [Cambridge, Massachusetts]; recaptured.

66. Mayer, Johannes
    Age: 31
    Birthplace: Neuenheim,
      Mainz. Territory
    Company: Lenz

    Deserted on 10 Nov 1778 from Winterhill [Cambridge, Massachusetts].

67. Klinckerfus, Esaias
    Age: 30
    Birthplace: Nauheim
    Company: Scheel

    Deserted on 12 Nov 1778 while on march to Siedboury [Sudbury].

68. Lehr, Johannes
    Age: 28
    Birthplace: Bockenheim
    Company: Scheel

    Deserted on 12 Nov 1778 while on march to Siedboury [Sudbury].

69. Roth, Johannes
    Age: 25
    Birthplace: Holzhausen
    Company: Scheel

    Deserted on 12 Nov 1778 while on march to Siedboury [Sudbury].

70. Braumann, Joh[ann]
    Age: 20
    Birthplace: Preungesheim
    Company: Scheel

    Deserted on 12 Nov 1778 while on march to Siedboury [Sudbury]; recaptured and sent to Canada.

71. Krebs, Valent[in]
    Age: 27
    Birthplace: Cleestadt?
    Company: Scheel

    Deserted on 12 Nov 1778 while on march to Siedboury [Sudbury].

72. Obrick, Wilh[elm]
    Age: 27
    Birthplace: Rodheim
    Company: Scheel

    Deserted on 12 Nov 1778 while on march to Siedboury [Sudbury].

73. Dietrich, Nicol[aus]
    Age: 25
    Birthplace: Marjoss
    Company: Vacant

    Deserted on 12 Nov 1778 while on march to Siedboury [Sudbury].

74. Ziewe, Conrad, Private
       First Class
       Age: 22
       Birthplace: Hetternheim,
         Mainz. Territory
       Company: Grenadier

Deserted on 12 Nov 1778 while on march from Sudbury to Maulborough [Marlborough].

75. Roth, Andreas
       Age: 25
       Birthplace: Seckbach
       Company: Grenadier

Deserted on 12 Nov 1778 while on march from Sudbury to Maulborough [Marlborough].

76. Lauckhard, Wilh[elm]
       Age: 24
       Birthplace: Fechenheim
       Company: Grenadier

Deserted on 12 Nov 1778 while on march from Sudbury to Maulborough [Marlborough]; recaptured and sent to Canada.

77. Klöber, Franz
       Age: 24
       Birthplace: Steinbach
       Company: Grenadier

Deserted on 12 Nov 1778 while on march from Sudbury to Maulborough [Marlborough].

78. Reitz, Henr[ich]
       Age: 26
       Birthplace: Bieber
       Company: Scheel

Deserted on 13 Nov 1778 while on march from Maulborough [Marlborough].

79. Bechtold, Fridr[ich]
       Age: 28
       Birthplace: Bergau
       Company: Leib [Bodyguard]

Deserted on 14 Nov 1778 from night quarters at Schrewsbury.

80. Hochstadt, Jacob
       Age: 27
       Birthplace: Windecken
       Company: Grenadier

Deserted on 19 Nov 1778 while on march from Wielbram? to Endfield.

81. Hochstadt, Wilh[elm]
       Age: 26
       Birthplace: Windecken
       Company: Grenadier

Deserted on 19 Nov 1778 while on march from Wielbram? to Endfield.

82. Emmerichs, Marx
       Age: 28
       Birthplace: Windecken
       Company: Grenadier

Deserted on 19 Nov 1778 while on march from Wielbram? to Endfield.

83. Heidenreich, Henr[ich]
       Age: 27
       Birthplace: Eisenach
       Company: Grenadier

Deserted on 24 Nov 1778 at New Hartford.

84. Groner, Peter
    Age: 26
    Birthplace: Nieder-
        dorfelden
    Company: Scheel

    Deserted on 25 Nov 1778 while on march from Newfurth [New Hartford?]

85. Gackemus, Jac[ob]
    Age: 37
    Birthplace: Langstadt
    Company: Vacant

    Deserted on 7 Dec 1778 at Harlestown.

86. List, Martin
    Age: 26
    Birthplace: Hanau
    Company: Vacant

    Deserted on 7 Dec 1778 at Harlestown.

87. Haumann, Jacob, Free
        Corporal
    Age: 23
    Birthplace: Alt-Hanau
    Company: Leib [Bodyguard]

    Deserted on 10 Dec 1778 while on march from Sussex to Herkerstown? [Heckers-town?]; recaptured.

88. Ewald, Conrad, Corporal
    Age: 30
    Birthplace: Ferna, Hessen
    Company: Leib [Bodyguard]

    Deserted on 10 Dec 1778 while on march from Sussex to Herkerstown.

89. Adami, Michael
    Age: 21
    Birthplace: Bergau
    Company: Lenz

    Deserted on 18 Dec 1778 while on march from Bedmünster to Norwelsch.

90. Volst, Martin
    Age: 21
    Birthplace: Bergau
    Company: Scheel

    Deserted on 18 Dec 1778 while on march from Bedmünster.

91. Diehl, Balth[asar]
    Age: 24
    Birthplace: Rossbach
    Company: Scheel

    Deserted on 19 Dec 1778 while on march from Queckentownship.

92. Linck, Henr[ich]
    Age: 24
    Birthplace: Gaisslitz
    Company: Scheel

    Deserted on 19 Dec 1778 while on march from Queckentownship.

93. Scheerer, Henr[ich]
    Age: 31
    Birthplace: Eichen
    Company: Scheel

    Deserted on 19 Dec 1778 while on march from Queckentownship.

94. Köhler, Jost
    Age: 22
    Birthplace: Wertheim,
      Löwenstein. Territory
    Company: Scheel

    Deserted on 19 Dec 1778 while on march
    from Queckentownship.

95. Linck, Stephan
    Age: 19
    Birthplace: Cresebach?
    Company: Leib [Bodyguard]

    Deserted on 19 Dec 1778 while on march
    from Northwalles to Valliforge [Valley
    Forge].

96. Bruckmann, Phil[ipp]
    Age: 28
    Birthplace: Zeitlos in
      Thüringischen? [Thurin-
      gian Territory]
    Company: Leib [Bodyguard]

    Deserted on 19 Dec 1778 while on night
    [duty as] fusilier at Valliforge [Valley
    Forge].

97. Bügeler, Ludwig
    Age: 20
    Birthplace: Umstadt?
    Company: Scheel

    Deserted on 22 Dec 1778 while on march
    from Becke.

98. Cress, Henr[ich]
    Age: 26
    Birthplace: Breidenbach
    Company: Scheel

    Deserted on 22 Dec 1778 while on march
    from Becke.

99. Unger, Andr[eas], Junior
    Age: 21
    Birthplace: Windecken
    Company: Scheel

    Deserted on 24 Dec 1778 while on march
    from Langaster [Lancaster, Pennsylvania].

100. Metzler, Adam, Sergeant
    Age: 47
    Birthplace: Langstadt
    Company: Scheel

    Deserted on 24 Dec 1778 while on march
    from Langaster [Lancaster, Pennsylvania].

101. Dietrich, Lorenz
    Age: 22
    Birthplace: Flörsbach
    Company: Grenadier

    Deserted on 24 Dec 1778 while on march
    from Langaster [Lancaster, Pennsylvania].

102. Schuster, Henr[ich]
    Age: 27
    Birthplace: Nauheim
    Company: Grenadier

    Deserted on 24 Dec 1778 while on march
    from Langaster [Lancaster, Pennsylvania].

103. Linneberger, Adam
    Age: 27
    Birthplace: Rampfen-
      brunn? Kampfenbrunn?
    Company: Grenadier

    Deserted on 24 Dec 1778 while on march
    from Langaster [Lancaster, Pennsylvania].

104. Becker, Henr[ich]
     Age: 24
     Birthplace: Fechenheim
     Company: Grenadier

     Deserted on 24 Dec 1778 while on march from Langaster [Lancaster, Pennsylvania]; recaptured and sent to Canada.

105. Trostmüller, Fridr[ich]
     Age: 23
     Birthplace: Bieber
     Company: Grenadier

     Deserted on 24 Dec 1778 while on march from Langaster [Lancaster, Pennsylvania].

106. Köhler, Henr[ich]
     Age: 24
     Birthplace: Bruchköbel
     Company: Leib [Bodyguard]

     Deserted on 24 Dec 1778 while on march from Langaster [Lancaster, Pennsylvania].

107. Breidenbach, Paul
     Age: 27
     Birthplace: Grossenhausen
     Company: Leib [Bodyguard]

     Deserted on 24 Dec 1778 while on march from Langaster [Lancaster, Pennsylvania].

108. Diehl, Fridr[ich]
     Age: 27
     Birthplace: Rossbach
     Company: v. Gall

     Deserted on 24 Dec 1778 while on march from Langaster [Lancaster, Pennsylvania].

109. Stock, Michael
     Age: 26
     Birthplace: Lanzingen
     Company: v. Gall

     Deserted on 24 Dec 1778 while on march from Langaster [Lancaster, Pennsylvania].

110. Schumm, Henr[ich]
     Age: 28
     Birthplace: Breidenborn
     Company: v. Gall

     Deserted on 24 Dec 1778 while on march from Langaster [Lancaster, Pennsylvania].

111. Schöner, Joh[ann]
     Age: 32
     Birthplace: Lohrhaupten
     Company: Leib [Bodyguard]

     Deserted on 25 Dec 1778 from night quarters at Hamfield.

112. Lohberg, Henr[ich]
     Age: 20
     Birthplace: Neu-Hanau
     Company: Lenz

     Deserted on 29 Dec 1778 while on march from Lancaster to Helltownship.

113. Weber, Valentin
     Age: 24
     Birthplace: Bruchköbel
     Company: Vacant

     Deserted on 29 Dec 1778 at Lancaster [Pennsylvania].

114. Müller, Phil[ipp]   Deserted on 29 Dec 1778 at Lancaster
      Age: 28   [Pennsylvania].
      Birthplace: Marköbel
      Company: Vacant

115. Schäfer, Ernst   Deserted on 29 Dec 1778 at Lancaster
      Age: 25   [Pennsylvania].
      Birthplace: Mittelbruchen
      Company: Vacant

116. Lanz, Valentin   Deserted on 29 Dec 1778 at Lancaster
      Age: 30   [Pennsylvania].
      Birthplace: Ginnheim
      Company: Vacant

117. Seelig, Johannes   Deserted on 30 Dec 1778 at the Susque-
      Age: 22   hanna River while on the march to Vir-
      Birthplace: Bellings   ginia.
      Company: v. Gall

118. Wissenbach, Philipp, Drummer   Deserted on 31 Dec 1778 at Townitown
      Age: 22   [Tawneytown] while on march to Vir-
      Birthplace: Schlüchtern   ginia.
      Company: v. Gall

119. Deckmann, Henr[ich]   Deserted on 31 Dec 1778 at Townitown
      Age: 27   [Tawneytown] while on march to Vir-
      Birthplace: Bleichenbach   ginia.
      Company: v. Gall

120. Müller, Wilh[elm]   Deserted on 31 Dec 1778 at Yorcktown.
      Age: 34
      Birthplace: Rodheim
      Company: Lenz

121. Weber, Johannes, Drummer   Deserted on 31 Dec 1778 at Yorcktown.
      Age: 33
      Birthplace: Steinau
      Company: Lenz

122. Weibling, Carl   Deserted on 31 Dec 1778 at Yorcktown.
      Age: 26
      Birthplace: Rodheim
      Company: Lenz

123. Blümler, Johannes   Deserted on 31 Dec 1778 at Yorcktown.
      Age: 23
      Birthplace: Babenhausen
      Company: Lenz

124. Reges, Phil[ipp]   Deserted on 31 Dec 1778 at Yorcktown.
        Age: 21
        Birthplace: Neu-Hanau
        Company: Lenz

125. Rausch, Nicol[aus]   Deserted on 2 Jan 1779 at New Hannover.
        Age: 25
        Birthplace: Schlüchtern
        Company: Grenadier

126. Bender, Conr[ad]   Deserted on 2 Jan 1779 at New Hannover;
        Age: 30   recaptured and sent to Canada.
        Birthplace: Eschersheim
        Company: v. Gall

127. Schreiber, Henr[ich],   Deserted on 2 Jan 1779 on the march to
        Drummer   Townitown [Tawneytown].
        Age: 20
        Birthplace: Rommershausen
        Company: Scheel

128. Bender, Henr[ich]   Deserted on 2 Jan 1779 on the march to
        Age: 25   Townitown [Tawneytown].
        Birthplace: Nieder-
          dorfelden
        Company: Scheel

129. Baist, Georg   Deserted on 3 Jan 1779 at Tonitown
        Age: 23   [Tawneytown] on the march to Virginia.
        Birthplace: Gumfritz
        Company: v. Gall

130. Zeth, Ulrich   Deserted on 3 Jan 1779 at Tonitown
        Age: 21   [Tawneytown] on the march to Virginia.
        Birthplace: Bellings
        Company: v. Gall

131. Zeul, Conrad   Deserted on 6 Jan 1779 at Fridrichs-
        Age: 22   town [Frederick, Maryland] while on
        Birthplace: Kilianstädten   the march to Virginia.
        Company: v. Gall

132. Lotz, Nicol[aus]   Deserted on 6 Jan 1779 at Fridrichs-
        Age: 24   town [Frederick, Maryland] while on the
        Birthplace: Schlüchtern   march to Virginia.
        Company: v. Gall

133. Schmitt, Melchior   Deserted on 6 Jan 1779 at Fridrichs-
        Age: 21   town [Frederick, Maryland] while on
        Birthplace: Bellings   the march to Virginia.
        Company: v. Gall

134. Kuton? Henr[ich], Private
     First Class
     Age: 28
     Birthplace: Kilianstädten
     Company: Grenadier

Deserted on 6 Jan 1779 at Fridrichs-town [Frederick, Maryland] while on the march to Virginia.

135. Weitzel, Nicol[aus]
     Age: 23
     Birthplace: Schlüchtern
     Company: Grenadier

Deserted on 6 Jan 1779 at Fridrichs-town [Frederick, Maryland] while on the march to Virginia.

136. Seibert, Phil[ipp]
     Age: 34
     Birthplace: Hargershausen
     Company: v. Gall

Deserted on 7 Jan 1779 at Louisbourg in Virginia.

137. Bender, Jost
     Age: 22
     Birthplace: Bockenheim
     Company: v. Gall

Deserted on 7 Jan 1779 at Louisbourg in Virginia.

138. Mercker, Johannes
     Age: 23
     Birthplace: Bieber
     Company: v. Gall

Deserted on 7 Jan 1779 at Louisbourg in Virginia.

139. Heyl, Georg
     Age: 29
     Birthplace: Bockenheim
     Company: v. Gall

Deserted on 7 Jan 1779 at Louisbourg in Virginia.

140. Crass, Henr[ich]
     Age: 26
     Birthplace: Fechenheim
     Company: v. Gall

Deserted on 7 Jan 1779 at Louisbourg in Virginia.

141. Sensel, Johannes
     Age: 25
     Birthplace: Bieber
     Company: Scheel

Deserted on 7 Jan 1779 at Louisbourg in Virginia.

142. Koch, Daniel
     Age: 27
     Birthplace: Bischofsheim
     Company: Vacant

Deserted on 7 Jan 1779 at Louisbourg in Virginia.

143. Jung, Conr[ad]
     Age: 25
     Birthplace: Rodheim
     Company: Grenadier

Deserted on 8 Jan 1779 at Louisbourg in Virginia.

144. Blum, Georg
    Age: 25
    Birthplace: Ahlersbach
    Company: Grenadier

Deserted on 8 Jan 1779 at Louisbourg in Virginia.

145. Lottig, Daniel
    Age: 28
    Birthplace: Steinau
    Company: Grenadier

Deserted on 8 Jan 1779 at Louisbourg in Virginia.

146. Nenner, Frid[rich]
    Age: 24
    Birthplace: Babenhausen
    Company: Grenadier

Deserted during the night of 25-26 Jan 1779 from the barracks at Charlotteville.

147. Lucas, Phil[ipp]
    Age: 27
    Birthplace: Rodenbach
    Company: Grenadier

Deserted during the night of 25-26 Jan 1779 from the barracks at Charlotteville.

148. Finck, Carl, Fourier
    Age: 34
    Birthplace: Steinau
    Company: Grenadier

Deserted on 27 Feb 1779 from the barracks at Albemarle as a consequence of an incident with the Grand Provost.

149. Kohlepp, Melchior, Sergeant
    Age: 30
    Birthplace: Hohenzell
    Company: Lenz

Deserted on 27 Feb 1779 as a consequence of the same affair with the Grand Provost.

150. Koch, Andreas, Fourier
    Age: 24
    Birthplace: Bergen
    Company: Lenz

Deserted on 27 Feb 1779 for the same reason as the two previously named.

151. Sauer, Johannes, Corporal
    Age: 31
    Birthplace: Steinau
    Company: Lenz

Deserted on same date and for the same reason as the previously named.

152. Zehener, Nicolaus, Corporal
    Age: 29
    Birthplace: Marios [Marjoss]
    Company: Lenz

[Deserted], as above.

153. Grimm, Wilhelm
    Age: 40
    Birthplace: Bergen
    Company: Leib [Bodyguard]

Deserted on 26 Oct 1779 from the barracks at Albemarle; detained in Canada; deserted again on 7 Feb 1781.

154. Hess, Caspar
    Age: 28
    Birthplace: Bischofsheim
    Company: Vacant

Deserted on 26–27 Oct 1779 at Albemarle; recaptured.

155. Theobald, Ernst Phil[ipp], Chaplain
    Age: 28
    Birthplace: Dörnigheim
    Company: Intermediate Staff

Deserted on 2 Nov 1779 from his quarters in Albemarle County [Virginia].

156. Kohlepp, Johannes
    Age: 18
    Birthplace: Hohenzell
    Company: Scheel

Deserted on 2 Nov 1779 with Chaplain [Ernst Philipp] Theobald.

157. Knittel, Peter
    Age: 34
    Birthplace: Marköbel
    Company: Grenadier

Deserted during the night of 14–15 Mar 1780 from his barracks [in Virginia?]; recaptured on 26 Jun 1780 and sent to Canada.

158. Leypold, Daniel
    Age: 26
    Birthplace: Cressebach
    Company: Grenadier

Deserted during the night of 14–15 Mar 1780 from his barracks [in Virginia?]; recaptured and sent to Canada.

159. Koch, Georg
    Age: 32
    Birthplace: Hintersteinau
    Company: Grenadiers

Deserted during the night of 14–15 Mar 1780 from his barracks [in Virginia?]; recaptured and sent to Canada.

160. Eyrich, Johannes
    Age: 28
    Birthplace: Steinau
    Company: Grenadier

Deserted during the night of 14–15 Mar 1780 from his barracks [in Virginia?]; recaptured on 26 Jun 1781 and sent to Canada.

161. Hinckel, Philipp
    Age: 25
    Birthplace: Massenheim
    Company: Leib [Bodyguard]

Deserted on 20 Jun 1780 from his barrack at Albemarle.

162. Weingärtner, Frid[rich]
    Age: 27
    Birthplace: Neu-Hanau
    Company: Leib [Bodyguard]

Deserted on 21 Jan 1780 from Albemarle barracks.

163. Kratz, Leonhard
    Age: 25
    Birthplace: Dudenhofen
    Company: Lenz

Deserted on 31 May 1779[!] from Albemarle barracks.

164. Linck, Caspar
    Age: 30
    Birthplace: Reinhards
    Company: Lenz

Deserted on 1 Jul 1779[!] from Albemarle barracks.

165. Linck, Nicolaus, Corporal
    Age: 33
    Birthplace: Breidenbach
    Company: Vacant

Deserted on 11 Jan 1779[!] from the barracks at Albemarle.

166. Cress, Nicolaus
    Age: 27
    Birthplace: Hintersteinau
    Company: Grenadier

Deserted on 27 Aug 1779[!] from the barracks at Albemarle; recaptured and sent to Canada.

167. Krebs, Conrad
    Age: 27
    Birthplace: Litzelhausen
    Company: Leib [Bodyguard]

Deserted on 27 Aug 1779[!] from the barracks at Albemarle.

168. Weber, Caspar
    Age: [not given]
    Birthplace: [not given]
    Company: Scheel

Deserted on 1 Oct 1780 from the camp near Quebec.

169. Waitzel, Joh[ann]
    Age: 38
    Birthplace: Hohenzell
    Company: Leib [Bodyguard]

Deserted on 12 Feb 1781 while on leave.

170. Weygand, Peter
    Age: 23
    Birthplace: Marköbel
    Company: Lenz

Deserted on 23 Feb 1781 from the barracks at Albemarle.

171. Mauerer, Martin
    Age: 29
    Birthplace: Dauerheim,
      Darmstädt. Territory
    Company: Scheel

Deserted on 26 Feb 1781 while on leave.

172. Kalbfleisch, Joh[ann]
    Age: 35
    Birthplace: Cleestadt
    Company: Grenadier

Deserted on 5 Apr 1781 from night bivouac near Martensburg.

173. Knot, Conrad
    Age: 26
    Birthplace: Litzelhausen
    Company: Grenadier

Deserted on 5 Apr 1781 from night bivouac near Martensburg.

174. Walther, Conrad   Deserted on 5 Apr 1781 from night
         Age: 28   bivouac near Martensburg.
         Birthplace: Dudenhofen
         Company: Grenadier

175. Kohlepp, Caspar   Deserted on 5 Apr 1781 from night
         Age: 32   bivouac near Martensburg.
         Birthplace: Hohenzell
         Company: Leib [Bodyguard]

176. Lenz, Carl   Deserted on 5 Apr 1781 from night
         Age: 26   bivouac near Martensburg
         Birthplace: Alt-Hanau
         Company: Leib [Bodyguard]

177. Stein, Peter   Deserted on 10 Oct 1781 from night
         Age: 26   bivouac near Winchester.
         Birthplace: Dudenhofen
         Company: Leib [Bodyguard]

178. Mahr, Phil[ipp]   Deserted on 10 Oct 1781 from night
         Age: 27?   bivouac near Winchester.
         Birthplace: Dudenhofen
         Company: Leib [Bodyguard]

Serial No.: 23   *Language:* German   *Number of entries in*
                                                  MS: 239

Source: Marburg Staatsar- *Place:* not given
  chiv, Bestand 4h:415;46,
  pp. 71-72   *Date:* 14 Dec 1782   *Number of pages in MS:* 2

Name of Unit: Hessen-Hanau, first battalion, Infantry Regiment Erbprinz
             [Crown or Hereditary Prince]
MS Heading: List and condition of captured underofficers [illegible
             word], and soldiers of the first battalion, Illustrious
             Hessen-Hanau Infantry Regiment Erbprinz [Crown or Heredi-
             tary Prince], as of 14 December 1782
Dorso: Signed by -- v. Eschwege, Staff Captain

GRENADIER COMPANY	Rank	Remarks
1. Krill, --	1st Sgt	Interned in New York, August 1782
2. Donné, --	Sgt	Still prisoner at Reading [Penna.]
3. Albrecht, --	D	Entered American service 14 Oct 1782
4. Walter, --, Senior	P	Still in prison at Lancaster [Penna.]
5. Hahn, --	P	Still in prison at Lancaster [Penna.]

		Rank	Remarks
6.	Rüffer, --, Senior	P	Still in prison at Lancaster [Penna.]
7.	Rüffer, --, Junior	P	Still in prison at Lancaster [Penna.]
8.	Hachenberger, --	P	Still in prison at Lancaster [Penna.]
9.	Behr, --	P	Interned in New York, August 1782
10.	Krammer, --	P	Sold as hired hand, 12 Sep 1782
11.	Schlingloff, --	P	Sold as hired hand, 21 Oct 1782
12.	Walter, --, Junior	P	Sold as hired hand, -- Nov 1782
13.	Müller, --	P	Sold as hired hand, -- Nov 1782
14.	Dietrich, --	P	Sold as hired hand, -- Nov 1782
15.	Köhler, --	P	Sold as hired hand, -- Nov 1782
16.	Hofmann, --, Junior	P	Entered American service, -- Aug 1782
17.	Feick, --	P	Entered American service, -- Oct 1782
18.	Engel, --	P	Entered American service, -- Oct 1782
19.	Immich, --	P	Entered American service, -- Oct 1782
20.	Setler, --	P	Entered American service, -- Oct 1782
21.	Vetter, --	P	Entered American service, -- Oct 1782

LEIB [BODYGUARD] COMPANY

		Rank	Remarks
22.	Vaupel, --	1st Sgt	Interned in New York, 5 Dec 1782
23.	Lentz, --	Fourier	Interned in New York, 11 Dec 1782
24.	Weber, --	Cpl	Entered American service, 16 Jul 1782
25.	Gottschalck, --	Medic	Interned in New York, 11 Dec 1782
26.	Klee, --	D	Still a prisoner at Reading [Penna.]
27.	Müller, --	Clari-net Player	Still in Philadelphia
28.	Raabe, --	Ditto	Still in Philadelphia
29.	Andreé, --	Ditto	Still in Philadelphia
30.	Emmert, --	Ditto	Still in Philadelphia
31.	Justorff, --	Ditto	Still in Philadelphia
32.	Remmy, --	P	Interned in New York, 11 Dec 1782

		Rank	Remarks
33.	Mahr, --	P	Still a prisoner at Reading [Penna.]
34.	Pfaff, --	P	Still a prisoner at Reading [Penna.]
35.	Sickenberger, --	P	Still a prisoner at Reading [Penna.]
36.	Kempff, --	P	Still a prisoner at Reading [Penna.]
37.	Henzel, --	P	Still a prisoner at Reading [Penna.]
38.	Unger, --	P	Still a prisoner at Reading [Penna.]
39.	Sommerlad? --	P	Still a prisoner at Reading [Penna.]
40.	Zimmermann, --	P	Still a prisoner at Lancaster [Penna.]
41.	Krafft, --	P	Still a prisoner at Lancaster [Penna.]
42.	Meorler [Moerler] --	P	Still a prisoner at Lancaster [Penna.]
43.	Löhnung, --	P	Still a prisoner at Lancaster [Penna.]
44.	Köhler, --	P	Sold as hired hand, 3 Aug 1782
45.	Orth, --	P	Sold as hired hand, 11 Sep 1782
46.	Wald, --	P	Sold as hired hand, 11 Sep 1782
47.	Wiskemann, --	P	Sold as hired hand, 2 Oct 1782
48.	Stein, --	P	Sold as hired hand, 12 Oct 1782
49.	Schettel, --	P	Sold as hired hand, 12 Oct 1782
50.	Koch, --	P	Sold as hired hand, 12 Oct 1782
51.	Rauch, --	P	Sold as hired hand, 16 Oct 1782
52.	Maul, --	P	Sold as hired hand, 6 Oct 1782
53.	Fischer, --	P	Sold as hired hand from prison at Lancaster [Penna.], -- Nov 1782
54.	Fintzel, --	P	Sold as hired hand from prison at Lancaster [Penna.], -- Nov 1782
55.	Rüffer, --	P	Sold as hired hand from prison at Lancaster [Penna.], -- Nov 1782
56.	Lotz, --	P	Sold as hired hand from prison at Lancaster [Penna.], -- Nov 1782
57.	Trautt, --	P	Sold as hired hand from prison at Lancaster [Penna.], -- Nov 1782
58.	Beockel, --	P	Sold as hired hand from prison at Lancaster [Penna.], -- Nov 1782
59.	Lack, --	P	Sold as hired hand from prison at Lancaster [Penna.], -- Nov 1782

		Rank	Remarks
60.	Pohl, --	P	Sold as hired hand from prison at Lancaster [Penna.], -- Nov 1782
61.	Kohlep, --	P	Entered American service, 25 Oct 1782

COLONEL LENTZ' COMPANY

		Rank	Remarks
62.	Becker, --	Sgt	Interned in New York, 5 Dec 1782
63.	Zehner, --	Cpl	Interned in New York 11 Dec 1782
64.	Weber, --	D	Retaken on 15 May 1782 [formerly imprisoned at Reading, Pennsylvania]
65.	Heck, --	D	Still imprisoned at Reading [Penna.]
66.	Pettry, --, Senior	P	Still imprisoned at Reading [Penna.]
67.	Beck, --	P	Still imprisoned at Reading [Penna.]
68.	Schmitt, --, Junior	P	Still imprisoned at Reading [Penna.]
69.	Jahn, --	P	Still imprisoned at Lancaster [Penna.]
70.	Best, --	P	Still imprisoned at Lancaster [Penna.]
71.	Roth, --	P	Still imprisoned at Lancaster [Penna.]
72.	Bach, --	P	Still imprisoned at Lancaster [Penna.]
73.	Haffener, --	P	Still imprisoned at Lancaster [Penna.]
74.	Weill, --	P	Sold as hired hand, -- Oct 1782
75.	Epp, --	P	Sold as hired hand, -- Oct 1782
76.	Seib, --	P	Sold as hired hand, -- Oct 1782
77.	Seé, --	P	Sold as hired hand, -- Oct 1782
78.	Schilling, --, Junior	P	Sold as hired hand, -- Oct 1782
79.	Resch, Henrich	P	Sold as hired hand, -- Oct 1782
80.	Resch, Nicolaus	P	Sold as hired hand, -- Nov 1782
81.	Premer, --	P	Sold as hired hand, -- Nov 1782
82.	Hetterich, --	P	Sold as hired hand, -- Nov 1782
83.	Krieg, --	P	Sold as hired hand, -- Nov 1782
84.	Mehrbott? --	P	Sold as hired hand, -- Nov 1782
85.	Schröder, --	P	Sold as hired hand, -- Nov 1782
86.	Schmitt, Nicolaus	P	Sold as hired hand, -- Nov 1782

		Rank	Remarks
87.	Schwab, Peter	P	Sold as hired hand, -- Nov 1782
88.	Stickel? --	P	Sold as hired hand, -- Nov 1782
89.	Westphal, --	P	Sold as hired hand, -- Nov 1782
90.	Zorbach, --	P	Sold as hired hand, -- Nov 1782
91.	Horn, --	P	Sold as hired hand, -- Nov 1782
92.	Witteram, --	P	Entered American service, 18 Sep 1782
93.	Schwab, Adam	P	Entered American service, 20 Sep 1782
94.	Pettry, --, Junior	P	Took service aboard an American warship, 16 Oct 1782, and brought in [recaptured?] to New York, 24 Dec 1782
95.	Schilling, --, Senior	P	Ditto
96.	Solh, --	P	Ditto
97.	Schott, --	P	Ditto
98.	Müller, Conrad	P	Ditto
99.	Müller, Philip	P	Ditto
100.	Hüffner, --	P	Ditto
101.	Horn, --	P	Ditto
102.	Knoblauch, --	P	Entered American service, 22 Oct 1782
103.	Schenck, --	P	Entered American service, 22 Oct 1782
104.	Urlettig, --	P	Deserted, 23 Aug 1782
105.	Goertler? --	P	Deserted, 18 Oct 1782; became an American prisoner and brought to Philadelphia prison.

LIEUTENANT COLONEL PRINCE FRIEDRICH'S COMPANY

		Rank	Remarks
106.	Eiffert, --	Master Sgt	Still imprisoned at Reading [Penna.]
107.	Gnüge, --	Medic?	Still imprisoned at Reading [Penna.]
108.	Baist, --	Sgt	Interned in New York, 11 Dec 1782
109.	Eckel, --	Captain d'Armes	Interned in New York, 11 Dec 1782
110.	Schmitt, --	Cpl	Interned in New York, 11 Dec 1782
111.	Lahr? --	P	Imprisoned at Reading [Penna.]

		Rank	Remarks
112.	Gruner, --	P	Imprisoned at Reading [Penna.]
113.	Stamm? --	P	Imprisoned at Lancaster [Penna.]
114.	Dünges, --	P	Imprisoned at Lancaster [Penna.]
115.	Heill, --	P	Sold as hired hand, 3 Aug 1782
116.	Hess, --	P	Sold as hired hand, 10 Sep 1782
117.	Scheeffer, Christian	P	Sold as hired hand, 11 Sep 1782
118.	Westphal, --	P	Sold as hired hand, 12 Sep 1782
119.	Spahn, --	P	Sold as hired hand, 17 Sep 1782
120.	Arnold, --	P	Sold as hired hand, 18 Sep 1782
121.	Schmitt, --	P	Sold as hired hand, 8 Oct 1782
122.	Scheeffer, Martin	P	Sold as hired hand, -- Nov 1782
123.	Fehl, --	P	Sold as hired hand, -- Nov 1782
124.	Aumann, --	P	Sold as hired hand, -- Nov 1782
125.	Gunckel, --	P	Sold as hired hand, -- Nov 1782
126.	Klees, --	P	Sold as hired hand, -- Nov 1782
127.	Hentzel, --	P	Sold as hired hand, -- Nov 1782
128.	Booss, --	P	Sold as hired hand, -- Nov 1782
129.	Becker, --	P	Sold as hired hand, -- Nov 1782
130.	Bartmann, --	P	Entered American service, -- Oct 1782
131.	Klü? --	P	Entered American service, -- Oct 1782
132.	Wachtersheuser	P	Entered service aboard American warship, -- Oct 1782
133.	Lintz, --	P	Entered service aboard American warship, -- Oct 1782
134.	Kitz? --	P	Entered service aboard American warship, 16 Oct 1782
135.	Müller, Christian	P	Entered service aboard American warship, 16 Oct 1782
136.	Manckel, --	P	Entered service aboard American warship, 16 Oct 1782
137.	Hentzler, --	P	Entered service aboard American warship, 16 Oct 1782
138.	Fix, --	P	Entered American service, 22 Oct 1782

	Rank	Remarks
MAJOR v. GERMANN'S COMPANY		
139. Scheer, --	Master Sgt	Interned in New York, 5 Dec 1782
140. Lapp, --	Fourier	Imprisoned at Reading [Penna.]
141. Beck, --	Captain d'Armes	Interned in New York, 5 Dec 1782
142. Schumbert, --	D	Imprisoned at Lancaster [Penna.]
143. Hamburger, --	P	Imprisoned at Reading [Penna.]
144. Heyl, --	P	Imprisoned at Reading [Penna.]
145. Koch, --	P	Imprisoned at Lancaster [Penna.]
146. Hallatschka, --	P	Imprisoned at Lancaster [Penna.]
147. Scheeffer, Michel	P	Imprisoned at Lancaster [Penna.]
148. Pfeffer, --	P	Imprisoned at Lancaster [Penna.]
149. Leybold, --	P	Imprisoned at Lancaster [Penna.]
150. Justenar? --	P	Imprisoned at Lancaster [Penna.]
151. Bätter? [Bettes?] --	P	Imprisoned at Lancaster [Penna.]
152. Wagener, --	P	Imprisoned at Lancaster [Penna.]
153. Heyer, --	P	Imprisoned at Lancaster [Penna.]
154. Keysser, --	P	Sold as hired hand, 10 Sep 1782
155. Strohl? --	P	Sold as hired hand, 11 Sep 1782
156. Holl, --	P	Sold as hired hand, 13 Sep 1782
157. Müller, Leonhard	P	Sold as hired hand, 17 Sep 1782
158. Seybold, --	P	Sold as hired hand, 10 Oct 1782
159. Hinckel, --	P	Sold as hired hand, 16 Oct 1782
160. Emrich, --	P	Sold as hired hand, -- Nov 1782
161. Mager, --	P	Sold as hired hand, -- Nov 1782
162. Kratz, --	P	Sold as hired hand, -- Nov 1782
163. Schepp, --	P	Sold as hired hand, -- Nov 1782
164. Mebus, --	P	Sold as hired hand, -- Nov 1782
165. Jahn, --	P	Sold as hired hand, -- Nov 1782
166. Hild, --	P	Sold as hired hand, -- Nov 1782
167. Wichl? --	P	Entered American service, 24 Jul 1782

		Rank	Remarks
168.	Hartmann, --	P	Entered American service, 18 Aug 1782
169.	Neiter? [Neiler?] --	P	Entered American service, 16 Sep 1782
170.	Klinckerfus, --	P	Entered service aboard American warship, 16 Oct 1782
171.	Jost, --	P	Entered service aboard American warship, 16 Oct 1782
172.	Cress, Henrich	P	Entered service aboard American warship, 16 Oct 1782
173.	Sterlepp, --	P	Entered service aboard American warship, 16 Oct 1782
174.	Müller, Wilhelm	P	Entered service aboard American warship, 16 Oct 1782
175.	Holtzemar, --	P	Entered service aboard American warship, 16 Oct 1782
176.	Lohmüller, --	P	Entered service aboard American warship, 16 Oct 1782
177.	Lotz, Georg	P	Entered service aboard American warship, 16 Oct 1782
178.	Feorter? --	P	Entered service aboard American warship, 16 Oct 1782
179.	Müller, Caspar	P	Entered American service, -- Nov 1782
180.	Müller, Philipp	P	Entered American service, -- Nov 1782
181.	Traband, --	P	Deserted, 22 Aug 1782
182.	Kirchner, Adam	P	Written off as shot dead in report of 7 Oct 1777; he is [in fact] imprisoned in Philadelphia

CAPTAIN v. SCHEOLL'S COMPANY

		Rank	Remarks
183.	Kitz, --	Master Sgt	Interned in New York, 5 Dec 1782
184.	Stoppel, --	Sgt	Interned in New York, 5 Dec 1782
185.	Keysser, --	Captain d'Armes	Imprisoned at Reading [Pennsylvania]
186.	Becker, --	P	Imprisoned at Reading [Pennsylvania]
187.	Guttermuth, --	P	Imprisoned at Reading [Pennsylvania

		Rank	Remarks
188.	Bausum, --	P	Imprisoned at Reading [Pennsylvania]
189.	Hallatschka, --	P	Imprisoned at Reading [Pennsylvania]
190.	Schmitt, --	P	Imprisoned at Lancaster [Pennsylvania]
191.	Bauscher, --	P	Imprisoned at Lancaster [Pennsylvania]
192.	Schlauch, --	P	Imprisoned at Lancaster [Pennsylvania]
193.	Ferber, --	P	Imprisoned at Lancaster [Pennsylvania]
194.	Obrig, --	P	Imprisoned at Lancaster [Pennsylvania]
195.	Hagenberger, --	P	Imprisoned at Lancaster [Pennsylvania]
196.	Emrich, --	P	Imprisoned at Lancaster [Pennsylvania]
197.	Rüb, --	P	Imprisoned at Lancaster [Pennsylvania]
198.	Ruhlmann, --	P	Sold as hired hand, 8 Sep 1782
199.	Brüll, --	P	Sold as hired hand, 14 Sep 1782
200.	Bensing, --	P	Sold as hired hand, 16 Sep 1782
201.	Schalk? --	P	Sold as hired hand, 8 Oct 1782
202.	Ruppel, --	P	Sold as hired hand, -- Nov 1782
203.	Behr, --	P	Sold as hired hand, -- Nov 1782
204.	Scheeffer, --	P	Sold as hired hand, -- Nov 1782
205.	Ifland, --	P	Entered American service, 16 Sep 1782
206.	Unger, --	P	Entered service aboard American warship, 16 Oct 1782
207.	Müller, --	P	Entered service aboard American warship, 16 Oct 1782
208.	Treutter, --	P	Entered service aboard American warship, 16 Oct 1782
209.	Mertz, --	P	Entered service aboard American warship, 16 Oct 1782
210.	Hentzel, --	P	Entered service aboard American warship, 16 Oct 1782
211.	Seiler, --	P	Entered service aboard American warship, 16 Oct 1782
212.	Geobel [Göbel] --	P	Entered service aboard American warship, 16 Oct 1782
213.	Beorner [Börner] --	P	Entered service aboard American warship, 16 Oct 1782

		Rank	Remarks
214.	Zipf? --	P	Entered service aboard American warship, 16 Oct 1782
215.	Urbach, --	Provost	Imprisoned at Reading [Pennsylvania]

ARTILLERY COMPANY

		Rank	Remarks
216.	Müller, --	Master Sgt	Interned in New York, -- Aug 1782
217.	Hoff, --	Cpl?	Interned in New York, 11 Dec 1782
218.	Wall, --	Cpl?	Interned in New York, 11 Dec 1782
219.	Encke, --	Cpl?	Deserted, 4 Jun 1782
220.	Hoffmann, --	D	Entered American service, 30 Oct 1782
221.	Lochmann, --	P	Sold as hired hand, 5 Oct 1782
222.	Koch, --	P	Sold as hired hand, 7 Oct 1782
223.	Zorbach, --	P	Sold as hired hand, 21 Oct 1782
224.	Leonhard, --	P	Sold as hired hand, 24 Oct 1782
225.	Urbach, --	P	Sold as hired hand, 26 Oct 1782
226.	Seltzer, --	P	Sold as hired hand, 24 Oct 1782
227.	Rüffer, --	P	Entered American service, 18 Sep 1782
228.	Heyl, --	P	Entered American service, 19 Sep 1782
229.	Spahn, --	Wagon Attendant	Entered American service, 29 Sep 1782
230.	Lohra, --	P	Entered service aboard American warship, 5 Oct 1782
231.	Loss? [Lohs?] --	P	Imprisoned at Reading [Pennsylvania]
232.	Starnfenger? --	Wagon Attendant	Imprisoned at Reading [Pennsylvania]

SHORT LIST OF [SOLDIERS?] INTERNED AT NEW YORK, 15 Dec 1782

233.	Immich, --	P	Grenadier Regiment
234.	Knobelach [Knoblauch?]	P	Col. Lentz' Regiment

Serial No. 23 [continued]

		Rank	Remark
235.	Bartmann, --	P	Lt.Col. Prince Friedrich's Regiment
236.	Fix, --	P	Lt.Col. Prince Friedrich's Regiment
237.	Wächtershäuser, --	P	Lt.Col. Prince Friedrich's Regiment
238.	Klü, --	P	Lt.Col. Prince Friedrich's Regiment
239.	Müller, Caspar	P	Major v. Germann's Regiment

Serial No.: 24   *Language:* German   *Number of serial entries in MS:* 108

Source: Marburg Staatsar-   *Place:* not given
  chiv, Bestand 4h:415:46,
  pp. 75-76   *Date:* 16 Jul 1783   *Number of pages in MS:* 2

Name of Unit: Hessen-Hanau Infantry Regiment Erbprinz [Crown or Heredit-
    ary Prince], first battalion

MS Heading: List of troopers of the first battalion of the Illustrious
        Hessen-Hanau Infantry Regiment Erbprinz [Crown Prince] re-
        maining in Virginia after the prisoner-of-war exchange of
        12 May 1783

Dorso: Taken 16 Jul 1783. From town [jurisdictions]: 4; from Brucherthal
       District, 11; Bergen [District], 10.

		Rank	Place of Residence	Whether Recaptured
GRENADIER COMPANY				
1.	Albrecht, --[1]	D	Cassel	In New York from 21 Jun 1783
2.	Walter, --, Senior	P	Dudenhofen	
3.	Hachenberger, --	P	Schwalheim	
4.	Cramer, --	P	Schlüchtern	
5.	Walter, --, Junior	P	Schlüchtern	
6.	Müller, --	P	Steinau	
7.	Dieterich, --	P	Girheim	
8.	Hoffmann, --, Junior	P	Windecken	
9.	Engel, --[1]	P	Alt-Hanau	Interned from 22 Apr 1783
10.	Selter? --	P	Erkheim	Detained at New York from 21 Jun 1783

	Rank	Place of Residence	Whether Recaptured
11. Schlingluff, --[2]	P	Hinter-Stein[au?]	Exchanged prisoner of 3? Jun 1783 but again deserted.

LEIB [BODYGUARD] COMPANY

	Rank	Place of Residence	Whether Recaptured
12. Weber, --	Cpl	Babenhausen	
13. Koehler, --	P	Lanzingen?	
14. Orth, --	P	Marköbel	
15. Wald, --	P	Marköbel	
16. Wiskemann, --	P	Alt-Hanau	
17. Stein, --	P	Hochstadt	
18. Schettel, --	P	Ober-Eschbach	
19. Koch, --	P	Heuckelheim	
20. Maul, --	P	Steinau	
21. Rüffer, --[1]	P	Hintersteinau	Detained from 24 May 1783
22. Lotz, -- .	P	Grossenhausen	
23. Trautt, --[1]	P	Kiliansteden [Kilianstädten]	Detained from 6? Jun 1783
24. Pohl, --[1]	P	Fechenheim?	Detained from 24 May [1783]
25. Kohlepp, --[1]	P	Hohenzell	Detained at New York from 21 Jun 1783

COLONEL LENTZ'S COMPANY

	Rank	Place of Residence	Whether Recaptured
26. Roth, --	P	Langstädt	
27. Goertler, --	P	Nauheim	
28. Urletig, --	P	Bergen	
29. Weill, --	P	Hungen	
30. Epp, --	P	Steinbach	
31. Seip, --	P	Dudenhofen	
32. Seé, --	P	Bischofsheim	
33. Schilling, -- Jr.	P	Dorheim	
34. Resch, Henrich	P	Dudenhofen	
35. Resch, Nicolaus	P	Dudenhofen	

Serial No. 24 [continued]

		Rank	Place of Residence	Whether Recaptured
36.	Premer? Bremer? --	P	Oberissig-heim?	
37.	Hetterich, --	P	Marköbel	
38.	Krieg, --	P	Niederdor-felden	
39.	Merbott, --	P	Hochstadt	
40.	Schroeder, --	P	Hochstadt	
41.	Schmidt, --, Jr.	P	Bellings	
42.	Schwab, Peter	P	Preunges-heim	
43.	Stickel, --	P	Grossen-hausen	
44.	Westphal, --	P	Windecken	
45.	Zorbach, --	P	Preunges-heim	
46.	Korn, --	P	Aach? in Fulda Ter-ritory	
47.	Witteram, --	P	Eisenberg, Saxony	
48.	Schwab, Adam[1]	P	Rödgen	Interned from 22 Apr [1783?]
49.	Schenck, --[1]	P	Hinter-steinau	Interned from 9 Apr [1783?]

LIEUTENANT COLONEL PRINCE FRIEDRICH'S COMPANY

50.	Lehr, --	P	Redenbach?	
51.	Dünges, --	P	Mottelbachen?	
52.	Heyl, --	P	Eschersheim	
53.	Hess? --	P	Bischofsheim	
54.	Scheffer, Christian	P	Nauheim	
55.	Westphal, --	P	Windecken	
56.	Spahn, --	P	Dudenhofen	
57.	Arnold, --	P	Geislitz	

		Rank	Place of Residence	Whether Recaptured
58.	Schmidt, --	P	Nauheim	
59.	Schaeffer, Martin	P	Schlüchtern	
60.	Fehl, --	P	Wallrod	
61.	Aumann, --	P	Babenhausen	
62.	Gunckel, --	P	Bieber	
63.	Klees, --	P	Eckerheim?	
64.	Hentzel, --	P	Schwalheim	
65.	Booss, --	P	Neu-Hanau	
66.	Becker, --	P	Bergen	
67.	Lintz, --	P	Trastenberg? [Grassenberg?]	Detained at New York, 21 Jun 1783

MAJOR v. GERMANN'S COMPANY

		Rank	Place of Residence	Whether Recaptured
68.	Leybold, --	P	Niederzell	
69.	Kayser, --	P	Girheim?	
70.	Strohl, --	P	Rumpenheim	
71.	Stoll? [Holl?] --	P	Redheim	
72.	Müller, Leonhard	P	Steinau	
73.	Seybold? --	P	Niedereschbach	
74.	Hinckel, --	P	Rüdigheim	
75.	Emrich, --	P	Mittelbuchen	
76.	Mager, --	P	Dudenhofen	
77.	Kratz, --	P	Seekbach?	
78.	Schepp, --	P	Rodenbach	
79.	Jahn, --	P	Gumfritz?	
80.	Wiohl? --	P	Hanau	
81.	Hartmann, --	P	Hanau	
82.	Neiter? --	P	Altenhaslau	
83.	Rost? --	P	Cleestadt	
84.	Müller, Philipp[1]	P	Gelnhaar	Interned on 9 Apr [1783]

		Rank	Place of Residence	Whether Recaptured
85.	Traband, --	P	Steinau[3]	
86.	Kirchner? Adam	P	Dittelfried--?	

CAPTAIN v. SCHOELL'S COMPANY

		Rank	Place of Residence	Whether Recaptured
87.	Ferber, --	P	Windecken	
88.	Obrig, --	P	Rodheim	
89.	Hagenberger, --	P	Schwalheim	
90.	Emrich, --	P	Bergheim	
91.	Rieb, --	P	Hohenzell	
92.	Ifland, --[1]	P	Hutten auf Fulda. [Territory]	Interned from 22 Apr [1783]
93.	Ruhlmann, --	P	Nidda, Darmstädt. Territory	
94.	Brühl, --	P	Steinau	
95.	Bensing, --	P	Niederzell	
96.	Schath, --	P	Windecken	
97.	Ruppel, --	P	Mittelbuchen	
98.	Behr, --	P	Eichen	
99.	Schaeffer, --	P	Nauheim	

ARTILLERY COMPANY

		Rank	Place of Residence	Whether Recaptured
100.	Encke, --	Sgt?	Hanau[4]	
101.	Hoffmann, --	D	Neu-Hanau	
102.	Lochmann, --	G	Marköbel	
103.	Zorbach, --	G	Eckerheim? [Eckenheim?]	
104.	Koch, --	G	Cleestadt	
105.	Leonhardt, --	G	Hohenzell	
106.	Rüfer, --	G	Hohenzell	
107.	Heyd, --	G	Wallrod	

Serial No. 24 [continued]

	Rank	Place of Residence	Whether Recaptured
108. Spahn, --	Wagon Attendant	Breitenbach	

[1]Entire entry is stricken in the original manuscript.

[2]Information given in a marginal note.

[3]The village name Cressenbach is stricken out.

[4]Appended notation "von Bieber" [from Bieber].

Serial No: 25   Language: German   Number of serial entries
                                                in MS: 93

Source: Marburg Staats-   Place: not given
   archiv, Bestand 4h:415
   :46, pp 80-81   Date: 1 Aug 1783   Number of pages in MS: 2

Name of Unit: Hessen-Hanau contingent [all units]

MS Heading: List of troopers remaining in America, arranged accord-
               ing to administrative districts [Aemtern], as of 1 Aug
               1783

	Rating	District & Town	Company
1. Wisckemann, Christoph	P	Alt-Hanau[1]	Leib [Bodyguard]
2. Boos, Daniel	P	Neu-Hanau[1]	LtCol Prinz Friedrich
3. Wicht, Carl	P	Neu-Hanau[1]	Maj. v. Germann
4. Hartmann, Peter	P	Neu Hanau[1]	Maj. v. Germann
5. Hofmann, Georg	D	Neu-Hanau[1]	Artillery
		Bücherthal District	
6. Stein, Friedrich	P	Hochstadt	Leib [Bodyguard]
7. Traut, Conrad	P	Kilianstädte[n]	Leib [Bodyguard]
8. Bremer, Conrad	P	Ober-Issigheim	Col. Lentz
9. Meerbott? [Meerbolt?] Johannes	P	Hochstadt	Col. Lentz
10. Schröder, Peter	P	Hochstadt	Col. Lentz

Serial No. 25 [continued]

		Rating	District & Town	Company
11.	Lehr, Moritz	P	Rodenbach	Col. Lentz
12.	Dönges, Christoph	P	Mittelbuchen	LtCol Prinz Friedrich
13.	Strohl, Christian	P	Rumpenheim	Maj. v. Germann
14.	Hinckel, Philip	P	Rudigheim	Maj. v. Germann
15.	Emrich, Philip	P	Mittelbuchen	Maj. v. Germann
16.	Schepp, Conrad	P	Rodenbach	Maj. v. Germann
17.	Ruppell, Conrad	P	Mittelbuchen	Maj. v. Germann
18.	Dietrich, Johannes	G	Ginnheim	Grenadier
19.	Settler, Conrad	G	Enekheim? [Enckheim?]	Grenadier
20.	Urlettig, Henrich	P	Bergen	Col. Lentz
21.	See, Johannes	P	Bischofsheim	Col. Lentz
22.	Schwab, Peter	P	Breungsheim[2]	Col. Lentz
23.	Zorbach, Carl	P	Breungesheim[2]	Col. Lentz
24.	Heyl, Daniel	P	Eschersheim	LtCol Prinz Friedrich
25.	Hess, Caspar	P	Bischofsheim	LtCol Prinz Friedrich
26.	Klees, Georg	P	Eckenheim	LtCol Prinz Friedrich
27.	Becker, Wilhelm	P	Bergen	LtCol Prinz Friedrich
28.	Kayser, Adam	P	Ginnheim	LtCol Prinz Friedrich
29.	Kratz, Conrad	P	Seikbach	LtCol Prinz Friedrich
30.	Zorbach, Joh[ann] Georg	P	Eckenheim	LtCol Prinz Friedrich

Babenhausen District

		Rating	District & Town	Company
31.	Walter? [Waller?] Conrad, Junior	G	Dudenhofen	Grenadier
32.	Weber, Peter	Cpl	Babenhausen	Leib [Bodyguard]
33.	Roth, Conrad	P	Langstadt	Col. Lentz
34.	Seib, Wendel	P	Dudenhofen	Col. Lentz
35.	Resch, Henrich	P	Dudenhofen	Col. Lentz
36.	Resch, Nicolas	P	Dudenhofen	Col. Lentz

		Rating	District & Town	Company
37.	Spann, Henrich	P	Dudenhofen	LtCol Prinz Friedrich
38.	Aumann, Henrich	P	Babenhausen	LtCol Prinz Friedrich
39.	Mager, Georg	P	Dudenhofen	LtCol Prinz Friedrich
40.	Jost, Joh[anne]s	P	Cleestadt	Maj. v. Germann
41.	Leonhard, Jacob	Gunner	Cleestadt	Artillery
			Alten-Hasslau & Frey-Gemuth District	
42.	Lotz, Wilhelm	P	Grossenhausen	Leib [Bodyguard]
43.	Steikel? [Stickel?] Henrich	P	Grossenhausen	Col. Lentz
44.	Arnold, Wilhelm	P	Geisliz	LtCol Prinz Friedrich
45.	Neider? Henrich	P	Alten-Hasslau	Maj. v. Germann
			Bieber & Lors . . .? District	
46.	Köhler, Matheus	P	Lanzingen	Leib [Bodyguard]
47.	Kunckell, Henrich	P	Bieber	LtCol Prinz Friedrich
48.	Encke, Isa[a]c	?	Bieber	Artillery
			Steinau & Schlüchtern District	
49.	Cramer, Janas[3]	G	Schlüchtern	Grenadier
50.	Walter, Martin	G	Schlüchtern	Grenadier
51.	Müller, Nicolaus	G	Steinau	Grenadier
52.	Maul, Caspar	P	Steinau	Leib [Bodyguard]
53.	Kolepp, Caspar	P	Hohenzell	Leib [Bodyguard]
54.	Schmitt, Nicolaus, Senior	P	Bellings	Col. Lentz
55.	Schäffer, Martin	P	Schlüchtern	LtCol Prinz Friedrich
56.	Fehl, Johannes	P	Wallerod	LtCol Prinz Friedrich

	Rating	District & Town	Company
57. Linz, Johannes	P	Trassenberg	LtCol Prinz Friedrich
58. Leipold, Nicolaus	P	Niederzell	Maj. v. Germann
59. Müller, Leonhard	P	Steinau	Maj. v. Germann
60. Jahn, Friedrich	P	Gumfritz	Maj. v. Germann
61. Traband, Johannes	P	Steinau	Maj. v. Germann
62. Rub, Caspar	P	Hohenzell	Maj. v. Germann
63. Bröll, Johannes	P	Steinau	Maj. v. Germann
64. Bensing, Georg	P	Niederzell	Capt. v. Schöll
65. Rüffer, Friedrich	P	Hohenzell	Artillery
66. Heid, Georg	P	Wallerod	Artillery
67. Spahn? Caspar	Wagon Attendant	Breitenbach	Artillery

Ortenberg District

68. Emrich, Johannes	P	Heckenbergheim	Capt. v. Schöll

Windecken District

69. Hoffmann, Henrich	G	Windecken	Grenadier
70. Pettry? Conrad	P	Marköbel	Leib [Bodyguard]
71. Walt? [Wall?] Philip	P	Marköbel	Leib [Bodyguard]
72. Hellerich, Peter	P	Marköbel	Col. Lentz
73. Krieg, Henrich	P	Niederdorfelden	Col. Lentz
74. Westphal, Gottfried	P	Windecken	LtCol Prinz Friedrich
75. Färber, Friedrich	P	Windecken	Capt. v. Schöll
76. Schad, Thomas	P	Windecken	Capt. v. Schöll
77. Bär, Johannes	P	Eichen	Capt. v. Schöll
78. Lochman, Wilhelm	Gunner	Marköbel	Artillery

		Rating	District & Town	Company
			Dorheim District	
79.	Hackenberger, Jacob	G	Schwalheim	Grenadier
80.	Roth? Johannes	P	Heuchelheim	Leib [Bodyguard]
81.	Görtler, Christoph	P	Nauheim	Col. Lentz
82.	Schilling, Henrich, Junior	P	Dorheim	Col. Lentz
83.	Scheffer, Christian	P	Nauheim	LtCol Prinz Friedrich
84.	Schmitt, Johannes	P	Nauheim	LtCol Prinz Friedrich
85.	Hentzell, Conrad	P	Schwalheim	LtCol Prinz Friedrich
86.	Hachenberger, Georg	P	Schwalheim	Capt. v. Schöll
87.	Schäffer, Joh[anne]s	P	Nauheim	Capt. v. Schöll
			Rodheim District	
88.	Schädell, Georg	P	Ober-Eschbach	Leib [Bodyguard]
89.	Epp, Caspar	P	Steinbach	Col. Lentz
90.	Holle, Melchior	P	Rodheim	Maj. v. Germann
91.	Seybold, Johannes	P	Nieder-Esch-b[ach]	Maj. v. Germann
92.	Obrich, Johannes	P	Rodheim	Maj. v. Germann
93.	Koch, Christian	P	Niederesch-bach	Artillery

---

[1] The city of Hanau was not a dependency of any of the *Aemtern* (administrative districts).

[2] So spelled. Probably the village of Preungeshain is meant.

[3] So spelled.

Serial No.: 26   Language: German   Number of entries in MS: 94

Source: Marburg Staats-   Place: Nauheim
   archiv, Bestand: 4h:
   415:46, p. 82   Date: 24 Sep 1783   Number of pages in MS: 1

Name of Unit: Hessen-Hanau contingent [all units]

MS Heading: Demission [Abgangs-] list of petty officers and privates
   from the first battalion of the Princely Hessen-Hanau
   Illustrious Infantry Regiment Crown Prince, including
   Artillery, who remained behind in America, [Bad] Nauheim,
   24 Sep 1783

Dorso: Signed, Christian v. Eschwege, Staff Captain

Recapitulation:	Grenadier [Company]	7
	Leib [Bodyguard]	10
	Col. Lentz's [Company]	22
	LtCol Prinz Friedrich's [Company]	16
	Maj. v. Germann's [Company]	18
	Capt. v. Schöll's [Company]	12
	Artillery [Company]	9
	Total	94

		Rating	Remarks
GRENADIER COMPANY			
1.	Schlingluff, Georg	P	Deserted
2.	Kramer, Jonas	P	Sold
3.	Müller, Nicolaus	P	Sold
4.	Walther, Conrad, Junior	P	Sold
5.	Hachenberger, Jacob	P	Sold
6.	Walther, Marthin	P	Sold
7.	Dieterich, Johannes	P	Sold
LEIB [BODYGUARD] COMPANY			
8.	Weber, Peter	P	Entered service [with American forces]
9.	Wisckemann, Christoph	P	Sold
10.	Orth, Conrad	P	Sold
11.	Wall, Philip	P	Sold
12.	Lotz, Wilhelm	P	Sold
13.	Maul, Caspar	P	Sold
14.	Stein, Friedrich	P	Sold
15.	Schettel, Georg	P	Sold

		Rating	Remarks
16.	Koch, Johannes	P	Sold
17.	Köhler, Henrich	P	Sold

COLONEL LENTZ'S COMPANY

18.	Witram, Christoph	P	Entered service [with American forces]
19.	Resch, Henrich	P	Sold
20.	Epp, Caspar	P	Sold
21.	Krieg, Henrich	P	Sold
22.	Resch, Nicolaus	P	Sold
23.	Westphal, Henrich	P	Sold
24.	Urledig, Henrich	P	Sold
25.	Weill, Hartmann	P	Sold
26.	Bremer, Conrad	P	Sold
27.	Schreoder [Schroeder] Peter	P	Sold
28.	Seé, Johannes	P	Sold
29.	Hetrick, Peter	P	Sold
30.	Merbot, Johannes	P	Sold
31.	Stickel, Henrich	P	Sold
32.	Roth, Conrad	P	Sold
33.	Korn, Georg	P	Sold
34.	Schilling, Henrich	P	Sold
35.	Geortler [Goertler] Christoph	P	Sold
36.	Leib? [Seib?] Wendel	P	Sold
37.	Schwab, Peter	P	Sold
38.	Schmitt, Nicolaus	P	Sold
39.	Zorbach, Carl	P	Sold

LIEUTENANT COLONEL PRINCE FRIEDRICH'S COMPANY

40.	Boos, Carl	P	Deserted
41.	Klees, Georg	P	Sold
42.	Hess, Caspar	P	Sold

		Rating	Remarks
43.	Westphal, Gottfried	P	Sold
44.	Scheeffer, Christian	P	Sold
45.	Heyl, Daniel	P	Sold
46.	Arnold, Wilhelm	P	Sold
47.	Spahn, Henrich	P	Sold
48.	Schmitt, Johannes	P	Sold
49.	Hentzel, Conrad	P	Sold
50.	Aumann, Henrich	P	Sold
51.	Scheeffer, Marthin	P	Sold
52.	Gunckel, Henrich	P	Sold
53.	Becker, Wilhelm	P	Sold
54.	Dünges, Christoph	P	Sold
55.	Fehl, Johannes	P	Sold

MAJOR v. GERMANN'S COMPANY

		Rating	Remarks
56.	Jost, Johannes	P	Entered service [with American forces]
57.	Wicht, Carl	P	Entered service [with American forces]
58.	Hartmann, Peter	P	Entered service [with American forces]
59.	Neiter, Henrich	P	Entered service [with American forces]
60.	Traband, Johannes	P	Deserted
61.	Leybold, Nicolaus	P	Sold
62.	Keyser, Adam	P	Sold
63.	Strohl, Christian	P	Sold
64.	Holl, Melchior	P	Sold
65.	Müller, Leonhard	P	Sold
66.	Seybold, Johannes	P	Sold
67.	Henckel? [Hinckel?] Philip	P	Sold
68.	Emmerich, Philipp	P	Sold
69.	Mager, Georg	P	Sold

		Rating	Remarks
70.	Schepp, Conrad	P	Sold
71.	Jahn, Friedrich	P	Sold
72.	Kratz, Conrad	P	Sold
73.	Kirchner, Adam	P	Sold

CAPTAIN v. SCHEOLL'S [SCHOELL'S] COMPANY

74.	Bensing, Philipp	P	Sold
75.	Behr, Johannes	P	Sold
76.	Scheeffer, Johannes	P	Sold
77.	Emmerich, Johannes	P	Sold
78.	Obrich, Johannes	P	Sold
79.	Schath, Thomas	P	Sold
80.	Ferber, Friedrich	P	Sold
81.	Ruppel, Conrad	P	Sold
82.	Brüll, Johannes	P	Sold
83.	Rüb, Caspar	P	Sold
84.	Ruhlmann, Georg	P	Sold
85.	Hachenberger, Georg	P	Sold

ARTILLERY COMPANY

86.	Encke, Ludwig	?	Sold
87.	Hoffmann, Georg	D	Entered service [with American forces]
88.	Heyl, Georg	P	Entered service [with American forces]
89.	Rüffer, Nicolaus	P	Entered service [with American forces]
90.	Orbach, Johannes	P	Sold
91.	Lochmann, Wilhelm	P	Sold
92.	Koch, Christian	P	Sold
93.	Zorbach, Georg	P	Sold
94.	Leonhard, Jacob	P	Sold

Serial No.: 27   Language: French   *Number of entries in MS:*
                                         304

Source: London, Public   *Place:* St. Antoine
  Record Office, W.O.   [Canada?]
  28/8, pp. 205-208   *Date:* 25 Jan 1783 *Number of pages in MS:* 4

Name of Unit: Hessen-Hanau, first battalion

MS Heading: List of the non-commissioned officers and soldiers of the first battalion, Hessen-Hanau, with names, birthplaces, ages, measurements, and years of [military] service

Dorso: [Signed:] Lentz, Colonel, 25 January 1783

Columns below: *A = Rating; B = Birthplace; C = Age; D = Measurement in Pouce/Ligne; E = Years of military service*

		A	B	C	D	E
GRENADIER COMPANY, CAPTAIN v. BUTTLAR						
1.	Krill, Jost	Sgt	Rosdorf	40	10/-	19
2.	Hentzel, Henri	Sgt	Rodheim	43	6/2	5
3.	Klingel, Philipe	Cpl	Bergen	32	8/3	13
4.	Werner, Michel	Cpl	Eigen	37	7/1	15
5.	Walter, George	Cpl	Gronau	33	8/2	10
6.	Müller, Gottlieb	Cpl	Hallen	53	11/1	7
7.	Brust, Thomas	Cpl	Ostheim	30	6/3	11
8.	Fetzer, France [Franz]	Surgeon	Langen	30	–	5
9.	Drill, Conrad	Fifer	Hanau	28	1/1	5
10.	Goetz, Jacques	D	Windecken	29	5/1	8
11.	Hofmann, Henri	S	Strasburg	39	7/3	14
12.	Leonhardt, Jean	S	Steinau	41	6/-	4
13.	Eirich, Jean	S	Marckoebel	30	6/2	9
14.	Bender, Henri	S	Marckoebel	27	6/3	6
15.	Behr, Henri	S	Marcköbel	30	6/2	7
16.	Freundt, Adam	S	Bieber	28	6/1	7
17.	Heeger, Henri	S	Erfurt	44	6/-	5
18.	Auer, Philipe	S	Dudenhofen	30	6/1	8
19.	Klobetanz, Gottlieb	S	Brandenburg	27	5/-	5
20.	Freundt, Henri	S	Bieber	40	6/3	19
21.	Lindner, Jean	S	Babenhausen	30	5/-	5

Columns below: A - Rating;   B = Birthplace;   C = Age;   D = Measurement
                 in Pouce/Ligne;   E = Years of military service

		A	B	C	D	E
22.	Knittel, Piere	S	Marckoebel	35	8/-	17
23.	Koch, George	S	Hinter-Steinau	34	6/3	11
24.	Dümler, Conrad	S	Wasserminignau? [Wassermungenau]	24	5/1	5
25.	Gescheidle, Jean	S	Rodenburg	29	4/1	5
26.	Cress, Caspar	S	Wallerod	28	7/1	9
27.	Beroth, Henri	S	Haussen	41	4/1	5
28.	Müller, Michel	S	Vollmerts	21	3/1	5
29.	Deffner, Georg	S	Marios [Mar-joss]	34	5/3	12
30.	Fritz, Michel	S	Bischofsheim	27	7/1	9
31.	Mahr, André	S	Dutenhofen	35	6/1	12
32.	Putz, Joseph	S	Rosswangen	25	3/1	5
33.	Kirsch, Ludwig	S	Frankfurt	30	3/1	5
34.	Weitzel, Nicolas	S	Hohenzell	31	6/-	12?
35.	Hommel, Nicolas	S	Wallerod	25	6/2	7
36.	Leipold, Daniel	S	Cressenbach	28	7/-	11
37.	Werner, Jacques	S	Amersbach	29	3/-	5
38.	Meusch, Joachim	S	Romingen	35	3/-	5
39.	Rau, Conrad	S	Bürnheim	21	3/-	4
40.	Etzig, Michel	S	Rodenbach	24	6/-	6
41.	Lehr, Pierre	S	Rosdorf	28	5/3	8
42.	Gerlach, Philipe	S	Schlüchtern	38	8/-	19
43.	Lauckhard, Piere	S	Fechenheim	27	5/2	9
44.	Linneberger, Adam	S	Kempfenbrun	30	6/-	7
45.	Becker, Henri	S	Fechenheim	27	6/2	7
46.	Merling, Philipe	S	Ostheim	27	5/2	5
47.	Szlabinger, Bernhard	S	Closter Zwet-tel	25	3/-	5
48.	Wagner, Philipe	S	Hochstadt	30	4/3	6

Columns below: A = Rating; B = Birthplace; C = Age; D = Measurement
in Pouce/Ligne; E = Years of military service

		A	B	C	D	E
49.	Bügler, Nicolas	S	Bochenheim	29	7/1	6
50.	Hachenberger, Guillaume	S	Rödgen	31	5/-	6
51.	Eigler, Gottfried	S	Dorheim	28	4/1	6
52.	Cress, Nicolas	S	Hinter-Steinau	28	5/2	6
53.	Gaertner, Georg	S	Marckoebel	30	5/1	6
54.	Kremer, Henri	S	Frankfurt	33	3/-	5
55.	Lauckhard, Nicolas	S	Fechenheim	33	6/3	6
56.	Jenaut? Isa[a]c	S	Neu Ysenburg	26	5/1	6
57.	Hachenberger, Chretien	S	Schwalheim	27	5/2	6
58.	Wien, Philipe	S	Rodheim	29	7/-	6
59.	Liebergott, Henri	S	Bleichenbach	26	4/1	6
60.	Klingel, Bernhard	S	Bergen	26	6/-	6
61.	Stock, André	S	Flörschbach	28	5/-	6
62.	Puth, Piere	S	Bergen	28	4/-	6
63.	Grünewald, Caspar	S	Babenhausen	24	4/3	6
64.	Wagner, Henri	S	Daubringen	41	6/2	5
65.	Krautwurst, Jean	S	Babenhausen	32	6/2	11

CORPS COMPANY

		A	B	C	D	E
66.	Boeckel, Frederic	Capt d'Armes	Gronau	30?	12/-	11
67.	Haumann, Jacques	Port Ensign	Hanau	27	7/3	7
68.	Bellinger? [Bollinger?] Jean	Cpl	Steinau	29	8/3	10
69.	Tack, Jacques	Cpl	Rodenbach	31	9/1	7
70.	Sebach, Conrad	D	Schlüchtern	20	6/3	6
71.	Gewald, Jacques	D	Hanau	38	6/2	17
72.	Weingaertner, Frederic	S	Hanau	30	11/-	7
73.	Krieg, Conrad	S	Altenhasslau	35	11/-	18

Columns below: A = Rating;   B = Birthplace;   C = Age;   D = Measurement
                 in Pouce/Ligne;   E = Years of military service

	A	B	C	D	E
74. Lindt, Jean	S	Hochstadt	30	10/3	11
75. Schauberger, Jean	S	Seidenroth	34	10/2	15
76. Glaas, Jean	S	Seltzers	27	10/1	7
77. Eidebens, Henri	S	Babenhausen	31	10/-	11
78. Lapp, Johann	S	Usenborn	27	10/-	7
79. Fengel, Piere	S	Dutenhofen	26	10/-	7
80. Bevale, Jean	S	Loeven	51	10/-	7
81. Kling, Jacques	S	Haitz	23	9/3	6
82. Grimm, Guillaume	S	Bergen	48	9/3	6
83. Traut, Philipe	S	Windecken	33	9/2	14
84. Merckel, Renard	S	Giese	43	9/-	5
85. Bohlender, Adam	S	Schlüchtern	30	9/-	10
86. Breidenbach, Guillaume	S	Bockenheim	40	8/3	10
87. David, Henri	S	Pfalz [Pala-tinate]	39	8/3	5
88. Christ, Frederic	S	Obdrsiegheim	35	8/3	7
89. Deffner, Jean	S	Marios [Mar-joss]	29	8/2	16
90. Engelhardt, Guillaume	S	Berckenheim? [Benkenheim?]	27	8/2	7
91. Henrich, Christofore	S	Steinbach	25	8/2	7
92. Eiffert, Jacques	S	Babenhausen	24	8/2	7
93. Fleischmann, Jacques	S	Gerschheim	41	8/2	6
94. Schmidt, Jacques	S	Bellersdorf	34	8/2	6
95. Bechtel, Caspar	S	Steinbach	34	8/1	7
96. Marofsky, Joseph	S	Breidenfeld	31	8/1	5
97. Schauer, Theophil	S	Sohl	27	8/1	5
98. Deschmer, Georg	S	Rottingen	27	8/-	3
99. Schaefer, Jacques	S	Nauheim	27	7/3	7

Columns below: A = Rating;   B = Birthplace;   C = Age;   D = Measurement
in Pouce/Ligne;   E = Years of military service

		A	B	C	D	E
100.	Schmidt, Nicolas	S	Drassenberg	41	7/3	11
101.	Filtzinger, Jean	S	Eckenheim	31	7/2	6
102.	Spanier, Anselmus	S	Maintz [Mainz]	34	7/2	5
103.	Zeh, Caspar	S	Hanau	44	7/2	6
104.	Harmann? [Hermann?] Paul	S	Princk	61	7/2	6
105.	Hessler, Frederic	S	Berckersheim	49	7/1	6
106.	Bock, Piere	S	Hanau	29	7/-	7
107.	Kayser, Frederic	S	Fechenheim	30	6/3	7
108.	Cress, Jean	S	Breidenbach	34	6/3	5
109.	Hessler, Christofore	S	Frankfurt	40	6/1	5
110.	Kling, Theodore	S	Hasselheck [so spelled]	27	6/1	5
111.	Kühn, Christofore	S	Frankfurt	43	5/3	5
112.	Meyer, Frederic	S	Gebingen	29	5/2	6
113.	Bruchhausen, Chretien	S	Hanau	45	4/3	5

LIEUTENANT COLONEL PRINCE FRIEDRICH'S COMPANY

		A	B	C	D	E
114.	Kohlep, Adam	Fourier	Bellings	29	8/2	14?
115.	Förder, Conrad	Cpl	Ostheim	27	8/-	9
116.	Reichmann, Michel	D	Almuthshausen	29	7/3	9
117.	Schroeder, Jean	D	Bieber	22	7/2	7
118.	Treulieb, Guillaume	S	Rödigheim	32	7/2	16
119.	Ament? Adam	S	Steinau	35	6/3	14
120.	Alter, Frederic	S	Geisslitz	34	7/2	12
121.	Traut, Philipe	S	Bruchkoebel	27	7/1	10
122.	Metzler, Sebastian	S	Langstadt	28	8/1	8
123.	Zipf, Henri	S	Schlüchtern	28	8/-	8
124.	Kohnes, Stephan	S	Marcköbel	25	10/-	7

Serial No. 27 [continued]

Columns below: *A = Rating;*   *B = Birthplace;*   *C = Age;*   *D = Measurement*
                in Pouce/Ligne;   *E = Years of military service*

		A	B	C	D	E
125.	Schönberger, Piere	S	Marcköbel	31	7/–	6
126.	Diehl, Henri	S	Bergen	30	5/2	6
127.	Müller, Martin	S	Marios [Mar-joss]	30	7/2	6
128.	Engel, Peter	S	Dornigheim	31	5/2	6
129.	Conrad, George	S	Dudenhofen	27	7/1	6
130.	Werner, Nicolas	S	Beckheim	26	8/1	6
131.	Hinckel, Conrad	S	Massenheim	27	6/2	6
132.	Wile, Jean	S	Rodheim	27	8/1	6
133.	Cress, Nicolas	S	Rompelheim	29	5/2	6
134.	Beck, George	S	Gelnhaar	26	6/3	6
135.	Kessler, Lorentz	S	Lohrhaupten	32	6/2	6
136.	Durr, Nicolas	S	Eigen	26	6/3	6
137.	Kloeber, Caspar	S	Schlüchtern	26	6/2	6
138.	Bender, Conrad	S	Eschersheim	31	6/2	6
139.	Müller, Jean	S	Schlüchtern	27	5/–	6
140.	Werheim, Conrad	S	Rodheim	30	7/3	6
141.	Frischkorn, Friedric	S	Schlüchtern	26	7/3	6
142.	Traut, Christofore	S	Kilianstäd[t]en	30	6/1	6
143.	Velten, Augustin	S	Bleichenbach	23	9/3	6
144.	Hufner, Henri	S	Hintersteinau	25	7/2	6
145.	Freyensener, George	S	Hanau	27	5/2	6
146.	Menck, Philipe	S	Hanau	23	7/2	6
147.	Schmidt, Johan[n]es	S	Oberbreidenbach	26	9/–	6
148.	Krieg, Leonhard	S	Rodenburg	23	7/3	5
149.	Loeder, George	S	Schessersheim?	38	5/–	5
150.	Weipert, Siriacus	S	Meerstadt	25	7/–	5
151.	Schnetter, Nicolas	S	Wurtzburg	29	3/–	5
152.	Weber, André	S	Frankfurt	28?	3/3	5

Columns below: A = Rating;   B = Birthplace;   C = Age;   D = Measurement in Pouce/Ligne;   E = Years of military service

		A	B	C	D	E
153.	Niebel, Henrich	S	Lingfeld	22	9/3	5
154.	Zinck, Jean	S	Schweinfurt	25	3/2	5
155.	Hiller, Michel	S	Wail [Weil?]	30	2/2	5
156.	Schmol, Christofore	S	Wurtzburg	33	3/–	5
157.	Kertzner, Jean	S	Wurtzburg	24	3/–	5
158.	Bril, Jean	S	Metz	23	4/2	5
159.	Schneider, Henri	S	Obereschbach	24	3/2	5
160.	Prile, Jean	S	Wernern?	19	6/–	5
161.	Schumpf, Chretien	S	Einkirch	30	2/–	5
162.	Oehle? Joseph	S	Breena?	25	5/1	4

CAPTAIN v. SCHÖLL'S COMPANY

		A	B	C	D	E
163.	Metzler, Adam	Sgt	Langstadt	50?	8/–	19
164.	Faupel, Georg	Sgt	Reichensachsen	31	10/–	7
165.	Unger, André	Cpl	Ostheim	33	8/–	12
166.	Leonhard, Chretien	D	Seckbach	31	5/2	12
167.	Neunobel, Jean	D	Gronau	24	7/3	7
168.	Walter, Daniel	S	Berckheim	31	9/2	8
169.	Gimbel, Jean	S	Kilianstäd[t]en	30	9/1	8
170.	Ohl, Jean	S	Bleichenbach	24	9/1	7
171.	Velten, Adam	S	Dudenhofen	26	9/1	7
172.	Becker, Georg	S	Breungesheim [Breungeshain]	30	9/1	11
173.	Braumann, Jean	S	Alten Gronau	24	9/1	7
174.	Zehner, Adolph	S	Seidenroth	27	7/2	6
175.	Simon, Conrad	S	Selders [Selters]	33	7/1	7
176.	Krafft, Henri	S	Gimbach	28	7/1	7
177.	Schwaab, Henri	S	Bischofsheim	39	6/3	7
178.	Bauscher, Jonas	S	Ostheim	25	6/1	7

Serial No. 27 [continued]

Columns below: A = Rating; B = Birthplace; C = Age; D = Measurement
in Pouce/Ligne; E = Years of military service

		A	B	C	D	E
179.	Brust, Henri	S	Dorheim	30?	6/1	7
180.	Müller, Jean	S	Umstadt	41	5/3	7
181.	Stein? [Hein?] George	S	Dorfeld	25	5/2	7
182.	Bügler, Chretien	S	Langstadt	24	5/1	7
183.	Schaefer, Baltazar	S	Schlüchtern	36	5/1	7
184.	Roth, Philipe	S	Altenhasslau	31	5/1	7
185.	Orth, Johnas	S	Rathheim	25	5/1	7
186.	Schmidt, Georg	S	Bockenheim	26	5/1	7
187.	Werheim, Lorentz	S	Ratheim	31	4/2	7
188.	Bender, Siegmond	S	Bockenheim	28	10/-	7?
189.	Müller, Baltazar	S	Babenhausen	25	8/2	7
190.	Schaefer, Caspar	S	Hintersteinau	33	8/-	7
191.	Dechert, Doris	S	Kesselstadt	28	5/1	7
192.	Gans, Christofore	S	Wallerod	21	5/1	5
193.	Lotz, Jean	S	Greeweil?	29	4/-	7
194.	Lauck, Adam	S	As[c]haffenburg	41	4/-	5
195.	Knap, Anton	S	Hildburghausen [so spelled]	41	4/-	5
196.	Schaad, Caspar	S	Flörsbach	26	3/3	5
197.	Hofmann, Jean	S	Hilburgshausen [so spelled]	29	3/2	7
198.	Schmidt, Henri	S	Man[n]heim	23	3/2	5
199.	Franisca, Christofore	S	Zwic[k]au	52	3/2	5
200.	Hofmann, Frantz	S	Ledesbach	42	1/1	5
201.	Gerhard, Philipe	S	Breslau	29	3/1	5
202.	Reichenbach, Ludwig	S	Langen	24	3/1	5
203.	Nauheimer, Georg	S	Bruchkoebel	24	4/-	5
204.	Bechtel, George	S	Nidda	33	7/1	6
205.	Rulmann, Jean	S	Wassermingenau	24	3/2	5
206.	Dümler, Christophore	S	Hillboldstein [Hilpoltstein]	30	5/2	5

Columns below: A = Rating; B = Birthplace; C = Age; D = Measurement in Pouce/Ligne; E = Years of military service

		A	B	C	D	E
207.	Wilhelm, Jean	S	Hi[r]schhorn	35	2/-	5
208.	Kunckel, Jean	S	Goessnitz	24	1/1	5
209.	Kabitzky, Benjamin	S	Huttengesaess	25	3/1	5
210.	Porbach, Jean	S	Schwäbisch [Swabian]	25	3/2	5
211.	Kessler, Michel	S	Wallerod	36	2/-	5
212.	Lotz, Jean	S	Wallerod	33	6/-	7

MAJOR v. GERMANN'S COMPANY

		A	B	C	D	E
213.	v. Pape, --	Port Ensign	Wardstein	28	11/2	5
214.	Schoeckel, Jean	Cpl	Gelnhaar	33	7/-	18
215.	Heyder, Georg	Cpl	Neuwi[e]d	35	7/-	1
216.	Storck, Melchior	Cpl	Reinharts	25	8/2	7
217.	Bobart, --	Surgeon	Bremen	27	-	5
218.	Berger, George	D	Gutenspurg	25	10/-	11
219.	Lentz, Valentin	S	Günheim	35	7/2	16
220.	Bühliny? [Bühling?] André	S	Eisenfeld	26	8/-	6
221.	Bingel, Jean	S	Marcköbel	26	8/2	8
222.	Klerle? Jacques	S	Steinau	35	8/-	10
223.	Diehl, Nicolas	S	Langstadt	24	7/-	6
224.	Bender, George	S	Günheim	31	7/-	5
225.	Lotz, Caspar	S	Marios [Marjoss]	35	5/3	6
226.	Dietrich, Chretien	S	Babenhausen	33	6/2	10
227.	Hammann, Jacques	S	Langstadt	31	7/-	6
228.	Muth, Henri	S	Babenhausen	36	5/2	6
229.	Schneider, Jean	S	Neuses	25	5/2	6
230.	Bolt, Jean	S	Steinau	26	7/2	6

Columns below: A = Rating; B = Birthplace; C = Age; D = Measurement
in Pouce/Ligne; E = Years of military service

		A	B	C	D	E
231.	Brescher, Ludwig	S	Hanau	43	6/–	6
232.	Hoffmann, Krafft	S	Mainbernheim	35	4/2	5
233.	Krauss, George	S	Aschaffenburg	28	4/–	5
234.	Hentz, André	S	Mossborn	43	6/3	6
235.	Emmerich, Conrad	S	Frankfurt	43	4/–	5
236.	Weimer, André	S	Litzel	20	4/–	5
237.	Stole? Henri	S	Braunheim	26	4/2	5
238.	Rödiger, Nicolas	S	Rodburg	45	3/2	5
239.	Vicario, Jean	S	Venedig [Ven-ice, Italy]	44	3/–	5
240.	Cress, George	S	Rombersheim	24	5/–	6
241.	Weider, Jean	S	Windecken	25	5/–	6
242.	Moerschel, Philipe	S	Eichen	25	5/–	6
243.	Saust, Henri	S	Linneburg	35	8/2	1
244.	Bruss, Jean	S	Meinling	49	–/2	5
245.	Wentzel, Jacques	S	Einenhain	20	5/2	5
246.	Travant, Jean	S	Cressenbach	26	5/2	6
247.	Baro, Jean	S	Hergenhain	23	5/2	5
248.	Hencke, Henri	S	Breungshausen	31	3/2	5
249.	Gottner, George	S	Nürnberg	36	4/–	5
250.	Fail, Henri	S	Dobershausen	22	2/2	5
251.	Georgi, Frederic	S	Dressen	28	4/2	5
252.	Iffland, Jean	S	Gouten?	28	5/2	5
253.	Assmus, Michel	S	Frankfurt	23	6/–	5
254.	Barth, Jean	S	Heubach	25	5/–	5
255.	Dele? Jacques	S	Burgebersheim	39	4/3	6
256.	Mentzer, Joseph	S	Coburg	41	6/–	5

COLONEL LENTZ'S COMPANY

		A	B	C	D	E
257.	Knittel, George	Sgt	Hirtzbach	37	8/–	19

Columns below: A = Rating; B = Birthplace; C = Age; D = Measurement
 in Pouce/Ligne; E = Years of military service

		A	B	C	D	E
258.	Schmidt, Philipe	Sgt	Rodheim	41	9/2	18
259.	Koch, André	Four- ier	Bergen	27	6/2	9
260.	Bodt, Henri	Cpl	Seidenroth	39	8/1	19
261.	Orbig, Valentin	Cpl	Niedereschbach	30	7/-	15
262.	Spohn, Ferdinant	Cpl	Justingen	29	7/1	6
263.	Rohre, Leopold	Cpl	Milits	40	4/-	6
264.	Klemm, --	Sur- geon	Sachsen [Saxony]	30	-	5
265.	Carl, Frederic	D	Braunschweig	17	2/-	5
266.	Otto, Samuel	D	Sobenheim	23	2/-	5
267.	Behr, Henri	S	Marcköbel	31	8/-	14
268.	Volst, Henri	S	Enckheim	25	8/2	8
269.	Klee, Nicolas	S	Schlüchtern	28	8/-	12
270.	Hem[m]erle, Thedeus	S	Altmünster	34	8/3	6
271.	Rüb, Jean	S	Marios [Mar- joss]	28	8/1	14
272.	Zehner, Piere	S	Marios [Mar- joss]	25	8/-	10
273.	Kunckel, Henri	S	Flörschbach	31	8/-	13
274.	Goebel, George	S	Hanau	23	6/-	8
275.	Foltz, Conrad, Junior	S	Langstadt	31	6/-	7
276.	Werling, Jean	S	Grimburg	29	6/2	6
277.	Frantz, Philipe	S	Windecken	28	6/1	7
278.	Holl, Philipe	S	Hanau	28	7/-	7
279.	Kayser, Nicolas	S	Rompelsheim	25	6/-	7
280.	Uffelmann, Nicolas	S	Hohenzell	24	6/-	7
281.	Hartmann, Piere	S	Harreshausen	33	5/2	7
282.	Pulver, Henri	S	Ginnheim	28	5/1	7
283.	Malla, Piere	S	Harreshausen	26	4/3	7

Columns below: A = Rating; B = Birthplace; C = Age; D = Measurement
in Pouce/Ligne; E = Years of military service

		A	B	C	D	E
284.	Hammann, Nicolas	S	Dudenhofen	30	6/-	7
285.	Rüb, Adam	S	Seidenroth	22	5/1	7
286.	Sauerwein, Chretien	S	Langstadt	20	6/1	5
287.	Vogelsberger, George	S	Bergen	27	6/-	7
288.	Schwindt, Jean	S	Rodenbach	22	4/2	7
289.	Geschke, Michel	S	Berlin	26	4/2	5
290.	Fritzel, Deonisius	S	Obereschbach	25	6/1	7
291.	Kappes, Engelbert	S	Bischofsheim	28	5/-	7
292.	Völker, Henri	S	Beilstein	22	4/-	5
293.	Rasch, Henri	S	Frankfurt	22	4/-	5
294.	Kreckel, Nicolas	S	Coburg	27	3/1	5
295.	Hofmann, Gottfried	S	Frankfurt	37	3/-	5
296.	Hopfenrath, Frederic	S	Leibzig [Leipzig]	25	2/1	5
297.	Port, Jean	S	Eckenheim	25	3/-	5
298.	Lallua, Frederic	S	Hanau	28	3/-	5
299.	Klensch, Baltazar	S	Zweybrücken	22	5/-	5
300.	Zipf, Caspar	S	Schlüchtern	37	8/3	3
301.	Kemmeren? [Kemmerer?] Wendelinus	S	Harreshausen	29	7/-	7
302.	Diehl, Martin	S	Langstadt	22	3/-	5

PERSONS ATTACHED TO ETAT MAJOR [GENERAL STAFF]

		A	B	C	D	E
303.	Hayn, André	Arm-orer	Bereith	34	-	7
304.	Louis, Natan	*Prevot* [Provost?]	Virginia	15	-	1

SUBJECT INDEX

Citation is to muster
roll number (heading)

NAME INDEX

Citation includes muster roll and
number therein; for example, 12-33
means muster roll 12, position 33.

Adami, Michael, 22-89
Albrecht, Jacob, 5-7
Albrecht, --, 23-3; 24-1
Alter, Friedrich, 14-8; 22-43; 27-120
Amann, Martin, 2-23
Amend, Adam, 14-3; 27-119
Ammon, Gottfried, 2-16
André, Johann, 6-12
André, --, 23-29
Anschütz, Paul, 22-3
Appel, Christoph, 19-9
Arnold, Wilhelm, 8-43; 25-44; 26-46
Arnold, --, 23-120; 24-57
Asmus, Michel, 15-42; 27-253
Atlohn, Johann, 2-31
Auer, Philip, 11-9; 27-18
Aufleiter, Georg, 6-44
Aumann, Henrich, 8-45; 25-38; 26-50
Aumann, --, 23-124; 24-61
Awalt. See Ewald

Bach, Conrad, 10-7
Bach, Michel, 20-2
Bach, --, 23-72
Backes, Wilhelm, 2-4
Baer, Henrich, 5-21; 10-18
Baer, Johann, 7-14; 25-77
Bär. See also Behr
Bätter, --, 23-151
Bäumert, Georg, 9-2
Baist, Georg, 22-129
Baist, Nicolas, 8-5
Baist, --, 23-108
Bandel, Johann Georg, 1-22
Bangert, Conrad, 20-3
Baro, Johann, 27-247
Baro. See also Paro
Barth, Johann, 15-36; 27-254
Barthold, Michel, 8-32
Bartmann, Johann, 8-40
Bartmann, --, 23-130; 23-235

Bauer, Jacob, 2-42
Bauer, Leonhard, 19-37
Bauer, Peter, 1-21
Baumann, Philip, 10-37
Bauscher, Johann, 7-43
Bauscher, Jonas, 27-178
Bauscher, Valentin, 7-25; 13-13
Bauscher, --, 23-191
Bausum, Lorenz, 7-39
Bausum, --, 23-188
Bechtel, Caspar, 12-27; 27-95
Bechtel, Georg, 27-204
Bechtold, Friedrich, 22-79
Bechtold, Georg, 7-27
Beck, Georg, 14-13; 27-134
Beck, Johann, 10-27
Beck, Philip, 9-5
Beck, --, 23-67; 23-141
Becker, Conrad, 1-29; 7-18
Becker, Georg, 27-172
Becker, Henrich, 17-7; 22-104; 27-45
Becker, Ludwig, 10-3
Becker, Wilhelm, 8-29; 25-27; 26-53
Becker, --, 13-4; 23-62; 23-129;
   23-186; 24-66
Behr, Henrich, 27-15; 27-267
Behr, Johannes, 26-75
Behr, --, 23-9; 23-203; 24-98
Behr. See also Baer
Beil, Johannes, 14-33
Bellinger, Johann, 12-3; 27-68
Bender, Conrad, 17-10; 22-126; 27-138
Bender, Georg, 15-22; 27-224
Bender, Henrich, 11-14; 22-45; 22-128;
   27-14
Bender, Jost, 22-137
Bender, Mathias, 18-14
Bender, Philip, 10-19
Bender, Siegmund, 7-13; 27-188
Bensing, Georg, 7-20; 25-64
Bensing, Philip, 26-74
Bensing, --, 23-200; 24-95

Cress, Caspar, 9-50; 11-10; 27-26
Cress, Georg, 27-240
Cress, Henrich, 9-32; 22-98; 23-172
Cress, Johann, 27-108
Cress, Johannes, 12-32
Cress, Nicolas, 14-26; 22-166; 27-52; 27-133

Dacke, Conrad Henrich, 1-40
Däfner, Georg, 11-25
Däfner, Johann, 12-19
Däfner. *See also* Deffner
David, Henrich, 12-15; 27-87
Dechert, Doris, 27-191
Deckert, Theodor, 7-46
Deckmann, Henrich, 22-119
Deffner, Georg, 27-29
Deffner, Johann, 27-89
Deffner. *See also* Däfner
Dele, Jakob, 27-255
Dele. *See also* Döll
Denhard, Christoph, 8-4
Deschemer, Georg, 12-23; 27-98
Desselberger, Friedrich, 19-36
Dickhaut, Henrich, 4-3
Diefenbach, Wilhelm, 16-25
Diehl, Andreas, 22-21
Diehl, Balthasar, 22-91
Diehl, Christoph, 12-37
Diehl, Friedrich, 22-108
Diehl, Henrich, 14-29; 27-126
Diehl, Martin, 16-44; 27-302
Diehl, Nicolas, 15-15; 27-223
Dieterich, Johannes, 26-7
Dieterich, --, 24-7
Dietrich, Christian, 15-12; 27-226
Dietrich, Johann, 5-9; 25-18
Dietrich, Lorenz, 22-101
Dietrich, Nicolas, 22-73
Dietrich, --, 23-14
Döll, Jacob, 15-18
Döll. *See also* Dele
Dönges, Christoph, 8-24; 25-12
Dönges. *See also* Dünges
Dörr, Nicolas, 14-24
Dörr. *See also* Durr
Donné, Johannes, 5-5
Donné, --, 23-2
Drill, Conrad, 11-8; 27-9

Dümler, Christoph, 13-21; 27-206
Dümler, Conrad, 11-24
Dünges, Christoph, 26-54
Dünges, --, 23-114; 24-51
Dünges. *See also* Dönges
Dufais, Wilhelm, 18-1
Durr, Nicolas, 27-136
Durr. *See also* Dörr

Ebersbach, Peter, 2-21
Ebert, Johannes, 2-13
Eckel, Caspar, 8-6
Eckel, --, 23-109
Eckhard, Georg, 4-24
Eichelmann, Bernhard, 20-5
Eichler, Gottfried, 11-34
Eidebenz, Henrich, 12-11; 27-77
Eiffert, Georg, 8-3
Eiffert, Jacob, 12-26; 27-92
Eiffert, --, 23-106
Eigler, Gottfried, 27-51
Eipp, Caspar, 10-29
Eipp. *See also* Epp
Eirich, Johann, 27-13
Eirich. *See also* Eyrich
Elsässer, Ludwig, 4-6
Emmerich, Conrad, 15-34; 27-235
Emmerich, Johann, 7-8; 26-77
Emmerich, Philip, 9-43; 26-68
Emmerich. *See also* Emrich
Emmerichs, Marx, 22-82
Emmert, Leopold, 6-14
Emmert, --, 23-30
Emrich, Johannes, 25-68
Emrich, Philip, 25-15
Emrich, --, 23-160; 23-196; 24-75; 24-90
Emrich. *See also* Emmerich
Encke, Isaac, 25-48
Encke, Jacob, 18-5
Encke, Ludwig, 26-86
Encke, --, 23-219; 24-100
Engel, Henrich, 5-19
Engel, Peter, 14-28; 27-128
Engel, --, 23-18; 24-9
Engelhard, Wilhelm, 12-28; 27-90
Epp, Caspar, 25-89; 26-20
Epp, --, 23-75; 24-30
Epp. *See also* Eipp

Erdmann, August, 4-22
v. Eschwege, Christian, 6-1
Etzig, Michel, 11-21; 27-40
Ewald, Conrad, 22-88
Ewald, Peter, 12-4
Eyrich, Johannes, 22-160
Eyrich. *See also* Eirich

Faber, Henrich, 10-33
Fack, Carl, 8-20
Färber, Friedrich, 7-32; 25-75
Färber. *See also* Ferber
Fail, Henrich, 27-250
Fail. *See also* Fehl; Feul
Faulstroh (Fautstroh), Henrich, 1-6;
    19-6
Faupel, Georg, 27-164
Faupel. *See also* Vaupel
Fehl, Johannes, 8-44; 25-56; 26-55
Fehl, --, 23-123; 24-60
Fehl. *See also* Fail; Feul
Feick, --, 23-17
Felger, Henrich, 16-33
Felsenheim, Joseph, 1-20
Felton. *See* Velton
Fengel, Peter, 12-38; 27-79
Ferber, Friedrich, 26-80
Ferber, --, 23-193; 24-87
Ferber. *See also* Faber; Färber
Fetter. *See* Vetter
Fetzer, Franz, 16-38; 27-8
Feul, Henrich, 15-45
Feul. *See also* Fail; Fehl
Filtzinger, Johann, 27-101
Finck, Carl, 3-1; 22-148
Fintzel, --, 23-54
Finzel, Conrad, 6-31
Firres, Conrad, 22-4
Firres. *See also* Fuhr
Fischer, Bernhard, 19-34
Fischer, Henrich, 6-26
Fischer, --, 23-53
Fix, Peter, 8-39
Fix, Valentin, 16-27
Fix, --, 23-138; 23-236
Fleckstein, Rudolph, 19-26
Fleischmann, Jacob, 12-14; 27-93
Förter, Caspar, 9-23
Förter, Conrad, 14-6; 27-115

Foerter, --, 23-178
Foltz, Conrad, Junior, 27-275
Foltz. *See also* Voltz
Forrest. *See* Wald *[translation]*
Franisko (Franisca), Christoph,
    13-31; 27-199
Frantz, Philip, 27-277
Franz, Jacob, 16-30
Freund, Adam, 11-18; 27-16
Freund, Henrich, 11-6; 27-20
Freyburger, Alexander, 2-12
Freyensener, Georg, 22-36; 27-145
Friderici, Salomon, 2-25
Fridrich, Johann, 19-15
Frischkorn, Friedrich, 8-38; 27-141
Frischkorn, Johann, 4-20
Fritz, Michel, 5-18; 27-30
Fritzel, Dionysius, 15-14; 27-290
Fuchs, Jacob, 2-26
Fuhr, Henrich, 17-5
Fuhr. *See also* Firres
Funck, Georg, 22-62
Funck, Peter, 4-21
Fus, Johannes, 22-20

Gackemus, Jacob, 22-85
Gackemus. *See also* Kuckumus
Gärtner, Georg, 11-26; 27-53
Gärtner, Jost, 5-20
Gans, Christoph, 13-32; 27-192
Gauel, Conrad, 9-13
Gehring, Daniel, 18-18
Genaud, Isaac, 22-22
Genaud, Jacob, 11-27
Genaud. *See also* Jenaut
Georgi, Friedrich, 15-33; 27-251
Gergens, Anthon, 2-41
Gerhard, Philip, 13-36; 27-201
Gerlach, Philip, 5-8; 27-42
v. Germann, August, 5-1
Gescheidle, Johann, 11-38; 27-25
Geschke, Michel, 16-21; 27-289
Geschwind, Johann, 16-31
Gewald, Jacob, 6-17; 27-71
v. Geyling, Wilhelm, 7-2
Giese, Wilhelm, 6-16
Gimbel, Johann, 13-8; 27-169
Glaas, Johann, 27-76
Glas, Jonas, 12-18

Globedanz, Gottlob, 11-30
Globedanz. *See also* Klobetanz
Gnüge, Friedrich, 8-8
Gnüge, --, 23-107
Göbel, Friedrich, 16-19
Göbel, Georg, 22-34; 27-274
Göbel, Paul, 7-23
Goebel, --, 23-212
Görtler, Christoph, 25-81; 26-35
Görtler, --, 23-105; 24-27
Görtler. *See also* Gürtler
Goetz, Jacques, 27-10
Gottner, Georg, 27-249
Gottschalck, Wilhelm, 6-8
Gottschalck, --, 23-25
Grimm, Wilhelm, 6-40; 22-153; 27-82
Groner, Peter, 22-84
Groner. *See also* Gruner
Grossmann, Georg, 2-33
Grubenstein, Philip, 19-24
Gruber, Johannes, 22-56
Gruber, Xaverius, 22-57
Grünewald, Casper, 11-33; 27-63
Gruner, Conrad, 8-16
Gruner, --, 23-112
Gürtler, Christoph, 10-53
Gunckel, Henrich, 26-52
Gunckel, Johann, 13-45
Gunckel, --, 23-125; 24-62
Gutermuth, Johann, 7-38
Guttermuth, --, 23-187

Hachenberg, Christoph, 15-26
Hachenberger, Christian, 27-57
Hachenberger, Georg, 7-42; 25-86;
  26-85
Hachenberger, Jacob, 25-79; 26-5
Hachenberger, Jost, 5-36
Hachenberger, Wilhelm, 11-31; 27-50
Hachenberger, --, 23-8; 24-3
Haffener, --, 23-73
Hafner, Pancratz, 10-12
Hagenberger, --, 23-195; 24-89
Hahn, Conrad, 1-3
Hahn, Isaac, 5-31
Hahn, --, 23-5
Hallatschka, Johann, 6-39
Hallatschka, Peter, 9-18
Hallatschka, Philip, 7-10
Hallatschka, --, 23-146; 23-189

Hamann, Conrad, 1-27
Hamann, Jacob, 15-30; 27-227
Hamann, Peter, 7-17
Hamburger, Philip, 9-37
Hamburger, --, 23-143
Hammann, Nicolas, 16-17; 27-284
Handel, Johann, 1-1; 19-27
Harmann, Paul, 27-104
Harmann. *See also* Hermann
Harnischfeger, Christoph, 4-9
Hartmann, Paul, 4-11
Hartmann, Peter, 9-20; 16-22; 25-4;
  26-58; 27-281
Hartmann, --, 23-168; 24-81
Haumann, Jacob, 12-2; 22-87; 27-67
Haupt, Mathias, 1-18
Hausmann, --, 1-36
Hayn, André, 27-303
Hayn. *See also* Hein
Heck, Caspar, 15-46
Heck, Martin, 10-5
Heck, --, 23-65
Heckmann, Michel, 4-23
Heeger, Henri, 27-17
Heep, Georg, 1-15
Heerswagen, Friedrich, 6-3
Heicke, Ludwig, 13-39
Heid, Georg, 25-66
Heid. *See also* Heyd
Heidelbach, Justus, 21-5
Heidenreich, Henrich, 22-83
Heil, Daniel, 8-27
Heil, Philip, 13-14
Heil. *See also* Heyl
Heill, --, 23-115
Heim, Philip, 21-2
Hein, Georg, 27-181
Hein. *See also* Hayn
Heinzinger, Philip, 6-19
Heisterreich, Ludwig, 12-1
Held, Henrich, 9-34
Hellerich, Peter, 25-72
Hemmerle, Thadeus, 16-7; 27-270
Hencke, Henrich, 15-37; 27-248
Henckel, Philip, 26-67
Henckel. *See also* Hinkel
Henning, Daniel, 19-17
Henrich, Christoph, 12-30; 27-91
Hensler, Adam, 8-41
Hens (Hentz), Andreas, 15-23; 27-234
Hentzel, Henrich, 27-2

Hentzel, --, 23-210; 23-127; 24-64
Hentzler, --, 23-137
Henzel, Conrad, 8-36; 25-85; 26-49
Henzel, Henrich, 7-31; 11-2
Henzel, Johann, 6-33
Henzel, --, 23-37
Herber, Michael, 22-35
Herchenröder, Johann, 9-44
Hermann, Johannes, 22-46
Hermann, Paul, 12-31; 27-104
Hermann. *See also* Harmann
Hess, Caspar, 8-35; 22-154; 25-25;
   26-42
Hess, --, 23-116; 24-53
Hessler, Christoph, 27-109
Hessler, Friedrich, 27-105
Hessler, Friedrich, Junior, 12-40
Hestermann, Friedrich, 19-2
Hetterich, Peter, 10-48; 26-29
Hetterich, --, 23-82; 24-37
Heyd, Georg, 18-12
Heyd, Johann, 9-11
Heyd, --, 24-107
Heyd. *See also* Heid
Heyder, Georg, 27-215
Heyer, Conrad, 9-26
Heyer, --, 23-153
Heyl, Daniel, 25-24; 26-45
Heyl, Georg, 22-139; 26-88
Heyl, --, 23-144; 23-228; 24-52
Heyl. *See also* Heil
Hickmann, Michel, 4-23
Hild, --, 23-166
Hildner, Friedrich, 19-35
Hiller, Michel, 14-40; 27-155
Hinckel, Conrad, 14-15; 27-131
Hinckel, Philip, 9-41; 22-161; 25-14;
   26-67
Hinckel, --, 23-159; 24-74
Hinckel. *See also* Henckel
Hirschberger, Friedrich, 2-27
Hochstadt, Jacob, 22-80
Hochstadt, Wilhelm, 22-81
Hock, Conrad, 4-2
Höger, Henrich, 11-22
Hof, Johann, 18-3
Hoff, --, 23-217
Hoffmann, Georg, 26-8
Hoffmann, Henrich, 25-69
Hoffmann, --, 23-220; 24-101

Hoffmann, --, Junior, 24-8
Hofmann, Andreas, 1-5
Hofmann, Balthasar, 1-25
Hofmann, Franz, 13-40; 27-200
Hofmann, Georg, 18-6
Hofmann, Gottfried, 16-39; 27-295
Hofmann, Henrich, 5-10; 27-11
Hofmann, Johann, 5-29; 13-18; 27-197
Hofmann, Kraft, 15-20; 27-232
Hofmann, Peter, 7-15
Hofmann, --, Junior, 23-16
v. Hohorst, --, 14-1
Holl, Melchior, 9-14; 26-64
Holl, Philip, 16-32; 22-54; 27-278
Holl, --, 23-156; 24-71
Holle, Melchior, 25-90
Holtzemar, --, 23-175
Holzheimer, Jonas, 9-36
Hommel, Nicolas, 11-11; 27-35
Hopfenrath, Friedrich, 16-43; 27-296
Horn, Nicolas, 10-50
Horn, --, 23-91; 23-101; 24-46
Huber, Jacob, 19-19
Hüfner, Henrich, 22-8; 27-144
Hüfner, Urbanus, 6-47
Hüfner, --, 23-100
Hufschmidt, Jacob, 2-38

Ifland, Henrich, 7-48; 22-26
Ifland, Johann, 15-29; 22-17; 27-252
Ifland, --, 23-205; 24-92
Immich, --, 23-19; 23-233
Immig, Daniel, 5-37

Jacobi, Tobias, 22-59
Jaeger, Friedrich, 2-14
Jahn, Friedrich, 9-15; 25-60; 26-71
Jahn, Johannes, 19-39
Jahn, Nicolas, 10-6
Jahn, --, 23-69; 23-165; 24-79
Jenaut, Isaac, 27-57
Jenaut. *See also* Genaud
Jordan, Anthon, 2-45
Jost, Johann, 9-45; 25-40; 26-56
Jost, --, 23-171
Jung, Conrad, 22-143
Justemer, Johann, 9-16
Justenar, --, 23-150

Justorf, Friedrich, 6-13
Justorf, Wilhelm, 6-15
Justorff, --, 23-31

Kabitzky, Benjamin, 27-209
Kabitzky. *See also* Capitzky
Kämmerer, Wendel, 14-21
Kämmerer. *See* Kemmeren
Kaempf, Caspar, 6-41
Käster, Johannes, 22-47
Kalbfleisch, Johann, 5-23; 22-172
Kapitzky. *See* Capitzky; Kabitzky
Kappes, Adam, Junior, 19-11
Kappes, Engelbert, 16-36; 27-291
Kappes, Peter, 4-7
Karl. *See* Carl
Kayser, Adam, 9-7; 25-28
Kayser, Friedrich, 6-63; 27-107
Kayser, Henrich, 7-5
Kayser, Johann, 19-4
Kayser, Nicolas, 16-29; 27-279
Kayser, --, 19-41; 24-69
Kayser. *See also* Keyser
Keller, Henrich, 19-3
Kemmeren, Wendelinus, 27-301
Kempfer, --, 16-1
Kempff, --, 23-36
Kempff. *See also* Kaempf
Kenner, Peter, 9-38
Keppenhan, Christoph, 22-15
Kerzner, Johann, 14-37; 27-157
Kerzner. *See also* Kirchner
Kessler, Joseph, 2-11
Kessler, Lorenz, 14-20; 27-135
Kessler, Michel, 13-44; 27-211
Keyser, Adam, 26-62
Keysser, --, 23-154; 23-185
Kirchhof, Adam, 16-2
Kirchner, Adam, 22-5; 23-182; 24-86;
  26-73
Kirchner. *See also* Kerzner
Kirsch, Ludwig, 11-40; 27-33
Kitz, Augustin, 7-3
Kitz, Caspar, 8-26
Kitz, Georg, 6-18
Kitz, --, 23-134; 23-183
Kitzstein, Leonhard, 2-30
Klärle, Jacob, 15-9
Klärle. *See also* Klerle

Klee, Leonhard, 6-9
Klee, Nicolas, 16-11; 22-50; 27-269
Klee, --, 23-26
Klees, Georg, 8-23; 25-26; 26-41
Klees, --, 23-126; 24-63
Kleimbel, Georg, 1-41
Klein, Philip, 19-20
Klemm, Christian, 16-5
Klemm, --, 27-264
Klentsch, Balthasar, 16-26; 27-299
Klerle, Jacques, 27-222
Klerle. *See also* Klärle
Klinckerfus, Esaias, 22-67
Klinckerfus, Gottlob, 9-17
Klinckerfus, --, 23-170
Kling, Jacob, Senior, 12-39
Kling, Jacob, 27-81
Kling, Theodor, 27-110
Klingel, Bernhard, 5-28; 27-60
Klingel, Philip, 5-6; 27-3
Klobetanz, Gottlieb, 27-19
Klobetanz. *See also* Globedanz
Klöber, Caspar, 14-23; 27-137
Klöber, Franz, 22-77
Klotzbach, Martin, 15-16
Klü, --, 23-131; 23-238
Klüe, Georg, 8-15
Knapp, Anthon, 13-28; 27-195
Knaus, Balthasar, 22-41
Knittel, Georg, 17-2; 27-257
Knittel, Peter, 22-157; 27-22
Knoblauch, --, 23-102; 23-234
Knobloch, Carl, 10-8
Knoch, Ehrenfried, 22-19
Knorr, Conrad, 19-18
Knot, Conrad, 5-26; 22-173
Koch, Andreas, 17-3; 22-150; 27-259
Koch, Christian, 18-16; 25-93; 26-92
Koch, Daniel, 22-142
Koch, Georg, 22-159; 27-23
Koch, Johannes, 6-22; 9-40; 26-16
Koch, --, 23-50; 23-145; 23-222;
  24-19; 24-104
Köhler, Henrich, 22-106; 26-17
Köhler, Jost, 22-94
Köhler, Mathias, 5-34; 25-46
Köhler, --, 23-15; 23-44; 24-13
Körber, Caspar, 20-4
Koerber, Henrich, 1-2
Kohlepp, Adam, 14-2; 27-114

Kohlepp, Caspar, 6-51; 22-175; 25-53
Kohlepp, Georg, 12-7
Kohlepp, Johannes, 22-156
Kohlepp, Melchior, 22-149
Kohlepp, --, 23-61; 24-25
Kohnes, Stephan, 27-124
Korn, Georg, 10-40; 26-33
Korn, --, 24-46
Krämer, Henrich, 11-47
Kraemer, Lorenz, 22-30
Krafft, Henri, 27-176
Krafft, Nicolas, 2-32
Krafft, --, 23-41
Kraft, Andreas, 6-49
Kraft, Henrich, 13-11
Kraft, Justus, 22-1
Kramer, Jonas, 26-2
Kramer. *See also* Kraemer; Kremer
Krammer, --, 23-10
Kratz, Conrad, 9-25; 25-29; 26-72
Kratz, Leonhard, 22-163
Kratz, --, 23-162; 24-77
Kraus, Georg, 15-40; 27-233
Krautwurst, Johann, 11-15; 27-65
Krebs, Conrad, 22-167
Krebs, Valentin, 22-71
Kreckel, Nicolas, 27-294
Kreim, Christoph, 7-40
Kremer, Henrich, 27-54
Kremer. *See also* Kraemer; Kramer
Krencke, Gottlieb, 22-16
Kressel, Nicolas, 8-11
Kretzler, Friedrich, 16-42
Kreuzer, Sebastian, 1-7
Krieg, Conrad, 6-27; 27-73
Krieg, Henrich, 10-11; 25-73; 26-21
Krieg, Leonhard, 14-22; 27-148
Krieg, --, 23-83; 24-38
Krill, Johann, 5-4
Krill, Jost, 27-1
Krill, --, 23-1
Kropp, Jacob, 11-28
Krutsch, Henrich, 22-64
Kuckumus, --, 2-28
Kuckumus. *See also* Gackemus
Kühn, Christoph, 12-45; 27-111
Kühn, Conrad, 19-22
Kühorn, Johannes, 20-8
Külp, Carl, 2-8
Kunckel, Henrich, 16-8; 25-47; 27-273

Kunckel, Johann, 27-208
Kunes, Stephen, 14-12
Kuton, Henrich, 22-134

Lack, Johannes, 6-42
Lack, --, 23-59
Lahr, --, 23-111
Lake. *See* See [translation]
Lallua, Friedrich, 27-298
Laluwa, Philip, 16-40
Laluwa. *See also* Latuwa
Landwehr, Jacob, 2-7
Lantz, Henrich, 1-17
Lanz, Valentin, 22-116
Lapp, Adam, 9-4
Lapp, Johann, 12-12; 27-78
Lapp, --, 23-140
Latuwa, Philip, 16-40
Latuwa. *See also* Laluwa
Lauck, Adam, 27-194
Lauckhard, Nicolas, 11-13; 27-55
Lauckhard, Peter, 27-43
Lauckhard, Wilhelm, 22-76
Lehnung, Henrich, 6-54
Lehnung. *See also* Löhnung
Lehr, Johannes, 22-68
Lehr, Moritz, 8-14; 25-11
Lehr, Peter, 5-30; 27-41
Lehr, --, 24-50
Leib, Wendel, 26-36
Leick, Adam, 13-30
Leick, Philip, 5-22
Leimbach, Johann, 5-33
Leipold, Daniel, 27-36
Leipold, Nicolas, 25-58
Leipold. *See also* Leybold
Lempert, Friedrich, 1-33
Lentner, Jacob, 2-39
Lentz, Christoph, 10-1
Lentz, Valentin, 27-219
Lentz, --, 23-23
Lenz, Carl, 6-57; 22-176
Lenz, Christoph, 10-1
Lenz, Henrich, 6-5
Leonhard, Christian, 7-6; 27-166
Leonhard, Jacob, 18-13; 25-41; 26-94
Leonhard, Johann, 11-19
Leonhard, --, 23-224

Leonhardt, Johann, 27-12
Leonhardt, --, 24-105
Leybold, Johann, 9-9
Leybold, Nicolas, 9-47; 26-61
Leybold, --, 23-149; 24-68
Leybold. *See also* Leipold
Leypold, Daniel, 22-158
Lichmann, Peter, 4-5
Liebegott, Henrich, 11-36
Liebergott, Henrich, 27-59
Liller, Henrich, 8-34
Linck, Caspar, 22-164
Linck, Henrich, 22-92
Linck, Nicolas, 22-165
Linck, Stephan, 22-95
Lind, Johannes, 12-6
Lind. *See also* Lindt
v. Lindau, --, 17-1
Lindebauer, Johann, 22-58
Lindner, Johann, 11-23; 27-21
Lindner, Joseph, 2-37
Lindt, Johann, 27-74
Lindt. *See also* Lind
Linneberger, Adam, 22-103; 27-44
Lins, Johann, 8-33
Lintz, --, 23-133; 24-67
Linz, Friedrich, 22-28
Linz, Johannes, 25-57
List, Martin, 22-86
List, Wilhelm, 4-1
Lochmann, Balthasar, 1-16
Lochmann, Wilhelm, 18-11; 25-78;
  26-91
Lochmann, --, 23-221; 24-102
Loeder, Georg, 27-149
Löhnung, --, 23-43
Löhnung. *See also* Lehnung
Löter, Georg, 14-31
Löwenstein, Conrad, 8-37
Lohberg, Henrich, 22-112
Lohmüller, Nicolas, 9-35
Lohmüller, --, 23-176
Lohra, Georg, 18-7
Lohra, --, 23-230
Lohs, --, 23-231
Loos, Balthasar, 18-8
Losberger, Johann, 1-12
Loss, --, 23-231
Lottig, Daniel, 22-145
Lotz, Caspar, 15-24; 27-225

Lotz, Georg, 9-39; 23-177
Lotz, Johann, 13-27; 16-16; 27-193;
  27-212
Lotz, Nicolas, 22-132
Lotz, Wilhelm, 6-38; 25-42; 26-12
Lotz, --, 23-56; 24-22
Louis, Natan, 27-304
Lucas, Philip, 22-147

Mager, Georg, 9-42; 25-39; 26-69
Mager, --, 23-161; 24-76
Mahla, Peter, 16-20
Mahla. *See also* Malla
Mahr, Andreas, 11-20; 27-31
Mahr, Georg, 6-32
Mahr, Philip, 6-37; 22-178
Mahr, --, 23-33
Maisch, Joachim, 11-44
Major, Georg, 2-19
Malla, Peter, 27-283
Malla. *See also* Mahla
Manckel, Johann, 8-21
Manckel, Martin, 8-42
Manckel, --, 23-136
Marofsky, Anton, 12-25
Marofsky, Joseph, 27-96
Marshall. *See* Mörschel
Mauerer, Martin, 22-171
Maul, Caspar, 6-48; 25-52; 26-13
Maul, --, 23-52; 24-20
Mayer, Johannes, 22-66
Mayr, Joseph, 2-17
Mebus, Peter, 9-8
Mebus, --, 23-164
Meerbott, Johann, 10-44; 25-9
Mehrbott, --, 23-84
Mehrbott. *See also* Merbot
Mehrling, Philip, 14-34
Menck, Philip, 14-17; 27-146
Mencke, Conrad, 10-30
Menzer, Joseph, 15-17; 27-256
Merbot, Johannes, 26-30
Merbott, --, 24-39
Merbott. *See also* Meerbott; Mehrbott
Merckel, Reinhard, 12-16; 27-84
Mercker, Johannes, 22-138
Merling, Philip, 27-46
Mertz, Henrich, 7-37
Mertz, --, 23-209

Metzler, Adam, 13-1; 22-100; 27-163
Metzler, Peter, 1-26
Metzler, Sebastian, 14-5; 27-122
Meuer, Martin, 7-45
Meusch, Joachim, 27-38
Meyer, Friedrich, 10-47; 27-112
Meyer, Henrich, 22-39
Meyer, Leonhard, 19-21
Michel, Henrich, 15-5
Moebus. *See* Mebus
Möller, Martin, 14-7
Mörler, Conrad, 6-35
Moerler, --, 23-42
Mörschel, Johann, 1-31; 19-1
Mörschel, Philip, 9-46; 27-242
Mörschel, Wilhelm, 7-34
Montreal, Joachim, 2-40
Moyer. *See* Meuer
Mühl, Georg, 5-13
Müller, Adam, 6-11
Müller, Andreas, 1-42
Müller, Balthasar, 7-36; 27-189
Müller, Caspar, 9-49; 23-179; 23-239
Müller, Chritian, 8-13; 23-135
Müller, Christoph, 15-10
Müller, Conrad, 10-15; 23-98
Müller, Friedrich, 2-18
Müller, Gottlob, 11-3; 27-6
Müller, Henrich, 4-4; 7-7
Müller, Joachim, 15-35
Müller, Johann, 4-14; 8-30; 8-48;
  13-15; 18-4; 27-139; 27-180
Müller, Leonhard, 9-31; 23-157;
  24-72; 25-59; 26-65
Müller, Martin, 27-127
Müller, Michel, 11-41; 27-28
Müller, Nicolas, 5-35; 20-6; 25-51;
  26-3
Müller, Peter, 22-11; 22-24
Müller, Philip, 9-52; 10-23; 22-114;
  23-99; 23-180; 24-84
Müller, Wilhelm, 9-10; 22-120; 23-174
Müller, --, 23-13; 23-27; 23-207;
  23-216; 24-6
Müllner, Friedrich, 12-34
Müs, Wilhelm, 15-31
Muth, Henrich, 15-27; 27-228

Nantz, Henrich, 19-8
Nauheimer, Georg, 13-34; 27-203

Neider, Henrich, 9-19; 25-45; 26-59
Neiler, --, 23-169
Neiter, --, 23-169; 24-82
Nenner, Friedrich, 22-146
Neunobel, Johann, 27-167
Neunobel, --, 13-7
Niebel, Henrich, 27-153
Nübel, Henrich, 14-14

Obrich, Johann, 7-26; 25-92; 26-78
Obrick, Mathias, 2-22
Obrick, Wilhelm, 22-72
Obrig, --, 23-194; 24-88
Ochs, Georg, 2-44
Oehl, Henrich, 14-25
Oehle, Joseph, 27-162
Ohl, Johann, 13-20; 27-170
Ohl. *See also* Uhl
Orbach, Johannes, 26-90
Orbach. *See also* Urbach
Orbig, Valentin, 27-261
Orpel, Arnold, 19-12
Orth, Conrad, 6-25; 26-10
Orth, Johannes, 13-3
Orth, Jonas, 27-185
Orth, --, 23-45; 24-14
Otto, Samuel, 14-4; 27-266

Paeusch, Georg, 20-1
Pahr, Georg, 19-14
v. Pape, Franz, 17-4
v. Pape, --, 27-213
Parisch, Jonathan, 14-30
Paro, Johann, 15-32
Paro. *See also* Baro
Paul, Michel, 4-12
Peltzinger, Johann, 4-19
Penz, Martin, 2-36
Peter, Thomas, 10-34
Petri, Philip, 10-26
Pettry, Conrad, 25-70
Pettry, --, Junior, 23-94
Pettry, --, Senior, 23-66
Petzinger, Johann, 4-19
Pfaff, Jacob, 6-24
Pfaff, --, 23-34
Pfeffer, Henrich, 9-27
Pfeffer, --, 23-148
Pflug, Johann, 4-8

Pierri, Joseph, 2-1
Pohl, Nicolas, 6-62
Pohl, --, 23-60; 24-24
Porbach, Johann, 27-210
Porbach. *See also* Zorbach
Porth, Johann, 16-41; 27-297
Premer, --, 23-81; 24-36
Premer. *See also* Bremer
Prile, Johann, 27-160
Prile. *See also* Brill
Pulver, Henrich, 16-23; 27-282
Puth, Peter, 11-34; 27-62
Putz, Joseph, 27-32

Quelmann, Peter, 1-19

Raab, Johannes, 6-10
Raabe, --, 23-28
Raimond, Peter, 2-34
Rapp, Peter, 1-4
Ras[c]h, Henrich, 16-35; 27-293
Ras[c]h. *See also* Resch
Rau, Conrad, 11-45; 27-39
Rau, Johannes, 22-31
Rauch, Joachim, 6-45
Rauch, Ludwig, 10-4
Rauch, --, 23-51
Rausch, Nicolas, 22-125
Reges, Philip, 22-124
Reichenbach, Ludwig, 13-41; 27-202
Reichmann, Michel, 8-9; 27-116
Reift, Vitus, 19-30
Reitz, Henrich, 22-78
Remy, Michel, 6-36
Remmy, --, 23-32
Remshard, Johann, 19-10
Reppert, Georg, 22-38
Resch, Henrich, 10-21; 23-79; 24-34;
  25-35; 26-19
Resch, Nicolas, 10-25; 23-80; 24-35;
  25-36; 26-22
Resch. *See also* Ras[c]h; Rauch
Reschebach, Carl, 9-22
v. Richtersleben, Wilhelm, 5-3
Rieb, --, 24-91
Rieb. *See also* Rüb; Rüpp
Rödiger, Nicolas, 15-39; 27-238
Rohre, Leopold, 16-4; 27-263
Rosenberger, Johann, 22-27

Rost, --, 24-83
Roth, Andreas, 22-75
Roth, Conrad, 10-16; 25-33; 26-32
Roth, Johannes, 22-69; 25-80
Roth, Ludwig, 7-29
Roth, Philip, 13-23; 27-184
Roth, Thomas, 4-26
Roth, --, 23-71; 24-26
Rottner, Georg, 15-38
Rudiger. *See* Rödiger
Rüb, Adam, 16-24; 27-285
Rüb, Caspar, 7-35; 25-62; 26-83
Rüb, Johann, 27-271
Rüb, --, 23-197; 24-91
Rüb. *See also* Rieb; Rüpp
Rüfer, Daniel, 6-28
Rüfer, Johann, 5-24
Rüfer, Nicolas, 5-14; 26-89
Rüffer, Friedrich, 1-39; 25-65
Rüffer, --, 23-55; 23-227; 24-21;
  24-106
Rüffer, --, Junior, 23-7
Rüffer, --, Senior, 23-6
Rüpp, Henrich, 16-9
Rüpp. *See also* Rieb; Rüb
Ruhl, Philip, 12-9
Ruhlmann, Georg, 7-41; 26-84
Ruhlmann, --, 23-198; 24-93
Rulmann, Johann, 13-43; 27-205
Ruppel, Conrad, 7-24; 25-17; 26-81
Ruppel, --, 23-202; 24-97
Ruppert, Peter, 2-3

Sartorius, C. A., 21-1
Sauer, Johannes, 22-151
Saurwein, Christian, 27-286
Saurwein, Christoph, 16-34
Saust, Henrich, 27-243
Schaad, Caspar, 13-33; 27-196
Schad, Thomas, 7-49; 25-76
Schädel, Georg, 6-53; 25-88
Schäfer, Balthasar, 13-26; 27-183
Schäfer, Caspar, 9-12; 27-190
Schäfer, Christian, 8-46
Schäfer, Ernst, 22-115
Schäfer, Gregorius, 19-28
Schäfer, Jacob, 12-36; 27-99
Schäfer, Johannes, 7-11; 25-87
Schäfer, Martin, 8-47; 24-59; 25-55
Schäfer, Michel, 9-24

Seelig, Johannes, 22-117
Seib, Wendel, 25-34; 26-36
Seib, --, 23-76
Seib. *See also* Seip; Selb
Seibert, Balthasar, 2-43
Seibert, Henrich, 5-32
Seibert, Philip, 22-136
Seiffert, Georg, 11-1
Seiler, Johann, 7-33
Seiler, --, 23-211
Seip, --, 24-31
Seip. *See also* Seib
Selb, Wendel, 10-31
Selter, --, 24-10
Seltzer, --, 23-226
Selzer, Georg, 18-10
Selzer, Johannes, 6-56
Sensel, Johannes, 22-141
Sensel, Nicolas, 1-28
Sensel, Peter, Senior, 1-34
Senzel, Nicolas, Junior, 19-16
Setler, --, 23-20
Settler, Conrad, 25-19
Seybold, Johannes, 25-91; 26-66
Seybold, --, 23-158; 24-73
Shepherd. *See* Schäfer *[translation]*
Shower. *See* Schauer
Sickenberger, Wilhelm, 6-34
Sickenberger, --, 23-35
Siebert, Georg, 1-13
Siebert, Heinrich Adolph, 22-60
Simon, Conrad, 13-16; 27-175
Simon, Michel, 18-17
Smith. *See* Schmid; Schmidt; Schmitt
Sohl, Friedrich, 10-51
Sohl, --, 23-96
Sommerlade, Conrad, 6-58
Sommerlad, --, 23-39
Spah, Caspar, 18-20
Spahn, Adam, 2-29
Spahn, Caspar, 25-67
Spahn, Henrich, 8-28; 25-37; 26-47
Spahn, --, 23-119; 23-229; 24-56;
   24-108
Spahn. *See also* Spohn
Spanier, Anselm, 12-44; 27-102
Spengler, Georg, 22-40
Spielmann, Conrad, 22-32
Spohn, Ferdinand, 16-3; 27-262
Spohn. *See also* Spahn

Staaf, Henrich, 10-2
Staal, Henrich, 10-2
Stahrenfänger, Johann, 18-21
Stahrenfänger. *See also* Starnfenger
Stamm, Georg, 8-12
Stamm, --, 23-113
Starck, Caspar, 22-10
Starnfenger, --, 23-232
Starnfenger. *See also* Stahrenfänger
Steer. *See* Stier
Steikel, Henrich, 25-43
Stein, Conrad, 22-63
Stein, Friedrich, 6-30; 25-6; 26-14
Stein, Georg, 13-25; 27-181
Stein, Jost, 2-9
Stein, Peter, 6-59; 22-177
Stein, --, 23-48; 24-17
Steinmetz, Johannes, 22-12
Stelter, --, 19-42
Stenger, Adam, 1-9; 19-13
Sterlepp, --, 23-173
Sterlepper, Anthon, 5-27
Sterlepper, Philip, 9-33
Stickel, Henrich, 10-39; 25-43; 26-31
Stickel, --, 23-43; 23-88
Stier, Gottlieb, 14-36
Stock, Andreas, 11-29; 27-61
Stock, Johannes, 1-30
Stock, Michel, 22-109
Stoll, Henrich, 15-44; 27-237
Stoll, --, 24-71
Stone. *See* Stein *[translation]*
Stoppel, Nicolas, 7-4
Stoppel, --, 23-184
Storch, Melchior, 15-11; 27-216
Stroh, Martin, 19-32
Strohl, Christian, 25-13; 26-63
Strohl, Christoph, 9-48
Strohl, --, 23-155; 24-70
Strong. *See* Starck *[translation]*
Strott, Johannes, 2-10
Szlabinger, Bernhard, 27-47
Szlabinger. *See also* Zlabinger

Tack, Jacob, 12-21; 27-69
Taylor. *See* Schneider *[translation]*
Tempel, Georg, 22-6
Theobald, Ernst Philip, 22-155
Thöne, Henrich, 2-24

Traband, Conrad, 7-30
Traband, Johann, 9-21; 13-19; 19-33;
  27-246
Traband, Johannes, 25-61; 26-60
Traband, --, 23-181; 24-85
Traut, Christoph, 27-142
Traut, Conrad, 6-29; 25-7
Traut, Philip, 7-19; 14-10; 17-9;
  27-83; 27-121
Trautt, --, 23-57; 24-23
Treiter, Henrich, 7-9
Treulieb, Wilhelm, 17-8; 27-118
Treutter, --, 23-208
Trostmüller, Friedrich, 22-105
v. Trott, Friedrich, 5-2

Uffelmann, Nicolas, 16-14; 27-280
Uhl, Adam, 22-9
Uhl. See also Ohl
Unger, Andreas, 7-21; 27-165
Unger, Andreas, Junior, 22-99
Unger, Carl, 6-52
Unger, Eberhard, 1-10
Unger, Nicolas, 13-5
Unger, --, 23-38; 23-206
Urbach, Adam, 21-3
Urbach, Henrich, 4-17
Urbach, Johann, Senior, 18-9
Urbach, --, 23-215; 23-225
Urbach. See also Orbach
Urbig, Valentin, 15-4; 22-53
Urledig, Henrich, 10-14; 25-20; 26-24
Urledig, --, 23-104; 24-28

Vaupel, Georg, 13-2
Vaupel, Samuel, 6-4
Vaupel, --, 23-22
Vaupel. See also Faupel
Velten, Adam, 13-12; 27-171
Velten, Augustin, 22-29; 27-143
Vetter, Lorenz, 5-25
Vetter, --, 23-21
Vicario, Johann, 15-41; 27-239
Viltz, Thomas, 4-10
Völcker, Anton, 2-5
Völcker, Henrich, 27-292
Vogelsberger, Georg, 16-15; 27-287
Vogt, Peter, 4-25
Volmert, Nicolas, 19-29

Volst, Henrich, 27-268
Volst, Martin, 22-90
Voltz, Conrad, 16-18
Voltz, Henrich, 16-10
Voltz. See also Foltz
Vorbach, Johann, 4-18

Wächtershäuser, Johann, 8-31
Wächtersheuser, --, 23-132; 23-237
Wagener, --, 23-152
Wagner, Henrich, 11-17; 27-64
Wagner, Philip, 11-32; 27-48
Waitzel, Johann, 22-169
Waitzel. See also Weitzel
Walcer, Daniel, 13-9
Walcer. See also Walzer
Wald, --, 23-46; 24-15
Wall, Conrad, 18-2
Wall, Philip, 25-71; 26-11
Wall, --, 23-218
Waller, Conrad, Junior, 25-31
Walt, Philip, 6-20; 25-71
Walter, Conrad, 5-16
Walter, Conrad, Junior, 25-31
Walter, Daniel, 13-9; 27-168
Walter, Georg, 11-4; 27-5
Walter, Martin, 25-50
Walter, --, Junior, 23-12; 24-5
Walter, --, Senior, 23-4; 24-2
Walther, Conrad, 22-174
Walther, Conrad, Junior, 26-4
Walther, Martin, 26-6
Walther, --, 1-38
Walz, Philip, 6-20
Walzer, Georg, 11-4
Walzer. See also Walcer
Wayman. See Wegmann [translation]
Weber, Andreas, 14-32; 27-152
Weber, Caspar, 13-29; 22-168
Weber, Christian, 1-8
Weber, Johannes, 22-121
Weber, Peter, 6-7; 25-32; 26-8
Weber, Valentin, 22-113
Weber, --, 23-24; 23-64; 24-12
Wegmann, Peter, 1-24
Wehrling, Johann, 16-13
Wehrling. See also Werling
Weibling, Carl, 22-122
Weider, Johann, 27-241
Weigand, Johann, 10-36

Weigand, Peter, 10-42
Weigand. *See also* Weygand
Weil, Hartmann, 10-52; 26-25
Weil, Thomas, 4-16
Weil. *See also* Wile
Weill, --, 23-74; 24-29; 24-80
Weimar, Adam, 15-43
Weimar, Andreas, 27-236
Weingärtner, Friedrich, 17-6; 22-162;
   27-72
Weinlein, Johann Adam, 2-46
Weipert, Cyriacus, 14-19; 27-150
Weiss, Georg, 11-7
Weitzel, Johannes, 6-46
Weitzell, Nicolas, 22-23; 22-135;
   27-34
Weitzel, Valentin, 8-2
Weitzel. *See also* Waitzel
Welter, Caspar, 12-17
Wenzel, Jacob, 15-21; 27-245
Werheim, Conrad, 17-11; 27-140
Werheim, Lorenz, 7-50; 27-187
Werling, Johann, 27-276
Werling, Johannes, 22-51
Werling. *See also* Wehrling
Werner, Jacob, 11-43; 27-37
Werner, Michel, 11-5; 27-4
Werner, Nicolas, 4-18; 27-130
Westphal, Gottfried, 8-18; 25-74;
   26-43
Westphal, Henrich, 10-17; 26-23
Westphal, --, 23-89; 23-118; 24-44;
   24-55
Weyd, Johann, 7-44
Weygand, Peter, 22-170
Weygand. *See also* Weigand
v. Weyhen, Wilhelm, 6-2
v. Weyhers, Wilhelm, 6-2
Weyter, Johann, 9-51
Wichl, --, 23-167; 24-80
Wicht, Carl, 9-53; 25-3; 26-57
Wien, Philip, 11-37; 27-58
Wieteram, Christoph, 10-20
Wieteram. *See also* Witram; Witteram
Wile, Johann, 27-132
Wile. *See also* Weil
Wilhelm, Johann, 13-42; 27-207
Will, Johannes, 14-27
Willmann, Michel, 4-15
Winckler, Philip, 9-29
Winter, Michel, 22-14

Wiohl, --, 24-80
Wiskemann, Christoph, 6-23; 25-1;
   26-9
Wiskemann, --, 23-47; 24-16
Wissenbach, Philip, 22-118
Witram, Christoph, 26-18
Witteram, --, 23-92; 24-47
Witteram. *See also* Wieteram
Wolf, Christoph, 15-19
Wolf, Martin, 22-33
Wüst, Johannes, 2-6
Wuth, Carl, 2-20

Zeh, Caspar, 12-24; 27-103
Zehener, Nicolas, 22-152
Zehner, Adolph, 12-35; 22-2; 27-174
Zehner, Peter, 16-12; 27-272
Zehner, --, 23-63
Zelly, Johannes, 22-13
Zeth, Ulrich, 22-130
Zeul, Conrad, 22-131
Zicklam, Georg, 18-19
Ziegler, Georg, 6-60
Ziewe, Conrad, 22-74
Zimmermann, Johann, 6-21
Zimmermann, --, 23-40
Zinck, Johann, 14-38; 27-154
Zinckhan, Johann, 10-32
Zipf, Adam, 7-22
Zipf, Caspar, 27-300
Zipf, Henrich, 8-22; 27-123
Zipf, --, 23-214
Zischler, Georg, 4-13
Zlabinger, Bernhard, 11-46
Zlabinger. *See also* Szlabinger
Zorbach, Carl, 10-45; 25-23; 26-39
Zorbach, Georg, 26-93
Zorbach, Georg, Junior, 18-15
Zorbach, Johann Georg, 25-30
Zorbach, --, 23-90; 23-223; 24-45;
   24-103
Zorbach, --, Senior, 1-37
Zorbach. *See also* Porbach

www.ingramcontent.com/pod-product-compliance
Lightning Source LLC
Chambersburg PA
CBHW081434270326
41932CB00019B/3193